The Federal Courts, Politics, and the Rule of Law

The Federal Courts, Politics, and the Rule of Law

John C. Hughes

Saint Michael's College

HarperCollins*CollegePublishers*

Editor-in-Chief: Marcus Boggs
Project Coordination: Ruttle, Shaw & Wetherill, Inc.
Design Manager: Mary Archondes
Cover Designer: Mary McDonnell
Art Studio: FineLine
Electronic Production Manager: Valerie A. Sawyer
Desktop Administrator: Sarah Johnson
Manufacturing Manager: Helene G. Landers
Electronic Page Makeup: R. R. Donnelley & Sons Company
Printer and Binder: R. R. Donnelley & Sons Company
Cover Printer: The Lehigh Press, Inc.

The Federal Courts, Politics, and the Rule of Law

Library of Congress Cataloging-in-Publication Data

Hughes, John C.
        The federal courts, politics, and the rule of law / John C. Hughes.
                p.   cm.
        Includes bibliographical references and index.
        ISBN 0-06-501652-1
        1. Judicial process—United States. 2. Political questions and judicial power—United States. 3. Law and politics. I. Title.
        KF8775.H84 1995   94-1184
        347.73'2—dc20   CIP
        [347.3072]

94 95 96 97   9 8 7 6 5 4 3 2 1

Contents

Preface

". . . the very definition of a republic is an 'empire of laws, and not of men.'"

—John Adams, Thoughts on Government, 1776

The founders of the American republic were men who feared the excesses of political power and sought to erect barriers against its abuse. This might be expected behavior for a population that had only a few years earlier suffered political outrage at the hands of a transatlantic British monarchy. Alas, it is by no means inevitable behavior. The annals of political history are replete with past victims turned successful revolutionaries who, on gaining power themselves, resorted to tyranny as despicable as that which they had overthrown. Between 1781 and 1789, some Americans began to fear a similar denouement to the American Revolution. Those who had tasted British imperialism, and who had fought and bled for freedom, once assembled into a legislative majority proved to be as high-handed in their treatment of weaker groups as the monarchy they had rebelled against. The behavior of state legislatures led some to fear growing class conflict, civil unrest, political instability, and, ultimately, the degeneration of republican government into despotism, an ignominious end long predicted by opponents and feared by defenders of popular government. A new concept entered the public rhetoric, the "tyranny of the majority," and with it the recognition that democratic politics alone would not preserve freedom.

We seldom talk as openly of our suspicions of democratic excess as the founders did two centuries ago. Our political culture has changed since then, mostly in the direction of a greater commitment to democratic politics, and mostly for the better. Today, the unquestioned goodness of democratic politics has become an American shibboleth. Perhaps, however, with our lost candor we have grown naive about the risks of democratic politics. All politics involves risk, for in any political controversy somebody will win and somebody will lose. The losers may pay a heavy penalty in terms of lost material wealth, status, opportunities, or diminished control over important aspects of their lives. Sometimes the losers pay with their very lives. In a democratic nation, minority groups are constantly at risk, and in a heterogeneous society we are all potential members of minority groups. The question faced by Americans in 1787, and still present in the 1990s, is whether the risk of politics could be reduced and the rights of minorities protected against abuses by powerful majorities.

Even the most democratic among the founders were not unqualified optimists regarding the wisdom or moderation of majorities. The dangers of democracy, in their view, were akin to the dangers of all politics, sharing a common source in the human personality. While human beings might be capable of reason, virtue, temperance, and mercy, they remain fundamentally egoistic. That is to say, at bottom, people are self-interested, their reasoning about justice generally being little more than self-justification. At worst, people are capable of great selfishness, even to the injury of others whose interests stand in the way of their own immediate gratification. The founders knew that when selfishness combined with power, tyranny was never far behind. If a single individual could not always be trusted to employ power justly, the founders were becoming increasingly aware from their own experience that majorities of people also could not be relied on always to govern fairly.

Some sought to reduce the risk of politics by reducing the community's level of selfishness. Education of the citizen in civic virtue, those moral qualities of public spiritedness that would induce individuals temporarily to lay aside their egocentric interests and discuss politics solely in light of the common good, was their answer to tyranny. Others, ultimately the winning faction, were pessimistic about the possibilities for a sustained civic virtue. If the propensity for self-interestedness was inherent to the human personality, moral education would supply a very tenuous remedy. Over time, the lessons in virtue would be lost in the pursuit of private interest. To correct for what James Madison referred to as "the defect of better motives," they sought instead to create institutional restraints on the power of majorities.[1] If appeals to virtue might someday fall on deaf ears, divided and balanced institutions would stand firm against the worst excesses of majority power, thus providing some protection for minorities. Among these institutional arrangements was an independent judiciary enforcing legal standards limiting the powers of the majority.

If laws could be made just, and if their content could be known and enforced without fear or prejudice, they might stand above the self-interested impulses of individuals or majorities. They might provide impartial standards moderating the popular passions that endanger freedom in a democracy. Courts, knowing only these impartial laws, could be, in the words of Alexander Hamilton, "bulwarks of a limited Constitution against legislative encroachments."[2] Judges could "guard the Constitution and the rights of individuals from the effects of those ill humors, which the arts of designing men, or the influence of particular conjunctures, sometimes disseminate among the people themselves." The restrained politics that remained would enable the majority ample discretion to define and pursue the common good of the community, but only in a responsible manner that respected rights held by others. In this way, weak minority groups would be protected from the risk of politics.

In their hearts, the founders probably knew that replacing the rule of men (only with difficulty could they conceive of the rule of men and women) with the rule of law was to be only partially realized. It was the same fallible human beings who needed the restraint of law in their daily lives, who, in their self-governing capacities, would make and enforce laws. Of more immediate concern, the courts that would adjudicate disputes under law would be staffed by very human judges. The special nature of courts, however, as independent and principled agencies, seemed to promise a reasonable impartiality among the contending interests in the community, and at least offered the best hope of resisting the dangerous rule of fallible individuals. Americans have ever since believed mightily in law. After two centuries of increasing social heterogeneity, law has become one of the few remaining vehicles through which diverse American communities can express common social values and aspirations.[3] It is America's civil religion, in that legal concepts, to an unprecedented degree, have become the common touchstone of moral legitimacy in our public discourse.

How successfully has the judiciary performed its role in the framers' overall project? Can judges know and apply to a dispute the standards of the law, free of the corrupting influence of their own prejudices or partisan interests? Can law really discipline politics and reduce the risks of popular government? Can we have democratic politics without the danger of tyranny of the majority? Are the rights of minorities secure? Can the majority properly use its power to govern the community, free of undue interference by judges? These are questions of vital interest to contemporary Americans. They will be pursued doggedly throughout this book. However, the student in search of quick and simple answers to these questions should be warned: none will be found here, for these are among the most perplexing issues of American politics. Quick and simple answers to such questions do not exist. Generations of citizens and scholars (not mutually exclusive categories) have pondered and debated them. The halls of Congress and state legislatures have rung with denunciations of alleged judicial usurpations. Presidential candidates have fired rhetorical salvos against policies identified with the courts. Much ink has been spilt, and many trees reduced to pulp, in futile efforts to demonstrate to various publics the validity of this or that solution. Students at all levels of sophistication have nervously sought mastery of complex theories that, on close examination, must appear to the fair-minded observer as inchoate, contingent, and tentative.

This book will survey a number of questions about the role of courts in the United States, selected on the basis of their interest to politically literate citizens in a constitutional democracy. We will test the notion of law as a stabilizing force in the community and the ability of courts to restrain the excesses of democratic politics. To perform the role Americans assign to it, law must have a fixed meaning that can be known fully by judges, without resort to political values beyond those clearly set out in appropriate legal texts. We will see, however, that contemporary legal thought views law as, to some degree, indeterminate. It is this indeterminacy in law—its ambiguity, its lacunas, and its "open texture"—that creates opportunities for policy making by judges. The theme we will attempt to hold in focus throughout this book is that the resulting policy making by an unelected elite, especially when done in the promotion of minority rights, exists in tension with our democratic national self-image and is itself politically contested. As we shall see, this tension will raise normative questions regarding the very nature of our political community, questions in which the federal courts are deeply enmeshed.

In consequence of this focus on legal indeterminacy, several topics currently of interest to the scholarly community—juries, sentencing, plea bargaining, alternative dispute resolution, and the like—have been omitted or given cursory treatment here. While interesting, such subjects appear to have a sporadic and attenuated impact on policy making and therefore seem relatively peripheral to the citizen's priorities. These choices are not made to disparage political science, but reflect the observation that the great majority of students reading this book will not become professional researchers of politics. They will instead be called on to participate responsibly as citizens in the political process. The primary objective of this book is the student's preparation for that very demanding role. The difficult decisions of inclusion and exclusion that have been made here may not please all readers, but they have been guided by the desire to elucidate the seemingly anomalous relationship between democratic and judicial politics in the United States. Instructors may choose to supplement this book with any of a number of fine studies offering a concentrated treatment of subjects omitted here.

To the citizen's questions, this book will offer only tentative solutions, at least some of which will strike any conscientious reader as controversial. It is written in the belief that law can, and frequently does, moderate politics, albeit not in the simple, one-dimensional sense we often assume. At the same time, we shall see that politics drives the law. If this seems contradictory, let us suspend our immediate judgments and agree on a working hypothesis that law and politics exist in a reciprocal relationship but are frequently at odds with one another. The nature of this relationship is our subject; the tensions inherent in the relationship will drive our queries. In place of the pat answers often heard from political leaders, partisans, or the popular media, this book attempts no more than to shed some light into the dark corners of judicial politics and to offer an occasion for reflection and informed dialogue. It is hoped that one author and an uncertain number of students (the collective pronoun *we* that is used liberally throughout the text is literal, not royal) will together achieve a deeper understanding of the issues discussed. A sophisticated understanding of politics implies an appreciation for what we do not truly know, but only surmise, as well as a respect for those who have employed their own considerable intellects to arrive at tentative conclusions different from our own. Most of all, democratic citizenship requires us to be ever-willing to engage in further dialogue, even with those with whom we sharply disagree, in the hopes of further enhancing our always incomplete understanding of the political enterprise.

To assess the role of the federal courts in American politics, we will consider normative theories of politics and law, those that tell us what *ought* to occur in judicial decision making. This material will call on us to consider the moral dimension of politics, particularly concerning the reconciliation of democratic government with constitutional restraints and minority rights. But we will also be interested in much of the empirical social science regarding the courts. This ever-growing body of literature explores what actually does occur, insofar as we can measure and record it employing techniques that emulate the detachment and intellectual rigor of the natural sciences. The empiricist examines the judicial process and searches for regularities of behavior. The focus is on institutions and participants in judicial policy making, and the goal is to describe what *is*, separate from what *ought* to be. These two approaches to politics have in the past been artificially separated and too often viewed as mutually exclusive. Now generally recognized as outmoded, this schism has perhaps been perpetuated longer in the field of judicial politics than elsewhere by the academic tradition that distinguishes the study of constitutional law from that of judicial institutions. This distinction is merely an academic convenience, however, and should not be permitted to confine our inquiry.

This book is not concerned with the specifics of legal doctrine, but is written in the belief that courts cannot be understood apart form what they do, and that what they do is interpret law. Incidental to the process of interpreting law, courts also make public policy. Consequently, we will address issues of jurisprudence (a fancy word for philosophy of law) insofar as they determine how judges interpret law, and so define the role courts might play in the political process. We will also be mindful of the institutional topics more commonly included in textbooks of this nature, to see how institutional arrangements might facilitate or inhibit the fulfillment of our normative goals. The study of theory divorced from practice is arid, while the study of practice without theory is incoherent. Here, the student will encounter both, integrated, it is hoped, into a useful whole, and leading to a sophisticated appreciation of judicial politics in America.

The two approaches may at times present fundamentally different pictures of politics. This should not be a cause for cynicism, but it should inspire us to look further at political phenomena, perhaps after a thorough reassessment of our methods of study. When theory and practice, the *is* and the *ought,* diverge sharply, we may have to reconsider our normative goals, for politics is often said to be the art of the possible. Charting a successful political course requires a realistic assessment of the shoals. Alternatively, stark differences between aspiration and achievement may direct us to assume our responsibilities as citizens and act politically to bring about better fulfillment of our hopes and dreams. Politics is also a moral enterprise that requires us to strive for a society more perfect than any we have yet known, even if it means occasionally reaching for the stars. Call it the art of the impossible. Successful politics consists of a delicate balance between the two.

Let us begin, then. Chapter 1 will consider the nature of the judicial decision. We will be interested in the relationship between law and politics. To put it bluntly, we will want to know whether law is autonomous and separate from the political winds of society, or whether law is, in fact, politics carried on under a different name. Or perhaps it is somewhere in between. Chapter 2 will survey the structure and organization of the federal court system. The structure of an institution constrains its behavior, and if we agree that courts help to apportion social goods within the community, then we must look carefully at their floor plan. We will see that the federal judiciary has always been in a state of flux and has never been far from the political concerns of the larger society. To the degree that we erode the sharp distinction between law and politics still to be found in so much political and judicial rhetoric, we should also be increasingly concerned about who occupies judicial posts. Chapters 3 and 4 will examine those who populate the federal bench in the role of judges, and how they acquired that role. We will see that the recruitment of judges has always been politicized to a high degree. Chapters 5 and 6 will examine the meat and potatoes of what courts do by studying the process by which disputes arrive in court and how common and statutory law is applied in their resolution. Finally, Chapter 7 will survey classical and contemporary constitutional theory, in which the tensions between politics and law, between power and restraint, between the majority and minorities, are played out for some very high stakes. It is a rocky road that we must travel, but the journey is interesting.

ACKNOWLEDGMENTS

I would like to express my appreciation for the many helpful comments I received from those scholars who reviewed this textbook in manuscript form. Gregory Caldeira, the State University of Ohio; Anthony Champagne, the University of Texas at Dallas; Cornell Clayton, Washington State University; Joel Grossman, the University of Wisconsin at Madison; William Lasser, Clemson University; and Mark Miller, Clark University, through their careful reading and criticism of early drafts, have made this book much better than it would otherwise have been. I am equally indebted to those additional readers who remain anonymous to me, and to Ruttle, Shaw & Wetherill for their careful copyediting and production.

My colleagues at St. Michael's College, who have helped to create a supportive and congenial atmosphere in which to teach and study political science, have earned my gratitude and admiration. Finally, the many students who have taken my courses over the years have contributed in ways they do not know to shaping the questions that motivate this textbook. Naturally, all remaining shortcomings are my responsibility. I hope they are few.

John C. Hughes

NOTES

1. James Madison, Federalist #51, in Alexander Hamilton, James Madison, and John Jay, *The Federalist* (Modern Library, New York, 1937) p. 337.
2. Ibid., Alexander Hamilton, Federalist #78, p. 508.
3. Mary Ann Glendon, *Rights Talk: The Impoverishment of Political Discourse* (Free Press, New York, 1991) p. 3.

Chapter
1

Litigation and Politics

This book is an exploration of the role courts play in the American political process. Our emphasis will be on the federal court system, although state judiciaries also perform important political tasks, which we shall describe only briefly. We are concerned with the organization and staffing of our courts and with the functions they perform, or ought to perform, in the making of public policy. Along the way, we will encounter the traditional questions of American politics, including considerations that arise from the Madisonian system of separated powers with mutual checks and balances, or the tension between democratic accountability and the preservation of individual and minority rights, when accomplished through constitutional limitations on the majority's powers.

Courts are unusually powerful actors in American politics. While all nations have courts, or some courtlike structure, no society entrusts its courts with as much responsibility for resolving its most fundamental moral conflicts as we do in the United States. This eminence of the judiciary imparts a peculiarly legalistic flavor to American political discourse. Americans are likely to analyze moral and political issues, for better or worse, in terms of legal categories, such as rights and obligations, contract, or personal liability. Over a century and a half ago, the French judge and political theorist Alexis de Tocqueville noted the influence of courts and legal concepts in American politics:

> There is hardly a political question in the United States which does not sooner or later turn into a judicial one. Consequently, the language of everyday party-political controversy has to be borrowed from legal phraseology and conceptions. . . . So legal language is pretty well adopted into common speech; the spirit of the law, born within schools and courts, spreads little by little beyond them; it infiltrates through society right down to the lowest ranks, till finally the whole people have contracted some of the ways and tastes of a magistrate.[1]

1

Were Tocqueville to visit America today, he would have little cause to revise his observation. He would witness courts deciding such issues as how to rectify the legacy of three centuries of slavery and racial oppression, determining the role religion might play in public school curriculums, and defining the limits of freedom of speech, including expressive acts such as saluting or burning the American flag. He would find courts involved in setting national environmental policy, for example, delaying the completion of the massive Tellico Dam, for which billions of dollars had already been spent, when its backwater was found to threaten the extinction of a rare 2-inch fish known as the snail darter. He would find courts adjusting the balance of powers between the two coordinate branches of the national government, including, for example, deliberating on the permissibility of legislative vetoes or on appointments to special commissions having power to regulate national elections or to establish a uniform policy for sentencing convicts. Courts would also be found settling disputes between the national government and the states, or between several states, say a dispute between California and Arizona over the diversion of water from the Colorado River for irrigation. Perhaps most dramatically, he would hear the story of how the Supreme Court ordered one of the most powerful chief executives in U.S. history to comply with a subpoena, resulting ultimately in that president's forced resignation from office days later. Tocqueville would today be hard pressed to find an important political issue in which courts were not at least a peripheral actor. In many, judges would be in the very thick of controversy.

Unfortunately, the work of the American judiciary is easily misunderstood. As Tocqueville observed:

> The judicial organization of the United States is the hardest thing for a foreigner to understand. He finds judicial authority invoked in almost every political context, and from that he naturally concludes that the judge is one of the most important political powers in the United States. But when he then begins to examine the constitution of the courts, at first glance he sees nothing but judicial attributes and procedures. The judge seems to intervene in public affairs only by chance, but that chance recurs daily.[2]

Tocqueville's difficulty in comprehending the political role of American courts is not peculiar to foreigners. Most Americans seem to understand that courts are powerful actors in determining the shape of their politics. Few have a very profound appreciation for the reasons, historical and political, why this is so. For all their power and prestige, courts remain mysterious to most Americans. Indeed, their very mystery might be part of their power. Most Americans do understand that courts often do more than resolve private disputes between individual citizens, yet few manage to penetrate the veil that separates the judicial process from other and more familiar forms of political decision making. Our purpose here is to take a second glance at the judiciary and see beyond the "judicial attributes and procedures." We will see that judicial "intervention" in our political life is far from being a product of chance. It is instead deeply ingrained in the American scheme of governing and represents an impressive attempt to reconcile competing values of popular sovereignty with limited government, of majority rule with individual rights, and of stability with change. The tensions between these values characterize all of American politics, of course, but we shall see that they are particularly acute in the politics of the judiciary.

THE NATURE OF COURTS AND ADJUDICATION

Courts perform the function of adjudication, or the resolution of disputes between two persons according to previously established norms, which are usually written into some body of law. Under traditional separation of powers theory, such as that on which the American government is based, adjudication is distinguished from the making of legal norms, or legislation. It is also said to be different from the implementation of legal norms, or administration. Hence, it is through the distinct function of adjudication that we traditionally try to understand courts as institutions and through which we delineate the concept of "courtness" that we apply, at least implicitly, whenever we are called on to evaluate the performance of our judges.

Unfortunately, popular notions of courts and adjudication founder on close examination of the actual practice of those institutions we call courts. To see why this is so, let us break this notion of adjudication down into its component parts. We think of courts as forums presided over by a judge of some sort, a person who is highly trained in his or her profession, sagacious, fair-minded, and, most of all, independent from all external influences save the law. When we think of the law, we imagine a comprehensive and internally consistent body of rules governing the kinds of activities common among members of the community. The requirements of the law have been well settled in advance and are clearly known, at least to those whose profession it is to know them. If Mr. Smith and Ms. Jones have a dispute and are unable to resolve it by negotiation, compromise, or ceasing to speak to each other, they might approach and ask our learned judge to settle their dispute, applying the law without favoritism to either Smith or Jones. The judge will make a decision only after an elaborate proceeding in which both Smith and Jones are able to state their case pursuant to established rules of evidence and trial procedure. The judge's eventual decision will represent a victory for only one party, leaving the other disappointed with the result. However the decision may turn out, the judge will be entitled to render it only because either Smith or Jones asked him to. Courts respond only to issues raised in the course of lawsuits filed by properly qualified persons like Mr. Smith and Ms. Jones. No other issues interest the court, unless some future litigant raises them.

We might then summarize a basic definition for adjudication, and by extension for the concept of "courtness," by noting this essential passivity and adding the prototype for courts offered by Martin Shapiro, an authority on courts in many nations. Like all prototypes, Shapiro's is an admitted oversimplification, but it is a useful place to start. We might describe a typical American court as:

1. An essentially passive body, presided over by
2. An independent judge, applying
3. Preexisting legal norms, after

4. Adversary proceedings, to achieve

5. A dichotomous decision in which one of the parties was assigned a legal right and the other found wrong.[3]

We will elaborate on these five tenets of adjudication momentarily, but at the outset we should note that much of the work done by political scientists who study courts consists of demonstrating the many ways in which institutions we are used to calling courts depart from this prototype. The sophisticated understanding of American courts that is our goal will especially challenge the second and third of these tenets. However, all will eventually be in need of substantial qualification. Let us look at each, for together they lay an important foundation for our work.

Essential Passivity

The first characteristics distinguishing courts from other centers of power is that courts do not self-start. We expect legislators and executive officials to anticipate social problems before they acquire crisis proportion. They may reach out on their own initiative to remedy the injustices they perceive. Of course, they may also be selective in choosing the problems they will address. Most likely, they will respond to pressure from interest groups, bestowing benefits on the most powerful—those groups that are large, organized, vocal, and well-financed. Others, lacking these accouterments of political clout, will probably be overlooked, or at least treated as lower priorities. Weak minority groups, in particular, may experience detrimental effects of public policy. They may—quite correctly—perceive themselves to be the victims of abuse by legislators because of their weakness and unpopularity. The salient point here is that legislatures and executives are active bodies that set their own agendas. As individuals, judges respond to the same ambitions, fears, and passions, and show the same sympathies, that motivate others. But in court a judge cannot act on any injustice, cannot right any wrong, no matter how heinous, cannot offer any relief to an injured party until asked to by a properly qualified litigant who brings the issue before the court in the formal attire of a lawsuit within the court's jurisdiction.

Judicial Independence

Courts are insulated from those other actors, so that our judge may theoretically decide the controversy between Smith and Jones *solely* on the basis of the law. In short, to ensure that the judicial decision remains qualitatively different from the political decisions of the legislature or of the executive branch, the courts are independent, not under the control of or manipulated by either of those bodies. The dominant powers of society may make laws, but they are powerless to interfere in the fair application of those laws to the conflict between Mr. Smith and Ms. Jones. Hence, judges usually cannot be removed from office, at least not easily. On the federal bench, their appointment is effectively for life. Judges' salaries are also protected to prevent their being influenced by threats or inducements of a financial kind. Thus, Congress may not diminish, although it may raise, a federal judge's salary so long as he or she serves on the bench.

Preexisting Norms

Legislative decisions reflect the balance of power in society. A congressperson can defend his or her vote on a matter of importance simply by saying, "My constituents wanted me to vote that way." No further explanation is likely to be demanded. In contrast, courts may act only when they can demonstrate, often by lengthy and complex written opinions, that some previously existing legal rule, perhaps derived from an earlier judicial ruling known as a "precedent" or from a statute or constitution, requires this and only this decision. Mr. Smith and Ms. Jones will get an explanation and a justification for their fate from the court such as they are unlikely to receive in any other political forum. This requirement to justify results according to preexisting norms is often said to be one of the chief sources of restraint on the power of courts. However, the nature and degree of restraint supplied by preexisting norms is a sharply contested issue. To the degree that preexisting norms are ambiguous or incomplete, other factors, including politics, may come to play a role in our judge's decision.

Adversary Procedure

Nor can our judge be approached by Mr. Smith, Ms. Jones, or any of their friends or allies, except in the carefully structured context of judicial procedures. These procedures, mystifying to those not trained in the profession of law, are designed to ensure that Smith and Jones each has a fair opportunity to present to the judge the reasons why they think the law requires the court to award them a victory in this suit. Each will also have the opportunity to test the veracity of the evidence and to rebut the arguments presented by their opponent. Our assumption is that both Smith and Jones want very much to win this suit. Consequently, we expect that both Smith and Jones will bring before the court every relevant piece of information needed to render a legally correct decision. If the two litigants present complete and cogent arguments, the court will become fully informed about all of the issues in the case. Genuine adversity between Smith and Jones is necessary for American courts to function properly. If the relationship between Smith and Jones appears more cooperative than adversarial, the court will refuse a decision in their case.

Dichotomous Decision

Of course, only one of them can be the winner, for the court's decision will be dichotomous: a winner-take-all proposition that precludes mediation or compromise. Two friends who find themselves in a dispute might agree to split the difference if they value their friendship more than victory. Two litigants are no longer friends; each is after total victory. Approached by two women both claiming to be the mother of the same child, Solomon could offer to cut the baby in half, but even his verdict was only a ploy to determine the singular winner in the dispute. Once a decision is made, either Smith or Jones will go home very unhappy, for every judicial decision creates a complete winner and a complete loser, and the possibility of friendship may be lost forever.

Because only the decision justified by preexisting legal norms is a legitimate decision, we will take great pains to make sure that the judge has not committed some error in the course of the proceedings that has awarded victory to the wrong party. So if Ms. Jones wins the suit, Mr. Smith may be able to appeal the case to a higher court. Since there is only one correct outcome to the case, Smith's appeal must allege that the lower court judge made a decision other than that required by the law. Appellate courts exist only to correct mistakes made in the heat of trial, ultimately to guarantee a fair process, and not to give Smith further opportunity to drag out the case or to harass Jones.

In the ensuing chapters, we will have cause to challenge each of these tenets. They are not wrong so much as they are incomplete and, to that extent, misleading. In reality, courts are complex institutions. Their complexity is derived from the fact that they are not wholly passive, nor wholly independent. Their proceedings are not entirely adversarial, nor are their decisions necessarily as dichotomous as they might seem. For now, however, we will focus on what seems to be the most critical element to the traditional understanding of adjudication, the application of preexisting legal norms.

THE MYTH OF FORMALISM

If courts rendered decisions in lawsuits merely by the mechanical application of legal standards derived from another source of authority, political scientists would pay them scant attention. Judges would then merely be the messengers of public policy. The source of their message would lie elsewhere, and we would want to go directly to the source. The political investigator would look at the legislature, or perhaps an executive agency, to understand how policy was being made. Unfortunately for political scientists, and perhaps for judges as well, things are not so simple. Judges exercise considerable discretion in their role as oracles of the law. By discretion, we mean that the judge is of necessity making choices among values—among the legal theories Mr. Smith and Ms. Jones might favor—that are not previously determined by clear and unambiguous legal standards. Instead, the judge must choose what he or she thinks would be a wise or just result to the suit, acting at least to some degree as a free agent. If decisions are made on the basis of sources other than existing law, we would expect the judge's personal perceptions, experiences, values, and prejudices to play a role in the process. No matter how well intentioned the judge might be, his or her personal idiosyncrasies would affect the outcome. This is in fact true. Even so, the rhetoric commonly employed in judicial opinions, and some legal scholarship, tends to obscure this discretion. We will refer to the view that judges exercise no personal discretion, but merely apply the law as they find it, as *formalism*.

The term suggests that adherence to correct judicial form—an accepted style of reason, based on an agreed upon canon of legal principles—will produce the singularly correct answer for any dispute. Implicit in this view of judging is the assumption that a legal proposition, say a statute, a precedent, or a constitution, already contains the full measure of its meaning, which is available to all who apply the correct interpretive technique to uncover it. The text of a precedent, statute, or constitution means only what it says, and nothing more. A further suggestion of formalism is that a judge who reasons properly, who does adhere to correct form, will arrive at the same conclusion as any other properly reasoning judge. In this way, the decision of the court can be said to be a politically impartial one, unaffected by the shifting equations of power that may determine legislative policy. Hence, formalism portrays law as autonomous from politics.

A rather quaint statement of the formalist position, one that remains influential in spirit if not in the footnotes, is that of William Blackstone. In the 1760s, Blackstone completed his magisterial *Commentaries on the Laws of England,* a codification of the common law of the day into one coherent source. A work of great scholarship, *Commentaries* was a staple in the education of American lawyers for well over a century. Explaining the nature of the judicial decision, Blackstone described a judge as "being sworn to determine, not according to his own private judgement, but according to the known laws and customs of the land; not delegated to pronounce a new law, but to maintain and expound the old one."[4] Notice the assertion that the law on all matters was already "known and settled," so that it could be "expounded" free of any taint by the judge's "own private judgement." Blackstone viewed the English common law as the unfolding of pure logic applied to human relations, as the judge reasoned from previous judicial decisions, or perhaps an occasional statute, to a singularly correct solution to the case before him or her. Such subjective factors as the judge's personal values were banished from the process. Judges did not make up a correct answer to a case, they discovered a correct answer already there—an answer that was correct by virtue of its independent logical existence. We would expect all right-minded judges to arrive, by a similar process of discovery, at the same answer to a case, much as all right-minded mathematicians would discover an identical answer to the equation $X + 2 = 4$.

This view of the judge as merely discovering and giving voice to law already existing outside of his or her subjective predilections raised for Blackstone a difficult question: How does one account for the phenomenon of a court overturning or ignoring a previous decision by another court? If judges contributed nothing of themselves to a legal decision, why didn't judicial rulings exhibit greater uniformity, like the correct answers on an algebra test? Blackstone's answer will require some attention. Regarding a judge's duty to follow precedent, he wrote:

> Yet this rule admits of exception, where the former determination is most evidently contrary to reason; much more if it be clearly contrary to the divine law. But even in such cases the subsequent judges do not pretend to make a new law, but to vindicate the old one from misrepresentation. For if it be found that the former decision is manifestly absurd or unjust, it is declared, not that such a sentence was *bad law,* but that it was *not law;* that is, that it is not the established customs of the realm, as has been erroneously determined.[5]

So when a court ignored or overruled an existing precedent, it was not out of disagreement with the previous judge's values, but because the previous judge was wrong—so flagrantly wrong that the decision was demonstrably contrary to reason. Law suits were similar to an algebra problem after all, and the newer decision was rather like a math professor correcting a student's exam. But there is a problem here, for mathematicians confronting our problem will easily reach a consensus that X = 2. They probably can even convince Smith and Jones by logical proof that X = 2. This is because algebra involves tautological relationships (for purposes of this equation, X + 2 is but another way of writing 4) that are amenable to logical demonstration. In contrast, law inevitably involves moral choices and seeks to restrain the behavior of free-willing and often self-interested human beings by applying those moral standards to ever new forms of conduct. If the moral rule most conducive to producing good conduct could be proved by logical demonstration, we would have considerably less need for courts!

Alas, American courts depart from previous rulings, or previous interpretations of statutes, or especially from previous understandings of the Constitution, for many reasons. Sometimes it is clear that a previous court has erred. Often, however, the previous court has not erred at all. Rather, it is simply that the values of an earlier day (or an earlier judge) have been replaced by new values, necessitating an alteration in the law. Far from vindicating the law from a previous misrepresentation, the court is making new legal standards, even as it reinterprets the same clause in a legal text. We will explore this process further in Chapters 6 and 7. For now, we need to lay to rest the canard that judges ought merely to give voice to law already existing mysteriously, like a "brooding omnipresence in the sky"—or, at best, ought merely to interpret the law, and should never make new law. Those who interpret the law must in fact make law, even if not with a legislator's creative freedom of choice.

The myth of formalism has long been powerful because it is so comforting to judges and litigants alike. Consider Mr. Smith and Ms. Jones, locked in bitter dispute, and now turning to the courts for a settlement. The judge rules in favor of Jones. Previously, Smith and Jones both perceived the judge as impartial, and both believed that an impartial authority would side with himself or herself. Had either of them believed otherwise, they probably would have avoided litigation by surrendering to the other party's claims, or perhaps negotiating some compromise. But upon hearing the verdict, Smith feels that the judge and Jones are ganging up on him.[6] "Why," he would certainly demand to know of our judge, "do you support Jones against me, when I had such a just cause?" Recall that the court owes him an answer. The judge would understandably be comfortable in saying, "There, there, Mr. Smith. It is not I who sided with Ms. Jones. Rather, the law, to which both you and Jones consented when you chose to remain in our community and enjoy its benefits, requires me to award in favor of Jones. It really was not my choice at all, you see." Not only does the judge avoid personal responsibility for the decision, but the legitimacy of that decision, and hence the likelihood that Smith will comply without having to be coerced, will be considerably enhanced. Smith will direct his resentment elsewhere, and our judge will sleep well tonight, to awake fresh for another case tomorrow.

The public would prefer to believe in formalism as well, for it appears to resolve one of the paradoxes of American politics least appreciated by most citizens. We think of ourselves as a democratic society and expect persons making important decisions about our collective future to be held accountable in elections. Yet, as noted previously, judges are largely independent of political accountability.

Federal judges are not elected at all, but are appointed by persons who are elected. Once appointed, they remain on the bench for as long as they are willing. That frequently proves to be a long time. Even in those states in which judges are elected, they serve long terms and seldom campaign in any fashion that elucidates for voters the way they will rule in particular cases. So where do judges get their authority to fashion public policy?

Formalism answers this question by denying that they have any such authority. They do what reasonable courts have always done, or perhaps they do the bidding of the legislature, or they merely apply the Constitution, but they are not the authors of the legal standards they apply. So not only do judges frequently employ the rhetoric of formalism for their own needs, but such is also the expectation of the public. Politicians, especially politicians seeking the support of groups who perceive themselves to be the Mr. Smiths of society, the victims of judicial usurpation, will frequently condemn the courts for not following the dictates of formalism. One suspects, however, that they know better.

CHALLENGES TO FORMALISM

The myth of formalism has been challenged almost for as long as it has been articulated, perhaps dating back to fifth century B.C. Athens, where the sophists might have been the first legal skeptics. In the interest of space, we will note here only two loose, and in some ways related, schools of American legal thought that have challenged formalism's claim to be an adequate explanation of the judicial decision, on either descriptive or prescriptive grounds. Legal realism refers to a group of scholars, and later judges, who during the earlier part of the twentieth century attacked what they perceived as the judiciary's abuse of power under the cloak of formalism. More recently, a group of iconoclastic law professors formed the self-styled Critical Legal Studies movement and have carried forward the critique of the realists, with an added dose of radical egalitarian politics. The former have proven very influential in legal thought and judicial behavior since the 1930s. The latter have thus far generated mainly controversy, but we will see whether they offer anything of value to our understanding of courts in American politics.

Most realists claim as their spiritual father Oliver Wendell Holmes, Jr. Holmes, who never acknowledged paternity, was a distinguished judge on the Massachusetts Supreme Court and later an associate justice on the United States Supreme Court. In his book, *The Common Law,* Holmes was critical of the view that legal decision making was a strictly logical process, along the lines of algebra. Influenced by the philosophy of pragmatism, Holmes viewed law as a transient human convention, adapted by human will to meet historically unique human needs. He wrote:

> The life of the law has not been logic; it has been experience. The felt necessities of the time, the prevalent moral and political theories, intuitions of public policy, avowed and unconscious, even the prejudices which judges share with their fellow-men, have had a good deal more to do than the syllogism in determining the rules by which men should be governed.[7]

Not only was law an intensely practical affair for Holmes, law was inevitably made in the course of judicial decisions. In fact, law really had no existence apart from the judicial decision: "The prophesies of what the courts will do in fact, and nothing more pretentious, are what I mean by the law."[8] It was on the basis of such predictions of judicial response that individuals determined their mutual rights and obligations and patterned their conduct so as to avoid the punitive sanction of the state. They conditioned their behavior on the expectation that courts would respond in a certain way, favorably or not, should such conduct be brought before them. Of course, their prediction, like Mr. Smith's, could be wrong. It was the difficulty the average person experienced when making such predictions that drove them to lawyers, the expert seers of court behavior. But the law was emphatically not a system of clear rules that could be discovered logically by the meditative oracle Blackstone described.

One may ask at this point, what about statutes, constitutions, precedents, and similar legal instruments? Are not these written texts the vessels of the law? The realist's response would be to concede the importance of these legal instruments, but to caution against an easy equation of written text with law. Frequently, when a court is confronted with a case, there may be precedents that appear to favor both Mr. Smith and Ms. Jones. Alternatively, several statutes may appear to apply to a case, and courts must choose which one governs a particular situation. More often than the public realizes, statutes or other written texts are vague or ambiguous. Their terms are in need of definition. Or the court will have to determine whether or not a statute or constitutional provision applies to a certain set of events in the first place. All written sources of law require interpretation, which amounts to circumscribed rule making for the particular set of facts presented in a case. For the realist, this turns the judge into a significant lawmaker.

One example will suffice. New technologies often present new challenges for the legal system. Sometimes new technologies create new criminal opportunities. Disturbed by the rising frequency of auto thefts, Congress, in 1919, passed the National Motor Vehicle Theft Act, proscribing the transportation of a stolen motor vehicle across a state line. The statute defined a "motor vehicle" as including "an automobile, automobile truck, automobile wagon, motor cycle, or any other self-propelled vehicle not designed for running on rails." On the basis of this statute, several "prophesies of what the courts will do in fact" could easily be made for some factual situations. We could predict with confidence that a criminal conviction, followed by a fine or imprisonment, would befall one who transported over a state line a stolen Volkswagen, firetruck, bus, or electric golf cart. We also can be pretty sure one would not be prosecuted, at least not under this statute, for transporting into the next state a stolen baby carriage, skateboard, tricycle, or train.

In 1931, the United States Supreme Court received an appeal from one McBoyle, convicted for having flown a stolen airplane from Illinois to Oklahoma. The question the Court had to resolve, and an important one for McBoyle, was whether a stolen airplane was comprehended by the National Motor Vehicle Theft Act. Surely an airplane was "self-propelled" and did not run on rails. The word "vehicle" could have been used to describe an airplane. Yet the use of the word by the average person was more likely to connote a device that moved across land. To this day, we would probably use a word like "craft" to describe an airplane. So what was the law in McBoyle's case, and how did the Court know? Could they have "discovered" by logical cogitation a law that existed prior to judgment? Or did the Court, which incidentally included Justice Holmes, have to "make law" in the process of explicating the scope of the word *vehicle?*

It is not likely that McBoyle consulted a lawyer when filing his flight plan. Had he sought advice of counsel, however, the lawyer could have told him: "Every specific example of a 'vehicle' found in the statute refers to land-bound instruments. Surely Congress, in 1919, knew of the existence of aircraft, and had it intended stolen airplanes to be included in the law could have said so explicitly. Besides, there is a rule courts tend to observe in criminal cases that requires them to interpret the meaning of a penal statute narrowly. You run a risk of federal indictment, but odds are you'll beat it. Whether the state of Illinois could prosecute and convict you under one of its own laws is another matter." McBoyle's lawyer would have been making a prophecy of how a court would actually respond—in this case, an accurate one, for the Court reversed McBoyle's conviction for those very reasons, in an opinion authored by Justice Holmes.[9]

After the Court's decision in *McBoyle v. United States,* we would be better able to make confident predictions regarding airplanes. Of course, we would have to rethink our prediction after Congress, in 1945, amended the statute, adding: "Wherever motor vehicle appears in this Act it shall read motor vehicle or airplane." But now, consider the rule of law for one who flies to another state in a stolen helicopter, a blimp, or hang glider (suppose the hang glider had a small motor)? Could we merely discover an existing rule? Or do we once again need to make one up, taking our cue from the statute and from the *McBoyle* case?

If law is unclear until courts apply it to facts, we would have to consider the possibility that the subjective values of the judge might enter into the process of adjudication. This is not to say that judges make decisions arbitrarily, based on nothing more than personal whim. Were that so, a prediction of how a court would react to a set of facts would be impossible. Judges generally share a desire to make decisions that lend consistency and evenhandedness to the law. Decisions must also conform to the expectations of the legal community by exhibiting certain characteristics of technical excellence. These include a written justification of the decision demonstrating its conformity to the appropriate legal text, traditions, judicial precedents, and canons of legal thought.

Realists frequently agreed that decisions are respected by the legal community to the degree they can be shown to be consistent with, even if not derived from, premises drawn from previous judicial decisions. Another judge in the realist tradition, Benjamin N. Cardozo, wrote:

> One of the most fundamental social interests is that law shall be uniform and impartial. There must be nothing in its action that savors of prejudice or favor or even arbitrary whim or fitfulness. Therefore in the main there shall be adherence to precedent. There shall be symmetrical development, consistently with history or custom when history or custom have been motive force, or the chief one, in giving shape to existing rules, and with logic and philosophy when the motive power has been theirs.[10]

Notice that in this formulation, adherence to precedent, or by implication the repudiation of precedent, was justified because it was useful, and not because it was the only solution to a case that some deified notion of reason will allow.

So there was an element of objectivity in the judicial decision, but it was put there by judges. The law might not determine the precise result in a hard case like *McBoyle,* but general agreement among judges on certain elements of proper legal technique did fix boundaries within which judicial discretion might be exercised. To the extent that some realists seemed to say that judicial decisions were mere products of subjective will, they overstated their case, but clearly the formalists' logical syllogism leading to wholly objective decision making did not accurately explain the judicial decision either. While judges might strive toward objectivity, the ideal of the impersonal decision was ultimately unobtainable. Cardozo portrayed the judicial decision as incorporating elements of discovery with elements of creativity, with the exact proportion of ingredients varying according to the specific case before the court:

> The traditions of our jurisprudence commit us to objective standards. I do not mean, of course, that this ideal of objective vision is ever perfectly attained. We cannot transcend the limitations of the ego and see everything as it really is. None the less, the ideal is one to be striven for within the limits of our capacity.
>
> If you ask how [the judge] is to know when one interest outweighs another, I can only answer that he must get his knowledge just as a legislator gets it, from experience and study and reflection; in brief, from life itself. Here indeed is the point of contact between the legislator's work and his. . . . Each is indeed legislating within the limits of his competence. No doubt the limits of the judge are narrower. He legislates only between the gaps.[11]

Cardozo's picture of a judge legislating "only between the gaps" —sometimes referred to as *interstitial legislating*—was an important one. It preserved some of the ideal of objectivity, for it suggested that the breadth of a judge's discretion was narrowly confined by previously existing legal standards. Yet it also recognized that to a significant degree judges made hard decisions when rules were vague, when multiple rules seemed to apply to a case and produced differing results, when a rule seemed outdated or resulted in manifest injustice, or when no applicable rule could be found. For Cardozo, there remained a substantial difference between a judge and a legislator, even if at times their respective roles intersected.

The scope of a judge's choice was narrower than that of a legislator. Further, the judge remained passive, whereas the legislator was a self-starting activist:

> The judge, even when he is free, is still not wholly free. He is not to innovate at pleasure. He is not a knight-errant roaming at will in pursuit of his own ideal of beauty or of goodness. He is to draw his inspiration from consecrated principles. He is not to yield to spasmodic sentiment, to vague and unregulated benevolence. He is to exercise discretion informed by tradition, methodized by analogy, disciplined by system, and subordinated to "the primordial necessity of order in the social life."[12]

Judges were not mere technicians, but from time to time had to make political choices. Consequently, not only should political scientists care about judges, but judges should care equally about politics. Holmes chided judges for not being more sensitive to the political ramifications of their decisions:

> I think that the judges themselves have failed adequately to recognize their duty of weighing considerations of social advantage. The duty is inevitable, and the result of the often proclaimed judicial aversion to deal with such considerations is simply to leave the very ground and foundation of judgments inarticulate, and often unconscious, as I have said.[13]

Formalism viewed law as a set of neutral standards that, if dispassionately applied by a correctly reasoning judge, would mediate relations between individuals and among groups in society without favor or prejudice. Law was an impartial umpire. Realists challenged this view by showing how legal decisions reflected competing conceptions of the mores and politics of the times, as the interests and values of judges seeped into the reasoning process. Logic, rather than guaranteeing impartial applications of preexisting legal concepts, served to rationalize, and sometimes only to obscure, the political choices that judicial decisions represented. Since judges were inevitably social engineers, Holmes and Cardozo called on them to make their values explicit and to settle disputes in a way conducive to the needs of social justice.

Much legal writing after the initial wave of realist criticism consisted of various attempts to rescue the legal objectivity promised by Blackstone's formalism, even if only to a partial degree. Many of these writers sought to build on Cardozo's balance of discretion and objectivity, often seeking to enhance the latter by confining the former. Thus, a kind of neoformalism became dominant, as legal theorists depicted courts as having a narrow range of creative choice, yet as bounded by overriding objective principles. Some advocated "neutral principles" as a guide for judicial discretion, the theory that judges perform a role in social engineering but must do so based on dispassionate principled argument, without regard for the individual parties of a dispute or the cause they represent. We will later encounter those who today contend that such neutral principles can be legitimately derived only from the specific intentions of those who framed the legal text applied to a case. Others found objective limits to judicial creativity in ideal moral principles that could be determined with relative certainty, or in economic models of analysis emphasizing efficiency in the social allocation of benefits and burdens.[14] All of these sought to confine subjective choice by judges, fearing that excessively freewheeling judicial policy making threatened the democratic nature of our politics.

The contribution of legal realism was to expose a myriad of ways in which the law was indeterminate and to describe the ways in which courts made a creative contribution to the shaping of public policy. Realists tended to explore the indeterminacy of the legal decision in terms of textual ambiguity, the multiplicity of rules pertinent to a given question, and the psychological predispositions of judges. Since the mid-1970s, heirs of the realist tradition, members of the Critical Legal Studies (CLS) movement, have explored further the creative role of political values in adjudication. In their view, the source of legal ambiguity is itself thoroughly political, and judicial discretion is exposed and criticized by CLS as part of their broader political agenda of restructuring the community along more egalitarian and democratic lines.

Scholars of CLS accept much of the realist critique of formalism and go on to repudiate the rescue efforts of the neoformalists. In the view of CLS, neutral principles, moral speculation or economic analysis are not useful in guiding the judicial decisions toward objectively correct answers, since they are themselves ambiguous. We are left to wonder what content will be embodied in the neutral principles or moral concepts. Economic analysis will produce results that appear objective, but only after one has chosen from among competing political visions the variables to be subjected to a cost/benefit calculation and the values to be assigned to them. Thus, attempts to reassert limited formalism serve to push ambiguity to a higher level of analysis, but they do not eliminate the need for creative choice by judges.

Even worse from the CLS perspective, such attempts to reintroduce objectivity into the law are not politically neutral. Rather, they reflect ideological values that often advance specific class interests. By pushing the value choice to a higher level of analysis, these theories succeed in obscuring the political foundations beneath judicial outcomes. Thus, political decisions are wrapped within the cloak of neutral legal principles more for purposes of mystification and diversion of public scrutiny than to achieve dispassionate justice. The result is an elitist decision making tending to preserve the dominant power and status of entrenched interests, insulated from criticism by others.

Critical Legal Studies scholars also go into new intellectual territory to portray law as constitutive ideology. That is to say, in addition to the by now commonplace assertion that judicial decisions are shaped to a substantial degree by politics, CLS views law itself as a product of politics in a more profound double sense. First, legal categories such as contract, tort, personal responsibility or individual constitutional rights are not timeless or politically neutral categories, as legal thought tends to portray them. They are in fact contingent products of particular political cultures that happen to exist at particular times and places. Whereas the formalist tends to see a legal rule as true simply because it is the logical outcome of correct reasoning, CLS treats rules as the temporary outcome of political struggles among competing groups in society, whether these are understood as socioeconomic classes, racial, or gender-based groups. Each group or faction has its own specific ideology, or way of understanding the world and constructing its own moral universe. Each seeks to impress its morality into law, but each succeeds only partially. As society is racked with conflict, or in the argot of CLS, "contradiction," so too the law is riddled with ambiguity, inconsistency, and tension.

Critical Legal Studies writers do not portray law as merely a product of pluralist bargaining. Not only is society ridden by factions, but the consciousness of groups, and even of individuals, reflects this same tension through inconsistent and self-contradictory thought processes. So law is ambiguous not only in its application, as depicted by realists, but ambiguity seeps into law at its very inception, as we think about the nature of society, of human needs, and of our goals of social justice. Most notably, conflicting yearnings for individual autonomy and communal solidarity produce legal thought that is inconsistent, and therefore indeterminate, at its most fundamental level.[15]

Rather than being the product of pure reason, law represents the relative power brought to bear on a certain issue by diverse groups, and consequently may be to some quite unreasonable. But these groups compete not only for the power to determine how a given kind of conflict—say a case alleging racial discrimination in the job market—will be settled. They compete over how that problem will be defined and understood. Courts are one forum in which this competition is played out, as attorneys for the two contending sides seek a determination favoring their client's interests. Discretion exists in the judicial decision not only because legal principles are vague, but because the law offers multiple and conflicting premises from which judges may construct a legal description of reality—say, as a case pitting one discrete individual's property rights against another discrete individual's desire for equal status and economic opportunity, rather than as a case of one group's subordination and economic exploitation of another group resulting in a kind of domestic colonialism. If law can be construed by courts in different ways, it can be used to reaffirm and legitimize some groups' ideological depiction of what is rational or politically conceivable and to disparage others'. Litigation, then, is not simply about the allocation of valued goods, opportunities, or status any more than it is the unfolding of pure reason. It is a conflict between various groups' preferred definitions of such values as liberty, equality, rights or interests, or conceptions of social justice. It is, at the deepest level, a contest over how we will describe ourselves and our complex social relationships.

Second, if law is a product of ideological conflict, it also helps to shape and limit the directions that ideological consciousness might take. In this sense, law is a powerful force in guiding the ways in which individuals may understand society and their place in it. Law and politics then exert a reciprocal influence on each other. As law reflects an underlying pattern of social relationships, so too it supplies intellectual blinders that cause us to construe social reality in certain ways and prevent us from seeing alternative possibilities. In this way, law contributes mightily to the maintenance of the status quo, although in ways not fully understood by realism. Not only does law preserve certain power relationships in society, it also limits the ways in which we can think about those power relationships (perhaps by denying that they involve power at all) and thus ensures the continued reproduction of existing social relations.

To return to the example of the discrimination suit, law limits our comprehension of racial discrimination, in a sense permitting us to understand it only as the prejudice-motivated acts of discrete individuals. This view is only one of a number of possible interpretations of reality, but having been placed in law it tends to eliminate all competing views. Not surprisingly, the view of racial discrimination as individual prejudice-motivated acts favors the interests of the white majority in perpetuating its status and power. It does this by focusing our attention on isolated acts of individual wrongdoers, rather than on broad social processes of group subordination, or "institutional discrimination." Thus, discrimination law might inhibit our comprehension of the problem of discrimination, and so too our ability to solve the problem it poses for the community.[16]

Notice that we are referring here to our ability to conceive of and understand a problem, even prior to developing a political strategy for its resolution. One prominent member of CLS, Robert Gordon, has described this power of law:

Many Critical writers would, I think, claim not only that law figures as a factor in the power relationships of individuals and social classes, but also that it is omnipresent in the very marrow of society—that law-making and law-interpreting institutions have been among the primary sources of the pictures of order and disorder, virtue and vice, reasonableness and craziness, realism and visionary naivete, and of some of the most commonplace aspects of social reality that ordinary people carry around with them and use in ordering their lives. To put this another way, the power exerted by a legal regime consists less in the force that it can bring to bear against violators of its rules than in its capacity to persuade people that the world described in its images and categories is the only attainable world in which a sane person would want to live.[17]

If the members of CLS are correct, then the judicial decision is even more deeply embedded in the political processes of society than previously supposed. Judicial decisions do more than authoritatively allocate valued goods for a society: they help to define that society in the eyes of its own members, and so condition the kinds of social possibilities that can be imagined, or deemed "respectable." In this sense, judicial decisions should be seen as moments in the creation (and recreation) of the collective consciousness of a community. Critical Legal Studies scholars contend that this creation of social consciousness, or ideology, is far from impartial. It tends to perpetuate a worldview favorable to the power of elite classes and obscures and mystifies the nature of their domination over others.

To expose this function of construing the intellectual categories of social reality, CLS writers engage in close and richly textured analysis of legal doctrine. This has the unfortunate—and for radical egalitarians, paradoxical—effect of making CLS literature exceptionally ponderous and obscure. So far, the insights generated by CLS analysis have been available only to law professors and similar academic elites. Also, the proposition that law helps to shape the social consciousness of society beyond the restricted legal community of lawyers, judges, and law professors is an empirical question that CLS has not investigated empirically. Instead, this fundamental tenet of the CLS critique of law is left to assumption. Nevertheless, even if we treat the insight tentatively, it must still cause political scientists to take renewed interest in the judicial process.

In this brief introduction to legal decision making, we have already seen that the judicial process is a complex one. Adjudication, the business of courts, occurs within the form of personalized dispute resolution. Yet, if the critics of formalism are correct, the ramifications of litigation reach deeply into the political process, helping to structure social conflict, affecting the outcome of political competition, and perhaps contributing to the ideological reflection a society carries of itself.

In the ensuing chapters, we will explore in greater detail the ways in which politics and litigation intersect. The next chapter will describe the structure of the national court system. We shall then explore, in Chapters 3 and 4, some of the politics of staffing the courts and the problem of reconciling the values of judicial independence and democratic accountability. This problem will not be resolved solely through the issues of judicial selection and discipline. Reconciling the political role of courts with the democratic postulates most of us assume form the basis of American society has become the focus of much scholarly activity over the past decade. In the final two chapters, we will explore further the nature of judicial decision making and the degree to which it might be determined by legal norms. There we will look inside the courts and examine how judges make their decisions as part of the common law tradition, as interpreters of statutes, and as stewards of the Constitution. The issue will be how deeply courts should intrude into politics. We shall see that in qualified form, formalism still has its proponents, and not without good reason.

Our discussion up to this point already causes us to qualify considerably Professor Shapiro's description of courts. We can see how the application of previously existing norms becomes problematic as a criterion defining "courtness." As Professor Shapiro concedes, such norms as exist are to some degree indeterminate. The result is that the distinction between judges and legislators is a bit more blurred than is commonly understood to be the case. This will call into question simple theories of the separation of powers. The intersections of adjudicating with legislating should be noted in the ensuing chapters. We shall also be challenging simple, unqualified assumptions of judicial passivity. For our limited purposes, less attention will be given to the more technical qualifications on adversity and to the dichotomous decision. The student should be warned at this point that many of the comfortable assumptions he or she may have lived with so far depend in some sense on the formalist model of judicial decision making. As we challenge formalism, the student must be willing to rethink much of what he or she currently understands about law, about government, and about society. The compensation will be a greater understanding of the way our society operates.

NOTES

1. Alexis de Tocqueville, *Democracy in America,* trans. George Lawrence, ed. J. P. Mayer (Anchor Press, New York, 1969) p. 270.
2. Ibid., p. 99.
3. The second through the fifth tenets of adjudication are from Martin Shapiro, *Courts: A Comparative and Political Analysis* (University of Chicago, Chicago, 1981) p. 1. Shapiro develops a framework for analyzing courts in many nations. The first tenet, essential for understanding American courts, is respectfully added for our narrower purposes.
4. William Blackstone, *Commentaries on the Laws of England,* vol. I (Robert H. Small, Philadelphia, 1825) p. 62.
5. Ibid., p. 63 (emphasis in original).
6. Shapiro, op. cit., p. 8.
7. Oliver Wendell Holmes, Jr., *The Common Law* (Harvard University Press, Cambridge, Massachusetts, 1963) p. 1.
8. Oliver Wendell Holmes, Jr., "The Path of the Law," 10 *Harvard Law Review* 457, 461 (1897).
9. *McBoyle v. United States,* 283 U.S. 25 (1931).
10. Benjamin N. Cardozo, *The Nature of the Judicial Process* (Yale University Press, New Haven, Connecticut, 1921) p. 112.
11. Ibid., pp. 106, 113.
12. Ibid., p. 114.

13. Oliver Wendell Holmes, Jr., "The Path of the Law," 10 *Harvard Law Review* 457, 467 (1897).

14. For a representative sample, see Herbert Weschler, "Toward Neutral Principles of Constitutional Law," 73 *Harvard Law Review* 1 (1959), Robert H. Bork, *The Tempting of America* (Free Press, New York, 1990), Ronald Dworkin, *Taking Rights Seriously* (Harvard University Press, Cambridge, Massachusetts, 1977), Richard Posner, *The Economics of Justice* (Harvard University Press, Cambridge, Massachusetts, 1981).

15. See generally, Duncan Kennedy, "Form and Substance in Private Law Adjudication," 89 *Harvard Law Review* 1685 (1976), "The Structure of Blackstone's Commentaries," 28 *Buffalo Law Review* 205 (1979), Umberto M. Unger, *The Critical Legal Studies Movement* (Harvard University Press, Cambridge, Massachusetts, 1983).

16. Alan Freeman, "Legitimizing Racial Discrimination Through Anti-Discrimination Law: A Critical Review of Supreme Court Doctrine," in Allan C. Hutchinson, ed., *Critical Legal Studies* (Rowman & Littlefield, Totowa, New Jersey, 1989) p. 120.

17. Robert W. Gordon, "Critical Legal Histories," in Allan C. Hutchinson, op. cit., p. 97.

Chapter
2

The Federal Court System

In this chapter our concerns will be primarily institutional. We will explore the structure and organization of the federal courts, with an eye toward how these might constrain or otherwise affect judicial policy making. We should note at the outset that political institutions do not spring forth whole, by a process of spontaneous generation. They are the products of political struggle. Since political conflict is a persistent part of social reality, we should expect institutions to be continuously recreated in the course of a society's political development. Political institutions do not solidify like concrete, but remain in dynamic flux. We shall see that throughout our history, discussion of the federal courts has been highly politicized. The direction in which the judiciary has developed has been a product of the shifting balance of power between state governments on one hand and the national government on the other. In more recent times, the development of federal courts has reflected the tension between legislative and executive power that was built into the Constitution. Although the power of the judiciary has waxed and waned over the two centuries of our national existence, courts have always been the subject of keen attention from other branches of the government. Interest groups seeking to influence the political, economic, and cultural development of the American community have also had a hand in shaping the judiciary. None of this should be surprising, for the courts of the United States exercise considerable influence in our national life and have never been far from the political fray for very long.

THE CONSTITUTIONAL CONVENTION OF 1787

Prior to American independence, the judges who presided over colonial courts were appointed by the king of England and served at his pleasure. Not only could a judge who displeased the king be removed from office by royal fiat, but their salaries were fixed annually. A judge's salary could be increased or reduced to pressure him to favor imperial interests in litigation. Not surprisingly, colonists viewed royal judges not as impartial adjudicators of disputes, but as an extension of British domination over colonial affairs, ruling on legal disputes in a prejudicial manner that denied justice to local interests. Bitterly resented by the local population, most royal judges fled to Nova Scotia or Britain when America finally gained independence.

After promulgating the Declaration of Independence in 1776, the Continental Congress called upon the 13 states to draft new constitutions establishing governments more conducive to "republican" principles. Some states made profound changes in their systems of government. Although these took several different forms, the general practice of the states was to concentrate enormous power in their legislatures. In revulsion against the years of heavy-handed administration of law by royal judges, state courts were considerably weakened. Judges were generally appointed by legislatures. Often, their continued tenure in office as well as their salaries were left to the annual discretion of legislative majorities. If adjudication had previously been unduly influenced by royal power, the effect of this legislative supremacy in the new state governments was to leave judges vulnerable to pressure by whatever factions held the upper hand in local politics. The wealthier classes, in particular, feared the loss of vested property rights through legislative interference in the adjudication of legal claims.

Despite his own subsequent suspicion of judicial power, Thomas Jefferson spoke for many when he complained about the politics of Virginia as early as 1781:

> All the powers of government, legislative, executive and judiciary, result to the legislative body. The concentration of these in the same hands is precisely the definition of despotic government. It will be no alleviation that these powers will be exercised by a plurality of hands, and not by a single one. 173 despots would surely be as oppressive as one. . . . An elective despotism was not the government we fought for. . . .[1]

For Jefferson, the cause of this legislative despotism was clear. In common with other states, Virginia's constitution was defective because its framers had:

> . . . laid its foundation on this basis, that legislative, executive and judiciary department ought to be separate and distinct, so that no person should exercise the powers of more than one of them at the same time. But no barrier was provided between these several powers. The judiciary and executive members were left dependent on the legislative, for their subsistence in office, and some of them for their continuance in it. If therefore, the legislature assumes executive and judiciary powers, no opposition is likely to be made; nor, if made, can be effectual. . . .[2]

Despite such difficulties, the task of governing the new nation between 1781 and 1789 was left almost exclusively in the separate and often competing hands of the 13 states. A very weak national legislature had been established under the Articles of Confederation, but this system failed to establish a unified nation able to administer its own policies in a consistent manner. Instead of a national entity, the Articles of Confederation created only a "firm league of friendship" between the states, with the latter retaining all "sovereignty, freedom and independence, and every Power, Jurisdiction and Right" that the Articles did not "expressly" delegate to "the United States, in Congress assembled."[3] Among the powers jealously withheld by the states was adjudication. There was no system of courts created under the authority of the national government, save one having a maritime jurisdiction only. Aside from captures of vessels during time of war or piracy or the commission of felonies on the high seas, the resolution of all legal disputes was to be obtained in state courts. One other minor exception was that the national legislature held a narrow authority to resolve boundary disputes between states. Adjudication of disputes between individuals that occurred on land could not be moved out of the reach of local majorities in each state, where to a large extent partisanship replaced justice.

Much of the motivation behind the Constitutional Convention of 1787 was to remove certain areas of policy from the hands of local interests that dominated state politics. A strong national government immune from state parochialism was advocated by federalists to promote the "disinterested" (we would today say "impartial") pursuit of the common good. Since one of the areas of policy where such disinterestedness was most lacking was in the adjudication of legal disputes, the solution was a national judiciary having jurisdiction over certain sensitive subjects.

Agreement on this much was simple. The hard question was whether Americans wanted a far-reaching system of national courts, with judges insulated from political pressure, supplanting a major portion the state courts' business. Federalists believed that only such a broad system of national courts would be able to insulate nationally protected rights from the abuses of local majorities. Alexander Hamilton was to write in Federalist Paper #22:

> [The consolidation of judicial power in a unified system of courts] is the more necessary where the frame of government is so compounded that the laws of the whole are in danger of being contravened by the laws of the parts. In this case, if the particular [state] tribunals are invested with a right of ultimate jurisdiction, besides the contradictions to be expected from the difference of opinion there will be much to fear from the bias of local views and prejudices and from the interference of local regulations. As often as such an interference was to happen, there would be reason to apprehend that the provisions of the particular [state] laws might be preferred to those of the [national] laws; from the deference which men in office naturally look up to that authority to which they owe their official existence. . . . The faith, the reputation, the peace of the whole Union are thus continually at the mercy of the prejudices, the passions, and the interests of every member [state] of which it is composed.[4]

Although the exact nature and scope of judicial powers would remain controversial for nearly a century, the delegates to the Constitutional Convention favored the creation of some kind of national judiciary, one that could at a minimum decide appeals on questions of national law in cases previously tried in the state courts. But would they go further? Would a complete system of national courts be created, one with lower courts that could try federal cases and remove all questions of national law entirely from the grasp of the state courts? Early in the convention's deliberations, the leader of the Virginia delegation, Governor Edmund Randolph, introduced a set of proposals (largely authored by James Madison) that became a sort of working draft for the Constitution eventually to be created. Included among Randolph's proposals was Resolution #9, which stated:

> Resolved that a National Judiciary be established to consist of one or more supreme tribunals, and of inferior tribunals to be chosen by the National Legislature, to hold their offices during good behavior; and to receive punctually at stated times fixed compensation for their services, in which no increase or decrease shall be made so as to affect the persons actually in office, at the time of such increase or diminution.[5]

The Virginia Plan, as it became known, also included a broad statement of jurisdiction for the national courts, ultimately including all legal "questions which may involve the national peace and harmony."

The Virginia Plan was quite sweeping in its transfer of powers from the states to the national government. Among its other provisions was a bicameral national legislature, with both houses apportioned by population, and with authority to legislate on all matters on which it deemed the separate states to be "incompetent" or where "the harmony of the United States may be interrupted by the exercise of individual legislation."[6] This provision would have created a congress of virtually unlimited jurisdiction. Furthermore, the national legislature was to veto all state laws that it believed to contravene the Constitution. Viewing such proposals, it did not take long for the smaller states to begin to fear domination by larger states such as Massachusetts, Pennsylvania, or, not coincidentally, Virginia. In response to the sweeping proposals offered by the Virginia delegation, New Jersey delegate William Paterson offered a hastily prepared counterproposal. While not adopted by the convention, Paterson's proposal did serve to unite sufficient opposition to the Virginia Plan to force concessions from the larger states, moderating considerably the powers of the national government.

Significantly, even Paterson's proposal, known today as the New Jersey Plan, included a provision for a national judiciary on which judges would have secured tenure and salary.[7] However, the New Jersey Plan proposed a supreme court only, absent any system of lower courts created by the national government. Prosecutions for the violation of national laws, and presumably civil lawsuits involving claims under national law, would be heard first in state courts. Their decisions would be subject to appeal to the national tribunal. The scope of valid national law was itself narrowly confined to the regulation of commerce between states and with foreign nations and to the raising of revenue, but without the potentially limitless legislative powers of the Virginia Plan.

With the two proposals now on the table, battle lines among the convention's delegates were sharply drawn. The New Jersey Plan envisioned a national government that would be a much smaller presence in the life of the nation and a judiciary that would be a smaller presence in the national government than was called for by the Virginia Plan. The proponents of decentralization and state power faced off against proponents of centralized national power. The former included John Rutledge, of South Carolina, Roger Sherman, from Connecticut, and the ever-cantankerous Luther Martin, of Maryland. These delegates preferred to have most adjudication performed by the state courts, which remained under the control of local majorities represented in the state legislatures. Rutledge, for example, argued that the creation of lower national courts by the Virginia Plan would pose "an unnecessary encroachment on the jurisdiction of the States." Appeal from the state courts to a single national supreme court would be adequate "to secure the national rights & uniformity of Judgments."[8] The states, he warned, would surely resist any invasions of their prerogatives such as that posed by the Virginia Plan's system of lower national courts.

Federalists such as James Madison, representing Virginia, Alexander Hamilton, from New York, and James Wilson, of Pennsylvania, advocated a complete national judiciary that would insulate the settlement of legal disputes from the very local power delegates like Rutledge sought to protect. Madison argued that "an effective Judiciary establishment commensurate to the legislative authority, was essential. A government without a proper Executive & Judiciary would be a mere trunk of a body without arms or legs to act or move."[9] Lower national courts were seen as necessary to avoid an impossible multiplication of appeals to the supreme tribunal. Implicit in Madison's argument was a distrust of the quality of justice to be had in local courts.

Votes were cast in the Constitutional Convention on a state-by-state basis. When Rutledge's motion to omit all reference to lower national courts from the Virginia Plan passed by a margin of five states to four (the delegations of New York and Massachusetts were divided and unable to vote), Madison and Wilson were forced to offer a compromise, one that effectively put off the question of lower national courts until another day. Observing that "there was a distinction between establishing such tribunals absolutely, and giving a discretion to the Legislature to establish or not to establish them," Madison proposed that a supreme court be created by the Constitution, while Congress would subsequently wrestle with the question of whether or not to create lower national courts.[10] This measure was adopted, resulting in the permissive language now included in Article III:

> The judicial Power of the United States, shall be vested in one Supreme Court, and in such inferior Courts as the Congress may from time to time ordain and establish.

For good measure, Article I provided that Congress shall have the power to "constitute Tribunals inferior to the supreme court." What Congress might create, Congress might also choose not to create, but no decision would have to be made at the moment. Delay was only a temporary form of compromise, however, and the arguments against a national judiciary first heard at the Constitutional Convention were not abandoned. They would soon be taken up by the opponents of the Constitution, today known as antifederalists, and still later by the state's rights followers of Thomas Jefferson. Remnants of the friction between these two camps can be found in contemporary American politics as well, in the tension between centralization and localism that still animates relations between the state and federal judiciaries. Even the internal politics of the federal judiciary are not immune from the conflict that erupted that summer of 1787, as we shall see in Chapter 3.

If the federalists had to duck and weave on the question of the structure of the national judiciary, they carried the day on the question of the scope of judicial powers. Article III extends judicial power to:

> . . . all Cases, in Law and Equity, arising under this Constitution, the laws of the United States, and treaties made, or which shall be made, under their authority.

Federal jurisdiction might be exercised according to the nature of the issues present in a case—whenever rights or duties were claimed under the Constitution, federal laws, and treaties and in all maritime cases. Alternatively, jurisdiction was authorized according to the nature of the parties to a lawsuit—ambassadors or other foreign ministers and consuls, states, a state and a citizen of a different state, citizens of different states, the United States, or a foreign nation or a citizen of a foreign nation—even if the legal questions present would normally be tried under state law.

In addition, Article VI incorporated a provision first offered by Paterson's New Jersey Plan, providing that:

> This Constitution, and the Laws of the United States which shall be made in pursuance thereof; and all treaties made, or which shall be made, under the Authority of the United States, shall be the supreme Law of the Land; and the judges in the several states shall be bound thereby, any Thing in the Constitutions or Laws of any State to the Contrary notwithstanding.

The purpose of this "supremacy clause" was to ensure state conformity to valid assertions of national power. Significantly, the clause assigned to courts the role of guaranteeing such conformity, although it was left unclear whether "the judges in the several states" referred exclusively to state judges, or whether it included judges on lower federal courts that happen to be convened "in the several states." At any rate, since Article III gave the Supreme Court appellate powers in all cases "arising under this Constitution," subject to exceptions that might be created by Congress, it was clear that the interpretation of national laws by either state or lower federal courts could be made subject to ultimate supervision by a single supreme court, as even the New Jersey Plan had allowed.

Another issue the Constitutional Convention chose not to decide was the size and composition of the Supreme Court, deferring another potentially divisive question to future legislative politics. Even with these concessions, many Americans greeted the creation of a national judiciary with something falling short of unbridled enthusiasm. Antifederalists feared that a nationally supported judiciary would become an instrument for the gradual expansion of national powers, to the diminution of the states. One prominent writer, known to us only by the pseudonym Brutus, foresaw the dangers of a politicized judiciary. The judges, he warned, "will not confine themselves to any fixed or established rules, but will determine, according to what appeals to them, the reason and spirit of the constitution."[11] Not trusting the formalist depiction of judicial decision making we examined in Chapter 1, Brutus feared the politicized decisions of a national judiciary with no appeal to legislative authority to correct their abuses. Thus, federal courts would:

> . . . operate to effect, in the most certain, but yet silent and imperceptible manner, what is evidently the tendency of the constitution;—I mean, an entire subversion of the legislative, executive and judicial powers of the individual states. Every adjudication of the supreme court, on any question that may arise upon the nature and extent of the general government, will affect the limits of the state jurisdiction. In proportion, as the former enlarge the exercise of their powers, will that of the latter be restricted.[12]

In addition, the more populist elements among the antifederalists saw in the judiciary the seeds of a professional aristocracy of lawyers and judges. Then as now, court hearings followed complex procedures not well understood by the lay public. To the extent courts came to be relied on for the resolution of disputes, ordinary people would become dependent on this highly paid and self-interested professional cadre to determine the direction of social policy. Some states had experimented with simplified forums for dispute resolution, similar to modern small claims courts, in an attempt to make legal remedies more available regardless of the social status, education, or wealth of the aggrieved. Several states had even gone so far as to consider outlawing the practice of law. Virginia delegate George Mason, later a committed antifederalist, sounded very contemporary when he observed:

> The Judiciary of the United States is so constructed and extended, as to absorb and destroy the judiciaries of the several states; thereby rendering law as tedious, intricate and expensive, and justice as unattainable, by a great part of the community, as in England, and enabling the rich to oppress and ruin the poor.[13]

Upon ratification of the Constitution, most antifederalists pledged their loyalty to the new government, some even running for office. Many, however, remained suspicious of national power and sought to limit the extent of national judicial authority. In large respect, the tensions of the Constitutional Convention were brought to the First Congress that assembled in New York City in 1789. The novel governmental structure outlined by the new Constitution had to be completed and launched by legislation. Along the way, many of the divisive conflicts of the Constitutional Convention were reignited.

THE JUDICIARY ACT OF 1789 AND SUBSEQUENT DEVELOPMENTS

The new Constitution was so sketchy in many of its provisions that the questions remaining to be decided by the First Congress must have been daunting. Article II, for example, created a president and vice president, but referred only obliquely to the "principle Officer[s] in each of the executive Departments." While such officers might be required to report in writing to the president, Congress was left to decide what executive departments (i.e., Treasury, War, State, etc.) would be created to fill out the president's cabinet. Similarly, Article III obligated Congress to create a single supreme court. Congress was left such nagging questions as: How large should this supreme court be? Will there be lower federal courts, or would all questions of federal law be decided in the first instance by state courts? If lower federal courts were to be created, how would they be staffed? What procedures would they follow in adjudication? Would their jurisdiction include the full sweep of cases and parties indicated in Article III, or would they be restricted to some narrower ambit of power?

For the present discussion, we will confine our attention to two questions: the existence and composition of lower federal courts and the scope of their jurisdiction. We have already noted a consensus in favor of a national supreme court. Those defenders of local autonomy who feared the intrusion of a distant national government into their local affairs sought to confine the national judiciary to this court exclusively. Those in favor of an active national government were anxious to wrest adjudication under national laws away from the state courts altogether. They feared the supreme court alone would be unable to guarantee uniformity in the interpretation of national law or to provide impartial justice in cases affecting the parochial interests of local majorities. Discussion of the question of whether to create lower federal courts would be followed inevitably by the second question, involving the same division of partisans: How broad should the lower courts' jurisdiction be? These two questions occupied much of Congress's attention between April and September of 1789. The culmination of this debate was an extraordinary piece of legislation, the Judiciary Act of 1789.

Authored by Representative Oliver Ellsworth, who would later briefly occupy the office of chief justice of the Supreme Court, and strongly supported by fellow congressman and future justice William Paterson, who must have had a change of mind since the Constitutional Convention, the Judiciary Act of 1789 established in nascent form the three-tiered system of federal courts that we have to this day. It organized the Supreme Court, which would consist of a chief justice and five associate justices. It also created U.S. district courts as courts of first instance, or trial courts that would hear suits under federal law. There would be one such court for each of 13 districts, designed to be coterminous with the boundaries of each state. Each district court would have a single federal judge. In addition, the act created three circuit courts that would each travel throughout their respective circuit, each multistate circuit containing a number of federal districts. Circuit courts had significant trial jurisdiction and also some jurisdiction to decide appeals from district courts. To the consternation of Supreme Court justices for a century to come, these intermediate courts had no permanent staff or location for conducting business. Instead, one district judge would be joined by two Supreme Court justices (later changed to two district court judges and one justice) to twice annually ride between distant cities, over some of the worst roads nineteenth century America had to offer, to preside over trials. The premature death of at least one Supreme Court justice, James Iredell in 1799, was blamed on conditions endured while riding the very extensive and disease-ridden Southern Circuit. Nevertheless, circuit riding remained part of the life of a federal judge until the very end of the nineteenth century.

Creation of these lower federal courts represented a commitment to a system of parallel courts. This means a litigant whose case involved questions of federal law might commence a suit in state court, appeal through the state system, and then from an adverse judgment by the state's highest court appeal to the United

States Supreme Court. Alternatively, the litigant might commence the suit in the federal court having jurisdiction to hear such a case. The avenue of appeal might then lie to the circuit court, or from there to the Supreme Court. Thus, on federal questions, there would be two separate and metaphorically parallel routes to the Supreme Court. Viewed another way, the citizen was subject to the jurisdiction of two competing court systems, a consequence of federalism that makes American law a complicated affair to this day. However, the victory won by nationalist forces in creating this extensive system of federal courts was paid for with concessions on the scope of lower federal court jurisdiction.

Proponents of state power, the ideological descendants of the antifederalists, managed to secure a restricted federal court jurisdiction that would remain until after the Civil War. Although Article III of the Constitution created a very broad jurisdiction for federal courts, the district courts created by the act were confined to a very narrow field that included only maritime cases, import regulations, naturalization, counterfeiting, and treason. The circuit courts were given trial jurisdiction over certain criminal and civil matters as well as appellate jurisdiction over some of the matters triable in the district courts. However, the all-important issue of resolving clashes between state and federal laws was reserved for initial resolution by state courts. Under Section 25 of the Judiciary Act, state court judgments would be subject ultimately to appeal to the United States Supreme Court in cases involving a value in excess of $3000, a sizable sum for the time that kept most such suits firmly within the grasp of the state courts. Even where appeal was taken to the Supreme Court, that federal bench was still left in a position of responding to issues previously framed and decided by the state courts.

Even this compromise did not go far enough to satisfy some ardent state's rights advocates. The Supreme Court of Virginia would later attempt to block United States Supreme Court review of one of its controversial judgments by ruling that Section 25 of the Judiciary Act of 1789 was unconstitutional. In effect, the Virginia Court claimed that it was sovereign on all legal matters occurring within the boundaries of Virginia, even those concerning the meaning of federal laws. This attempt to insulate state courts from national appellate review was rebuffed by the United States Supreme Court in Martin v. Hunter's Lessee, decided ultimately in 1816.[14] Even this case did not end conflict between the federal and state benches.

Not until Congress enacted the Removal Act of 1875 did the federal district courts acquire full jurisdiction over cases raising federal questions. As used in law, "removal" refers to the power of a defendant who is claiming a federal right to take the case out of the state court and place it before a federal district court. This power of removal would be most desirable in circumstances where a defendant had reason not to trust local courts to provide a fair hearing on a federal claim. Given the suspicion of local politics shared by many of the federalists, the lack of removal prior to 1875 must be seen as a major concession indeed.

After the Civil War, Congress was confronted with the problem of protecting the rights guaranteed to the newly emancipated African-American population by Reconstruction civil rights acts. State courts in the vanquished confederacy could not be relied on adequately to protect such newly acquired rights as voting, the right to hold property, or the right to enter into contracts when these were asserted by former slaves. Hence, it was deemed necessary to enable litigants to transfer cases involving these rights to the federal courts, which were expected to be more sympathetic. In addition, the Removal Act created, for the first time, the possibility that litigation involving clashes between federal and state laws could commence in U.S. district courts. Hence, only in 1875 do we find the United States adopting a truly parallel court system, in practice as well as in theory. Since then, state and lower federal courts have shared power to interpret the meaning of federal laws.

One final legislative innovation needs to be mentioned. In 1891, Congress finally created permanent positions for judges on the intermediate circuit courts, thus relieving Supreme Court justices of their onerous circuit-riding duties. This was motivated by a problem still very much with us, the burgeoning caseload of the Supreme Court. Abolition of circuit riding not only gave justices more time to devote to the work of the Supreme Court, but also avoided the potentially embarrassing prospect of a justice having to hear an appeal from one of his own judgments in the lower court. In such frequently occurring circumstances, a justice who upheld himself would be viewed as prejudiced, while one who overruled himself would be viewed as incompetent! With this legislation, the United States acquired a fully developed three-tiered system of courts. Each level of courts had its own permanent judges and meeting places. Some years later, the circuit courts were renamed U.S. courts of appeals, although their geographic venues continued to be called circuits. Subject to some future revisions in procedure, we can date the modern federal court system from 1891. We have enjoyed its presence for only a century, or half of our existence as a nation.

Courts are likely to become the subject of political controversy to the degree that we mistrust formalism as an accurate depiction of judicial decision making. In Chapter 1, we saw that theoretical challenges to formalism were primarily a product of the late nineteenth and twentieth centuries. However, the suspicion that formalism did not accurately describe what judges were doing seems to have long been part of American politics, for courts have been controversial from the start. We see in this brief historical survey that while some important decisions concerning the judiciary were made at the Constitutional Convention of 1787, many more had to be put off for future legislative consideration. The framers of the Constitution were faced with a tension between the need for stability that could be provided by a strong central governing authority and the demand for local control over people's daily affairs. This tension remains characteristic of American politics, so we should not be surprised to learn that the conflict between national power and localism is very much part of contemporary judicial politics. Not only is there frequent tension between federal courts and state court systems, but the politics of judicial appointments to district and appeals courts, discussed in Chapter 3, build considerable localism into the federal judiciary itself. This localism sometimes places the lower federal courts in conflict with the policies of the Supreme Court. In the following sections, we will examine each level of federal court, with a view toward understanding the different role each plays in contemporary American legal (and political) affairs.

CONTEMPORARY LOWER FEDERAL COURT STRUCTURE

The greater responsibility for governing American society continues to lie in the states. While it has expanded its activities over the past half century to become a much greater presence in our lives, the federal government remains a government of limited functions. Similarly, federal courts carry only a small fraction of the burden of litigation in America. We can see this most clearly by comparing data on court filings—the total number of cases commenced before all trial courts or appeals brought to all higher courts—for the federal and state systems. A recent study of state courts by Harry Stumpf and John Culver found that of the 98 million cases filed in all American courts in 1988, 99.7 percent were filed in state and local courts![15] For every case filed in federal trial court that year, there were 100 state trial court filings, and for every federal appeal, 5 state appeals were lodged. However, these figures must be treated cautiously, particularly for trial courts. Not all filings constitute an equal demand on judicial resources. Many filings never go to trial at all. A large portion of the state trials represented here are traffic and minor ordinance violations that are quickly litigated before municipal tribunals. But not including those, state trials still outnumber federal trials by a ratio of nine to one. According to the same study, the caseloads of several states, California, New York, and Texas, to cite the three biggest, each exceed that of the federal courts several times over. Again, much of the workload of state courts of general jurisdiction consists of misdemeanors, divorces, and small claims cases, a large portion of which are uncontested and handled through a summary process that resembles administration more than adjudication. Qualitative comparison of the federal and state judiciaries is a risky enterprise, at best. The point here is simply to suggest that the federal bench is one of limited jurisdiction, and that most routine litigation affecting the lives of most people occurs before the state courts.

Fortunately, there are more state courts and state judges than there are federal courts and federal judges, thus enabling them to process all of this state litigation. State courts outnumber federal courts by a ratio of 150 to 1.[16] States, however, tend to have more complex judicial structures than the federal government has, with a great deal of fragmentation and duplication of forums. State systems include all municipal courts and courts of limited jurisdiction, such as family court, surrogate court, and a place some readers many have been, traffic court. State judges on trial courts outnumber their federal counterparts by 13 to 1, and state appeals judges outnumber their federal counterparts by 7 to 1. If these numbers sound surprisingly lopsided, recall that we are comparing 50 state judiciaries to one federal system.

Many important issues concerning the ways in which members of society relate to one another—everything from the definition and punishment of most crimes, to contractual arrangements on which our economic system depends, to the law of property, of family relations, and of torts (a body of law that regulates the level of care and consideration individuals must show for one another as they go about their daily lives)—are dealt with almost exclusively by the law of the 50 separate states. Except in unusual circumstances noted later, legal conflicts concerning these important but fairly routine areas of life are settled exclusively in state courts. The conflicts under federal laws most likely to be litigated in federal court concern an important but relatively narrow range of issues.

Having paid tribute to the importance of state judicial systems, we will now concentrate on the federal courts. Most of the great issues of the day that become the subject of extensive political controversy—from abortion, to church/state relations, to rights of the accused, to free speech and press, to environmental policy, to antitrust policy, to school desegregation—are subjects of federal litigation. When citizens think of courts as controversial political actors, they tend to think of the federal courts, and their perception tends to be correct. It is also difficult to generalize about 50 independent systems at any level of sophistication. The subject is worth a book in itself, but this is not it. Henceforth, we will consider only the federal judiciary.

As noted above, the United States has a three-tiered court structure. We will begin at the lowest level, the district courts, and proceed through the appellate courts. It should be stated immediately that the term lower court is not intended to signify any diminution of importance. To the contrary, the district courts and courts of appeals play very significant roles in legal policy making. In some ways, they may even overshadow the influence of the more visible Supreme Court.

United States District Courts

The United States has been divided by Congress into 89 districts, each of which has one district court. There is at least one district for each state, although some of the large and populous states are subdivided into several districts. In addition, there is a district court for the District of Columbia and one for the Commonwealth of Puerto Rico, for a total of 91 district courts having limited jurisdiction for the kinds of cases described in Article III of the Constitution. Finally, there is one district court for each of the territories of Guam, the Virgin Islands, and the Northern Mariana Islands. These last three are distinguished by the fact that they have jurisdiction over the local law of the territory as well as federal jurisdiction. They operate rather like a hybrid of state and federal courts. This brings the total to 94 district courts, each of which hears cases that arise within its geographic district. This plan represents a continuation of the scheme we saw originally adopted in the Judiciary Act of 1789, whereby districts were wholly contained by states. There is only one minor exception to this rule—the district for Wyoming includes all of Yellowstone National Park, small portions of which extend into Montana and Idaho.

There is considerable cultural diversity among the districts, so even as they are all part of the same network of federal courts, we should expect each to acquire a distinctly local character. For example, the United States District for Vermont, composed of two judges holding court in Burlington and Rutland, has accommodated the needs of a small, thinly populated, mainly rural state. During a single recent fiscal year (October 1, 1991–September 30, 1992), the district court received 454 civil and 135 criminal cases.[17] Since Vermont shares a border with Canada, its district court received a number of immigration cases—7. For much the same reason, drug trafficking is also a prominent part of the court's business, at 31 cases during that period. The 13 firearms cases further reflect something of the culture of Vermont. Other federal matters, such as tax questions, bankruptcies, or financial regulations, might come up as well, but infrequently. So far as federal law is concerned, there is not a great deal happening in Vermont.

Contrast Vermont with the United States District Court for the Southern District of New York, a densely populated district that includes boroughs of New York City (excluding Queens and Brooklyn) and some of its northern suburbs. Like Vermont, this is a northeastern district. Both are part of the Second Circuit and share the same appellate court. But there are obvious differences as well. New York City is a major port of entry and trade, creating heavy caseloads in the fields of immigration, import/export, and maritime law. As New York is a major financial center, housing much of the federally regulated banking system as well as the stock exchange, we would expect the caseload to reflect a heavy economic emphasis. For example, during the same fiscal year, the Southern District of New York outnumbered Vermont in embezzlement cases by a ratio of 77 to 2, in fraud by 272 to 21, and in civil contract cases by 2317 to 79. Broadcasting and publishing are concentrated in New York, reflected in the ratio versus Vermont for copyright, patent, and trademark cases of 564 to 15. Drug trafficking is also a part of the local culture, with 258 cases, dwarfing Vermont's 31.

The district court in Vermont can get by with only two judges. In contrast, the court in downtown Manhattan's Federal Plaza is the largest district court, with 28 judges. And with 10,038 civil and 1,131 criminal filings during the same year, the court in New York frequently had to borrow a judge from another district or rely on the part-time services of a retired judge to help process its heavy caseload.[18] Vermont's total of 589 filings is a light load when compared with the Southern District of New York's 11,169 filings. So both the volume and the subject matter of the district courts' work will vary according to local characteristics of population, economic conditions, and litigiousness. Both the number of judges and the type of cases that fill the docket of each court will affect its overall efficiency in processing cases.

Currently, a total of 649 U.S. district court judges are authorized by federal statute.[19] They are aided by 479 U.S. magistrate judges, who since 1968 have been authorized to conduct pretrial conferences, issue warrants or temporary restraining orders, try certain petty offenses, and perform other essentially administrative tasks, to free up more time for the district court judges to devote to litigation. A bevy of law clerks, bailiffs, secretaries, probation officers, public defenders, administrative officers, court reporters, librarians, and miscellaneous personnel round out the roster. Special judges and their support staff have been authorized to handle the burdensome bankruptcy jurisdiction of the federal courts.

For all that, the reality district courts face is an ever-expanding caseload that strains available resources to the breaking point. Particularly since the mid-1970s, the caseload of all federal courts has been growing at an unprecedented rate,

TABLE 2.1   U.S. DISTRICT COURT FILINGS: 1940–1990

Year	Number of Authorized Judgeships	Total Filings	Filings Per Jugdeship
1940	190	68,135	359
1950	215	92,382	430
1960	245	89,112	364
1970	401	127,288	317
1980	516	197,710	383
1981	516	211,907	411
1982	515	238,875	464
1983	515	277,714	539
1984	515	298,330	579
1985	575	313,170	545
1986	575	296,318	515
1987	575	282,477	491
1988	575	281,219	489
1989	575	279,524	486
1990	575	266,783	464
1991*	649	258,013	398
1992*	649	278,875	430

*In 1992, the Administrative Office shifted its statistical year from July 1 to June 30, to October 1 to September 30. Figures for the last two years reflect this change. They still reflect judicial business for a period of one year, even if the time frame of that year is different.

Source: Annual Report of the Director of the Administrative Office of the United States Courts (U.S. GPO, Washington, D.C.) for 1985, pp. 122, 129; for 1990, pp. 8, 10. 1991 and 1992 from the preliminary draft of the 1992 Annual Report, pp. 4, 6.

causing concern that the system may be stretched beyond its capacity. Between 1960 and 1983, the number of cases filed in all of the district courts rose by 250 percent. This rise was steepest during the early 1980s. Between 1978 and 1983, a period of only five years, the number of cases filed in the district courts rose 60 percent![20] The legislative response to this increased pressure on the district courts has been primarily to increase the number of judges available to process cases. However, even as more judges were added the number of case filings continued to rise. We saw a drop in civil filings during the late 1980s and early 1990s, but even this short reversal offered little relief and seems to have ended in any event.

Table 2.1 illustrates this trend during the past half century, for all district court filings, criminal and civil. The number of authorized judgeships is also indicated. The actual number of judges working will depart from this figure slightly, due to illness or a delay in replacing a judge who leaves the bench. On the other hand, some retired judges continue to work part-time to help reduce the backlog in busy jurisdictions. As a rough indicator of workload, we include the average number of filings per judgeship. Not all cases demand equal attention, of course, as some are more complicated than others, but this is the best simple indicator of workload we have.

Note that these numbers refer to filings—cases commenced in the district courts—and not the number of trials conducted. The total number of trials completed in all federal district courts during 1988 was only 19,901, so slightly more than 1 filing in 14 actually went to trial. Some plaintiffs drop their suits and some cases are dismissed on various grounds by the courts. Most suits are settled out of court when the parties come to some sort of negotiated agreement prior to trial, sometimes at the last minute, which the court then ratifies by entering a consent decree. This is an order by the court that accomplishes the result agreed upon and is binding in law as a judgment. A similar phenomenon occurs in criminal cases, where most convictions result from guilty pleas that avoid trial. Usually, defendants enter these guilty pleas in exchange for a lighter sentence, a practice referred to as plea bargaining. It is doubtful that our court system could long function if all cases filed actually had to complete the lengthy trial process. Often, filing a civil lawsuit is merely part of a negotiating strategy by the weaker party, since nothing gets the attention of a large and unresponsive entity quite like the arrival of a subpoena to appear in court. The settlement usually represents some compromise position between the litigants' respective claims. We might, therefore, view this phenomenon of settlement as a major qualification of the rule presented in Chapter 1, that courts render dichotomous decisions.

Despite their inherent limitations, case filings still represent important data, for every filing represents a formal request for a court to adjudicate a legal claim. Thus, they remain the best indicator we have to measure the business of courts. Some variations in the rate of filings occurring after 1986 are the result of a drop in civil suits filed in district court. Since then, the number of civil filings has risen only modestly. Much of the annual variation in filings in recent years resulted from suits by the government to recover for overpayment of veterans benefits, social security disability claims, and defaulted student loans. However, we continued to witness a rise in criminal charges brought in district courts during the late 1980s, partially nullifying the relief obtained as a result of fewer civil suits. A growing emphasis on federal drug prosecutions has burdened the courts even further, threatening their ability in some jurisdictions to hear civil cases at all. Whether the rate of federal civil filings will continue to increase slowly or at an accelerated rate more consistent with the past decade as a whole remains to be seen.

There are many complex reasons for this increase in federal cases. Obviously, the increased role of the federal government in society is partly to blame, but the past decade has not been a period of regulatory growth at the national level. An increase in rights-creating legislation, such as laws against employment discrimination on the basis of race, religion, sex, or disability, would increase the opportunities for citizens to turn to the federal courts for relief, but the last decade was not a period of innovation in such legislation, except for the recent amendment to federal civil rights law prohibiting employment discrimination against the disabled. There has been some debate among scholars about the propensity of Americans to sue one another. The claim frequently heard that Americans are unusually litigious appears doubtful.[21] At any rate, the importance of the district courts can be illustrated by noting that they handle about 97 percent of all litigation in the federal court system at any one time. The question of how U.S. district courts can process the growing number of cases presented to them, while still delivering the quality of justice Americans have come to expect from their courts, will likely be with us for a long time.

District courts are described as "trial courts" or "courts of first instance" because they are the point of entry into the federal system for most cases. But district courts will also be the last court to deal with most suits, since only a very small number of litigants appeal a trial court decision. Trials are presided over by a single judge and offer the familiar spectacle of opposing lawyers interrogating witnesses, presenting evidence, and arguing passionately on behalf of their clients, each of whom wants to be the single party who will leave court victorious. It should be understood that the stakes in a trial are very high, for people turn to courts to resolve only their most significant disputes, and only after other attempts at reconciliation have failed. Recall also that trial decisions for cases where settlement was impossible are dichotomous—at least half of the litigants will go home very disappointed with the results. Actually, even the winner is seldom jubilant, for they have probably spent a good deal of money and time, and have suffered considerable psychological trauma, on their way to victory. A lawsuit is an eventuality never to be undertaken lightly.

The conduct of most trials is remarkably more low-key than is portrayed in movies or on television. Dramatic last-moment confessions by sobbing witnesses are rare exceptions. However, the essential idea of adversarial combat between a plaintiff and a defendant is accurate enough for our purposes. In criminal cases, the active party is the government, represented by a prosecutor, who must file a criminal charge against the accused and then offer evidence to establish guilt beyond a reasonable doubt.[22] Both civil and criminal trials are heard before a passive and, it is hoped, impartial judge. Civil or criminal cases may be tried with a jury present, but today the great majority of both kinds of trials do not use a jury. A trial without a jury is called a "bench trial," because it requires the judge to determine the issues of fact that a jury would have determined had one been present. In a jury trial the judge's role is that of a referee, to enforce the rules of order and to protect the integrity of the trial process in a way that is fair to both sides. He or she may be called on to make rulings concerning the admissibility of certain evidence or of the precise definition of certain crimes or other legal categories in civil trials. At the conclusion of a jury trial, the judge will have to "charge" the jury, that is, instruct the jury in whatever factual determinations it has been called on by the litigants to make. If no jury was present, the judge will have to decide whether or not the evidence introduced by the parties was sufficiently convincing to establish their claim. In a criminal case, the judge will have to decide whether the government has proven the accused guilty beyond a reasonable doubt. Finally, the judge may have to render an award whereby one party will have to pay compensation for damages suffered by the other, may have to order certain kinds of conduct on the part of a losing party, or may have to sentence a convicted felon to a term in prison. In federal court, sentencing is always by the judge, the role of the jury being confined to a determination of guilt or innocence.

Trials are conducted according to formal rules of evidence and procedure. The litigants are responsible for raising issues before the court and for bringing forward evidence to substantiate their claims. The judge remains a passive participant. He or she cannot initiate litigation and normally plays only a limited role in shaping the nature of a suit or determining exactly what issues will be explored once it has begun. The assumption is that if two parties are locked in real combat before the court, each will bring forward all available evidence and make all pertinent legal arguments in support of its own case. In the process, the court will receive a full canvassing of all issues present in the controversy and will be able to render a fully informed decision. After each side has presented witnesses or physical evidence that supports its side of the argument, the opposing side will have an opportunity to impeach the evidence or cross-examine adverse witnesses. This is done in an attempt to uncover inconsistencies, irregularities, perhaps even lies in the testimony given. The goal is to test the reliability of the evidence presented by the adversary. At the very least, each side will want to correct any misinterpretations of the evidence that might result from only one side being heard. The responsibility this places on the parties, and hence on their lawyers, is considerable. The best case can be lost by poor trial advocacy.

One fairly technical distinction needs to be explained at this point. Every lawsuit starts out as a difference of opinion between two or more parties, be they individuals, corporations, or governmental entities. Few such conflicts result in litigation. However, those that do may present courts with two kinds of questions to be settled. First, the court may have to settle issues of fact. Here the court is investigating what happened: What set of events gave rise to the dispute now before the court? Resolution of questions of fact will involve an attempt to reconstruct history based on available evidence, mostly in the form of witness testimony. Did the defendant make a fraudulent representation through the U.S. mail? Did an employer discriminate against an employee on the basis of race or gender? Has a factory been discharging pollutants into a nearby river? Will the merger of two corporations create one firm with enough of a market share in its particular product area to constitute a "conspiracy in restraint of trade"?

We hope the judicial reconstruction of history resembles the actual set of past events (or, more rarely, a prediction of future events) to a high degree. We must recognize, however, that some discrepancy is inevitable. Courts are selective in the facts they will consider. Some critical evidence may not be available, or it may not be admissible into the trial under the rules of evidence the judge is bound to follow. Perhaps evidence is available and admitted but is misunderstood or ignored. A tendency toward oversimplification is present, as complex social relations are made to fit general-purpose legal categories of thought. "Facts" are things in need of interpretation, and no human being given the task of figuring out what evidence means can completely escape his or her own subjectivity in the process. Persons with different moral values might perceive the same "facts" differently. Whether by a jury or by the judge, one possibility for trial courts to fail to deliver justice is in the determination of facts.

Alternately, the parties to a suit may agree on the facts but argue questions of law. In such a case, both sides would be giving essentially the same historical account of their conflict but would disagree on the legal consequences of those facts. The employer might say, "I did not hire the plaintiff because of her race or gender, but so what? At least in the circumstances of this decision it was alright for me to pursue such a policy." The factory owners might say, "We are dumping waste water into the nearby river, but so what? We are in full compliance with the federal Clean Water Act." The solicitation for contributions mailed by a self-proclaimed prophet of God might seem fraudulent to the nonbeliever, but the right of others to believe his prophecy and to raise money for the propagation of their faith may be constitutionally protected from government interference. Perhaps the near monopoly will unfairly restrain trade and cost consumers millions of dollars, but not in the precise manner that has been proscribed by law. It comes as a surprise to the uninitiated, but laws are often not crystal clear, as we saw in Chapter 1. We shall further develop this point in Chapters 6 and 7, but for now we need only understand that such questions of law are decided solely by the trial judge.

Parties to litigation may agree on facts and fight over the legal consequences of those facts. More likely, they will agree on the meaning of the laws but fight over their competing versions of history, each side presenting an interpretation most favorable to its own interest in winning the case. Or they may fight over both. Trial courts, and only trial courts, have jurisdiction over both kinds of questions. They will hear witnesses or examine physical evidence in an attempt to uncover what actually did happen. They will also apply their understanding of the law to those facts and determine what legal consequences should follow. Will the prophet go to jail? Must the employer make compensation to the victim of discrimination? Will the factory be enjoined from discharging any more waste water, and perhaps fined for its past pollution? Will the corporate merger be permitted?

It is well known by the lay public that a litigant who loses at trial might appeal that court's judgment to a higher court. What is not generally recognized is that this may be done only if the losing party claims that the trial court misunderstood or misapplied the law. A misunderstanding of facts cannot be appealed. Since most trials actually are arguments over facts, decisions are often effectively insulated from any possibility of appeal. Also, recall all of those cases, more than 90 percent, that are filed in federal district court but never go to trial. They are dropped or dismissed or settled out of court by negotiated agreement of the litigants. In such cases, litigants finally agree on a common description of the facts and of their respective legal obligations. If the court accepts the settlement, as it usually does, then there can be no appeal. Cost is yet another factor limiting the availability of appellate review. In addition to lawyers' time in preparation of an appeal and court filing fees, the appealing party is responsible for the costly production of a trial transcript. Even a favorable decision on appeal may simply mean that another trial must be had, consuming even more of the litigant's resources. Weighing these costs against uncertain benefits, the parties may be reluctant to drag out their dispute for an uncertain period of time, preferring instead to accept the trial court's judgment, lick their wounds, and retire from the battlefield.

These considerations help to explain the low volume of appeals beyond the district courts. If a judgment of the district court has been appealed, all subsequent discussion of the case in the higher courts will be confined to the record of facts assembled by the trial court. One exception to this so-called "two court" rule, more notorious than common, used to occur in obscenity trials. Because of the peculiar way in which issues of fact and law were intermingled in obscenity cases between 1963 and 1971, the justices on the Supreme Court had to read every book and view every film alleged to be obscene as a part of the appellate review. In general, however, the trial court's examination of evidence will not be repeated by the higher court, and no new evidence bearing on the case may be considered. Hence, we can see another reason why U.S. district courts are important. As the gatekeepers of the federal judiciary, they alone determine the factual portrayals that may come under appellate review.

United States Courts of Appeals

Permanent intermediate appellate courts with their own judicial personnel have been a part of the federal court system for only the past century. However, just as the United States has been divided by Congress into districts, so has it also been divided into circuits since the Judiciary Act of 1789. Each circuit includes a number of districts and has one U.S. court of appeals. For example, appeals from all federal district court decisions in Maine, New Hampshire, Rhode Island, Massachusetts, and Puerto Rico will go to the United States Court of Appeals for the First Circuit, which meets in Boston. Appeals from federal district courts in Vermont, New York, and Connecticut are heard by the United States Court of Appeals for the Second Circuit, in New York. Pennsylvania, New Jersey, Delaware, and the Virgin Islands comprise the Third Circuit, from which appeals will go to Philadelphia. The rest of the country is similarly divided into a total of 11 circuits, with 11 U.S. courts of appeals, as illustrated in Figure 2.1. There is also a United States Court of Appeals for the District of Columbia, because the District of Columbia has a heavy volume of cases arising from suits against the government and appeals from regulatory agencies, such as the Federal Communications Commission, and specialized administrative courts, such the United States Tax Court. Finally, there is in Washington a Court of Appeals for the Federal Circuit. This court was created in 1982 with a specialized jurisdiction to hear appeals from the United States Claims Court, the Court of International Trade, the Court of Veterans Appeals, and appeals from the United States Court of Customs and Patent Appeals. (These specialized courts will be explained presently and need not concern us deeply at this time.) In all, there are 13 intermediate appellate courts, having 167 judges. Twelve more judges sit on the specialized Court of Appeals for the Federal Circuit. The number of judges assigned to each court varies depending on the caseload and size of its circuit.

The burden of appealing falls on the losing party in the lower court. The winning party has little interest in further proceedings, and in a criminal case the prosecutor is prohibited from appealing an acquittal. Appellate courts exist solely for the purpose of correcting errors committed in law by the trial courts. Factual determinations made in the trial courts will not be disturbed by an appellate court. Thus, the appealing party, called an appellant, may by right file an appeal if he or she can argue that the trial judge misunderstood the law. The trial judge may have made an erroneous ruling on the admissibility of evidence or committed some other procedural error, such as providing a jury with inadequate instructions. The judge's ruling may have gone beyond what the law allows, perhaps by

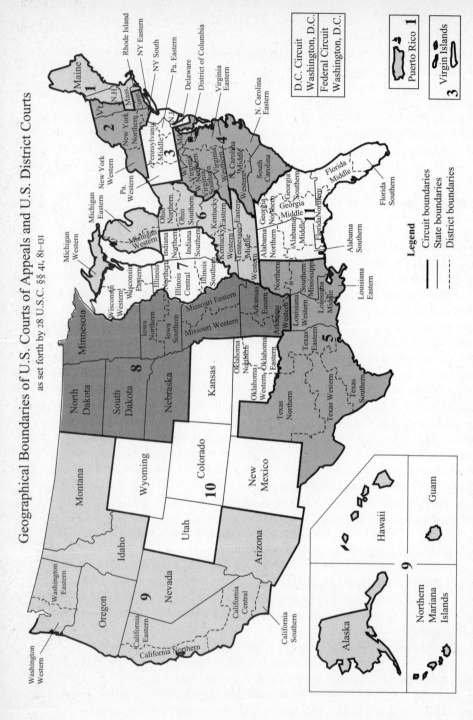

Geographical Boundaries of U.S. Courts of Appeals and U.S. District Courts

as set forth by 28 U.S.C. §§ 41, 81–131

Legend

— Circuit boundaries

— State boundaries

----- District boundaries

D.C. Circuit
Washington, D.C.

Federal Circuit
Washington, D.C.

Puerto Rico **1**

Virgin Islands

3

Figure 2.1 The 13 federal judicial circuits. In addition to the 11 circuits shown there are the United States Court of Appeals for the District of Columbia and the Court of Appeals for the Federal Circuit, also in Washington, D.C.

sentencing a convict to a longer term than the maximum indicated by the appropriate federal sentencing guidelines. Perhaps a civil rights law does not proscribe the personnel policy demonstrated at trial.

Since factual issues are not reopened on appeal, there will be no interrogation of witnesses or examination of physical evidence by the appellate court. No jury will be present. Instead of a trial, appellate courts have a hearing, in which attorneys representing each side may present written and oral arguments in support of the interpretation of law they would like the court to adopt. In the U.S. courts of appeals, most hearings are before a panel of three judges. Only in unusually important cases may an en banc, or "full bench," hearing take place before all of the appeals judges who serve on that circuit. This exceptional procedure may be requested after a party has lost an appeal before a three-judge panel. In all proceedings, after studying written arguments or hearing oral arguments, the judges will vote on the result. Most decisions by three-judge panels on the appellate courts are unanimous, but a vote of two to one is sufficient for a decision.

Recall that few trial court decisions are appealed. Although a party dissatisfied with the ruling of the trial court has a right to file an appeal, few choose to do so. In practice, district court decisions are final in all but a small number of cases, for only about 13 percent of their decisions are appealed. This, however, is up from a 4 percent rate of appeals only 20 years ago. One study of appellate court dispositions found that district courts were upheld in 67 percent of appeals. This statistic may help to discourage some litigants from appealing. Nevertheless, the U.S. courts of appeals face a burgeoning caseload similar to that faced by the district courts. The year 1940 saw only 3,446 filings in the appellate courts. That figure had risen to more than 6,000 by 1964, but the 1980s saw a significant acceleration in the rate of appeals, reaching 47,013 in 1992. Table 2.2 indicates the growth in appeals filed during the past half century. We include the number of authorized judgeships, again cognizant of the fact that the actual number of judges working may vary somewhat. Judges may get sick or leave the bench, sometimes leaving a seat open for some period of time. Since most appeals are heard in panels of three, we have calculated an average number of filings for each panel. Not all cases are alike, however, so this is only a rough estimate of workload. The continued rise in the number of appeals filed has been accommodated by expanding the number of appellate judges available to hear them. However, each gain was soon nullified by the continued expansion of the number of appeals filed. Thus, the crisis some commentators see in the district courts is shared with even greater urgency by the appellate courts.

Just as the trial courts have had to rely on shortcuts such as plea bargaining or the active encouragement of settlements to manage their heavy caseloads, the appellate courts have had to resort to summary proceedings. A minority of appeals today result in oral argument. Increasingly, the courts have issued judgments based solely on written briefs submitted by the litigants and the record of the trial court. Again, this raises difficult questions about the quality of justice litigants receive in the U.S. courts of appeals.

If few litigants appeal their cases to the U.S. courts of appeals, fewer still succeed in appealing from them, for the highest court, the United States Supreme Court, remains a remote presence in the judicial structure. One study found that

TABLE 2.2   U.S. COURTS OF APPEALS FILINGS: 1940–1990

Year	Authorized Judgeships	Total Filings	Filings Per Panel of Three
1940	57	3,446	184
1950	65	2,830	131
1960	68	3,899	172
1970	97	11,662	361
1980	132	23,200	527
1981	132	26,362	599
1982	132	27,946	635
1983	132	29,630	673
1984	132	31,185	716
1985	156	33,360	642
1986	156	34,292	659
1987	156	35,176	676
1988	156	37,524	722
1989	156	39,734	764
1990	156	40,898	787
1991*	167	43,027	768
1992*	167	47,013	840

*The Administrative Office has recently shifted its statistical year from July 1 to June 30, to October 1 to September 30. The last two years relect this change. They still measure business for a one-year period, although the year begins and ends on a different date. This table excludes appeals filed in the specialized U.S. Court of Appeals for the Federal Circuit, which was established in 1982.

Source: Annual Report of the Director of the Administrative Office of the United States Courts (U.S. GPO, Washington, D.C.) for 1980, p. 124; for 1990, p. 3. 1991 and 1992 are from the preliminary draft of the 1992 Annual Report.

one in five appellate court decisions were brought before the Supreme Court. However, we shall soon see that the Supreme Court is distinct from other courts in that it has the ability to choose which cases from among the many raised before it the Court will actually accept for consideration. This discretion is exercised by the Supreme Court very selectively, for less than 1 percent of decisions by the intermediate appellate courts are actually reviewed by the Supreme Court. This means that the U.S. courts of appeals are in practice the court of last resort for all but a very small number of appeals. Even if the Supreme Court were to overrule appellate court decisions three-quarters of the time, the U.S. courts of appeals would still be making decisions that formally prevailed in more than 98 percent of their cases.[23] This indicates that the role held by the intermediate appellate courts in shaping legal policy is significant. While the Supreme Court may indicate the broad outlines of a certain policy, much of the burden of giving detailed shape to that policy will be carried by the intermediate appellate courts. After the Supreme Court, in the mid-1950s, determined that racial segregation in public schools was contrary to the Constitution, it fell largely to the United States Court of Appeals for the Fifth Circuit to desegregate schools in the deep south.[24] Most of the law of desegregation was in fact made by this singularly extraordinary court. We shall see presently that the role of the Supreme Court is highly specialized. There are whole bodies of law that the Supreme Court avoids completely. The courts of appeals are the final arbiters for these areas of public policy.

Specialized Courts

While most federal litigation is conducted before district and appellate courts, there are a few federal courts of limited jurisdiction that should be noted. Most of these are trial courts established for specific kinds of cases.

Three-judge district courts are authorized by Congress for a narrow class of cases. These are ad hoc tribunals, assembled as a trial court for a specific case, then disbanded when their work is done. As one might guess, three judges preside over the trial, including at least one district judge and at least one judge from the federal appeals court. In practice, the third judge is usually another district court judge. One obvious advantage to such courts is to provide an avenue around a local district court that plaintiffs have reason to mistrust. The mix of judges may dilute the localism often found in district courts. Another advantage, especially from the perspective of a plaintiff challenging a government policy on constitutional grounds, is that an appeal from a three-judge district court ruling will lie directly to the United States Supreme Court. This expedited avenue to the Supreme Court made the three-judge district court an attractive option for civil rights litigators challenging southern state policies during the 1960s. Statutes such as the Civil Rights Act of 1964, the Voting Rights Act of 1965, and the Presidential Election Campaign Fund Act of 1974 have authorized the use of such courts. However, these courts were obviously unpopular with local power structures. They also add to the Supreme Court's burgeoning caseload. In recent years, both Congress and the Supreme Court have restricted the use of three-judge district courts, and they are of declining significance. Only nine such courts were convened in 1990, down from a high of 321 in 1973.

There are also several adjudicating bodies created by Congress under its Article I authority, which are considered separate from the Article III federal court system we have been discussing. These are known by the paradoxical term of legislative courts, or sometimes Article I courts. The line between Article I and Article III courts is problematic for constitutional theory. We shall only reiterate that the theory of separation of powers itself is not precise in delineating the functions assigned to different branches of government. Congress has created legislative courts with very specialized jurisdictions requiring considerable substantive expertise. An important example is the United States Tax Court, which operates within the labyrinthine Internal Revenue Service. The Court of Veterans Appeals is another recent innovation, to expedite adjudication of conflicts over benefits owed the nation's war veterans.

Besides their specialized jurisdiction, such courts differ from the Article III courts in several respects. They are not as independent of the political branches as are the Article III courts and are often given by statute explicit administrative or rule-making responsibilities. Judges serve for a specified term, rather than for the life tenure enjoyed by Article III judges. Appeals from legislative court decisions generally go the United States Court of Appeals for the District of Columbia and appeals from the United States Court of Claims or the Court of Customs and Patent Appeals to the newly created United States Court of Appeals for the Federal Circuit. Ultimately, an appeal may go before the United States Supreme Court. Such specialized courts, however, will occupy no more of our attention. We will proceed instead to the highest and most visible court in the land.

THE UNITED STATES SUPREME COURT

The most visible court in America, and the most powerful court in the world, is the United States Supreme Court. Recall that Article III mandates only this single court, but leaves its precise composition for Congress to decide. We are told, however, in no uncertain terms, that there shall be at minimum "one Supreme Court." The Judiciary Act of 1789 determined that the Supreme Court should have six justices. By 1869, the number of justices had been as small as 5 and as large as 10. Since then, however, the Court has had a stable population of nine justices. These include the chief justice of the United States, who is the highest administrative officer of the federal court system. The chief justice oversees the preparation of the budget for the whole of the federal judiciary and allocates tasks to the nonjudicial personnel who make up the support staff of the courts. All told, these comprise only about 0.4 percent of all federal employees. He or she also reports annually to Congress on the state of the judiciary. In the chief justice's role as a judge, he or she is joined on the Supreme Court by eight associate justices. We have seen that other courts have varying numbers of judges, but that trials are conducted before a single judge and the great majority of appeals are heard by panels of three judges. However, the Supreme Court hears all of its cases en banc—all nine justices participate on each case. Each has one vote, and a decision by the Supreme Court can be made by a simple majority of five votes, although most decisions result from a more lopsided vote.

One problem faced by the Supreme Court is immediately apparent. We have seen that Congress has responded to growing caseloads in the district courts and courts of appeals by expanding their size and number. An increase in the number of lower courts soon translates into more litigants seeking appeal before the Supreme Court. As we shall see in a moment, the past 40 years in particular have seen a staggering rise in the number of litigants seeking review of their cases by the Supreme Court, yet Congress cannot solve the problem of burgeoning Supreme Court caseloads by increasing the number of courts or judges. The reason for this is easily understood: the Constitution speaks of "one" Supreme Court. A second Supreme Court would violate the terms of Article III.

In addition, if there were more than one supreme court, all of them would cease to be supreme. A litigant who lost before one supreme court would still have reason to seek review before the other, where the chances of victory might appear greater. Such a multiplicity of supreme courts would be unable to fulfill the role of an ultimate court, to render a final authoritative judgment on all issues brought before it. Adding justices also would not help, since each justice must participate

TABLE 2.3   FILINGS IN THE UNITED STATES SUPREME COURT

Year*	Total Docket†
1900	406
1910	516
1920	565
1930	845
1940	977
1950	1181
1960	1940
1970	3419
1980	5144
1981	5311
1982	5079
1983	5100
1984	5006
1985	5158
1986	5134
1987	5268
1989	5746
1990	6319
1991	6770
1992	7245

*Term beginning in October, ending in June or July

†Includes new filings, plus unfinished cases carried over from previous term

Source: 1900–1970 from Gerhard Casper and Richard A. Posner, The Workload of the Supreme Court (American Bar Foundation, Chicago, 1976) p. 3. 1980–1989 from Annual Report of the Director of the Administrative Office of the United States Courts (U.S. GPO, Washington, D.C.) 1985, p. 243; 1990, p. 103. Filings for 1992 are from the Supreme Court Clerk, "Statistical Sheet #26 (Final)," June 28, 1993.

in every case, precluding a division of labor. Hearing cases in smaller panels would, in effect, create multiple supreme courts. Because we have only a single supreme court, it is the last court of appeal, and because it is the last court of appeal, it must be singular. And there is no court to overturn judgments—even the most flagrantly wrongheaded judgments—by the Supreme Court.

Case Selection

Can one supreme court adequately function as an appellate forum for an enlarged federal judiciary, in which caseloads seem to expand ever more rapidly? Consider the data on the number of cases filed before the Court during the twentieth century. Table 2.3 indicates the total number of Supreme Court filings for 10-year intervals from 1900 through 1980, followed by annual data for the rest of the decade. We can see clearly that the Supreme Court is a kind of a bottleneck and that expansion of the lower courts has put increased pressure on the Supreme Court.

The total rate of filings in some recent years has exceeded 6000 cases. It is safe to say that the Supreme Court is absolutely incapable of deciding this many cases in a single year. Congress has in the past instituted some structural reforms to relieve pressure on the Supreme Court. We noted previously that the intermediate appellate courts were intended in 1891 to provide a forum for appeals from erroneous trials, without each and every such case having to come before the Supreme Court. With the enactment of the Judges' Bill of 1925, however, the Supreme Court acquired a role quite distinct from that of an ordinary appellate court. This bill, the product of vigorous lobbying by Chief Justice William Howard Taft, greatly expanded the Court's control over its own docket through its certiorari jurisdiction. Under this jurisdiction, litigants who are unsatisfied with the result of an appeal to one of the U.S. courts of appeals or to a state supreme court where a federal question is present may request review by the Supreme Court. Technically, this is called a petition for certiorari. A writ of certiorari, (meaning "to be made certain") is an order from the Supreme Court to a lower court to send up the case for review. Certiorari is distinguished from ordinary appeals in that it is wholly discretionary. The Supreme Court may grant the writ if it wants to hear the case but may also deny it if the justices do not believe the case presents issues of sufficient national importance to warrant the Court's attention. Today, nearly all cases come before the Supreme Court on certiorari, and the Court denies certiorari for the majority of cases brought before it.

About half of petitions for a writ of certiorari come before the Court on the "appellate docket" and half on the "miscellaneous docket." In practice, the latter category of litigants almost entirely file in forma pauperis, meaning that because the petitioning party is without funds, Court filing and printing fees are waived. Some in forma pauperis cases are accepted by the Court and turn out to be very significant cases. Most, however, are prisoners' appeals that are more desperate than worthy. Through the early 1980s, only about 1 percent of these petitions were accepted for review, a figure that is down somewhat from earlier years when the caseload was not so pressing and when the Court was more sympathetic to defendants' rights. For the other half of the certiorari pool, the paid cases, the acceptance rate varies between 7 and 10 percent. The overall acceptance rate hovers around 5 percent.[25]

Parties who lose in the intermediate appellate courts or in state supreme courts have a limited period of time in which they may request a writ of certiorari. They must serve notice of their intention to do so with the other party to their suit, and that party, the "respondent," has the right to try to convince the justices not to accept the case. All such petitions and replies are filed with the Supreme Court, printed in 40 copies each. A copy of the record of lower court dispositions for the case is held by the clerk of the Court, should any justice desire to study it. For those not petitioning in forma pauperis, this documentation can become quite an expensive proposition, even before one is assured of Supreme Court review. In theory, materials filed are studied by all nine justices. As the number of petitions arriving at the Court annually began to increase at a rate making this impossible, the task of reviewing certiorari petitions was delegated, with varying degrees of supervision by individual justices, to the justices' law clerks. They prepare brief summaries of the issues raised and suggestions to "cert" the case or, more often, to deny review. In fact, all but Justice Stevens now rely upon a "cert pool," whereby the same memorandum prepared by a clerk is circulated among all of the participating justices. This allows for a more efficient allocation of the workload among the law clerks of participating justices.[26] Stevens has indicated that even he relies heavily on his clerks for screening of cases. His clerks select about 20 percent of the certiorari petitions for his personal attention.[27]

There is some controversy over just how much influence the law clerks have over the certiorari process. Clerks are hired for one- or two-year terms by individual justices. They tend to be recent honors graduates of the nation's most prestigious law schools. While obviously accomplished, their youth precludes the kind of worldly experience that we might like the gatekeepers of the Supreme Court to have. Since the justices are not likely to look at a certiorari petition their clerks have decided lacks substantial issues, some critics have raised the specter of the justices losing control over their docket to a bevy of transient neophytes. On the other hand, Supreme Court justices are also highly accomplished individuals, and usually of considerable professional and political experience. It is hard to imagine that they are manipulated by the assistants they hire (and fire) any more than they themselves choose to be.

Supreme Court justices do not often appear to be a weak-willed lot. Presumably, it is they, and not the clerks, who establish the criteria employed for certiorari review by each justice's office. Their transience also would most likely prevent the clerks from coming to dominate a justice. Perhaps it would be most accurate to portray the clerks as screening out only the most frivolous cases, sending the remainder to the justices, with comments and recommendations, for their personal scrutiny. The consistency of work produced by justices over time seems to support the thesis that it is they, and not the clerks, who control the business of the Court. However, an important impediment to our understanding of the certiorari process is that the Court seldom supplies an explanation for the case selections it has made. We are left to speculate as to who ultimately controls case selection.

The preparation of cert memos and their study by the justices is only the first stage in the certiorari process. Every Friday morning while the Court is in session, the justices assemble in a private conference room adjacent to the chief justice's chambers to discuss certiorari petitions. In practice, clerks for the chief justice will have previously prepared and circulated a "discuss list" of cases they think might be worthy of certiorari. The other justices may add to the discuss list any additional case they deem worthy of discussion at the conference. It appears that all cases not on the discuss list by the morning of the conference are denied certiorari en masse. They are estimated to include about 70 percent of all certiorari petitions.[28] Those petitions included on the discuss list will be considered in conference, leading ultimately to a vote by the justices. Under the informal "rule of four," an affirmative vote by four justices is sufficient to grant a writ of certiorari, placing the case on the Court's docket. This means the case has gotten through the courthouse doors and will be decided by the Supreme Court.

Obviously, the Court is very selective in choosing the cases it will hear, eliminating routine or frivolous cases and concerning itself only with the most significant. This is how it should be, for the role of the Supreme Court is not primarily to correct errors made in trial courts, for the benefit of individual litigants. The certiorari process reserves this role for the U.S. courts of appeals. The Supreme Court focuses on cases that raise legal and political issues of national importance. As Chief Justice Taft wrote, defending the Judiciary Act of 1925, which established the certiorari jurisdiction over most cases coming before the Court, "The function of the Supreme Court is conceived to be, not the remedying of a particular litigant's wrong, but the consideration of cases whose decision involves principles, the application of which are of wide public or governmental interest."[29] In short, the certiorari jurisdiction recognizes that the Supreme Court is primarily a policy-making body, rather then a forum for individual dispute resolution.

Now we must qualify the rule of judicial passivity introduced in Chapter 1. Along with other courts, the Supreme Court can only act on issues brought before it in the trappings of a lawsuit. Recall that this is one of the differences between a court and a legislature: courts are not self-starting. While the Supreme Court is dependent on litigants to shape its docket initially, it is distinguished from the district and appellate courts by the fact that it does not have to hear arguments on every issue raised before it. This enables the Supreme Court to choose the fields of public policy in which it will be a significant player for a given year. It may, for example, choose to hear cases raising questions of church and state relations and environmental issues, assuming such cases are among the certiorari petitions, while ignoring defendants' rights cases and cases alleging discrimination by race or gender. In the course of making this decision, the Court has the potential to decide what policies it will help to shape and what policies will be left to the legislative processes in Congress or the states or to litigation in the lower courts.

In large measure, the Court defines the role it will play in the political process through its selection of cases. The basis on which the justices choose cases to grant certiorari is, therefore, of considerable interest to political scientists. Unfortunately, since the justices do not explain their certiorari decisions, we are left to conjecture about their motives. Rule 10 (formerly Rule 17) of the Supreme Court rules of procedure, which describes the certiorari docket, supplies only the "character of reasons that will be considered" by the justices when reviewing petitions. These include:

a. When a federal court of appeals has rendered a decision in conflict with the decision of another court of appeals on the same matter; or has decided a federal question in a way in conflict with a state court of last resort; or has so far departed from the accepted and usual course of judicial proceedings, or so far sanctioned such a departure by a lower court, as to call for an exercise of this Court's power of supervision.
b. When a state court of last resort has decided a federal question in a way in conflict with the decision of another state court of last resort or of a federal court of appeals.
c. When a state court or a federal court of appeals has decided an important question of federal law which has not been, but should be, settled by this Court, or has decided a federal question in a way in conflict with applicable decisions of this Court.

These standards beg many questions and are meant only as guidelines rather than self-defining criteria. One dominant theme of Rule 10 is that the Supreme Court should supply uniformity to the law by resolving conflicts among the lower courts in the interpretation of federal laws. To some extent, this may encourage litigants seeking a Supreme Court hearing to magnify the degree of conflict among lower courts on a question pertinent to their case. Even so, mere conflict in legal interpretation does not, by itself, ensure a hearing by the Supreme Court. The most significant factor determining which cases will be granted review seems to be the justices' perception of the proper role of the Supreme Court in American politics and the kinds of issues important enough to merit the Court's attention.[30]

Inevitably, judgments of "importance" will be influenced by the political agendas of the members of the Court. One need only compare the indulgence shown by the Court to defendants' rights cases, including prisoners filing in forma pauperis, during the 1960s, with the relative lack of interest in the field shown by the Court since the appointment by President Nixon of four "law and order" justices to observe the influence of politics in the selection of cases. In particular, during the 1970s and 1980s the Court displayed a greater likelihood of accepting a civil liberties case if lower courts had ruled in favor of individual rights claims. Conservative justices were apparently motivated by a desire to reverse such policies with rulings favoring government powers.[31] On the other hand, the 1970s also witnessed a significant growth in the Court's sensitivity to complaints alleging sex discrimination, a subject that had seldom been presented prior to then and with which the Court had previously been rather uninterested.

Justices appointed by former Presidents Reagan and Bush have shifted the political center of gravity further to the right. While the annual number of certiorari petitions remains high, there has been a sharp drop in cases selected for review since the 1989 and 1990 terms. This may indicate that the Court is again revising its political definition of "important" cases. Alternately, it may reflect growing conservativism on the lower bench, obviating the need for reversal by a conservative Supreme Court. Whether the election of Democrat Bill Clinton to the White House in 1992 will affect this trend remains to be seen. The retirement of Justice Byron White presented Clinton with his first opportunity to influence the political composition of the Court when he appointed Justice Ruth Bader Ginsberg. Justice Harry Blackmun's announced retirement at the conclusion of the 1993 term and President Clinton's nomination of federal appeals judge Stephen Breyer as his successor do not seem likely to substantially alter the political conplextion of the Supreme Court very much. It will likely take several more appointments to influence Court behavior significantly.

Another important factor that seems to affect the likelihood of acceptance of a case for review by the Supreme Court is requests by the federal government. The solicitor general, in the Justice Department, is in charge of all appellate litigation for the federal government. Of the myriad of cases involving different federal departments and programs, the solicitor general decides which will be brought to the Court's attention. In this he or she is highly selective, asking for Supreme Court review in only one of every five or six cases in which the United States has lost. Among the cases the solicitor general asks the Court to review, certiorari is granted in about 70 percent.[32] Comparison of this figure with the acceptance rate of less than 3 percent for nongovernment litigants who request Supreme Court review reveals the solicitor general's influence in the certiorari process. The solicitor general's win rate also exceeds that of other litigants, perhaps a reflection of the ability to choose the strongest cases for appeal, whereas other litigants have only one case to appeal. Obviously, the Court relies heavily on the solicitor general to use good judgment in deciding which cases are worthy of Supreme Court review. His or her influence is such that he or she must be counted as an important actor in the Court's case screening process. Similarly, participation by interest groups seems to be taken by the justices as a reliable indicator of the importance of a case. It is unusual for interest groups to join a litigation at this early stage, but when they do, even to oppose certiorari, the likelihood of the Court accepting the case for review increases sharply.[33]

The Court has warned observers against reading too much meaning into a denial of certiorari,[34] that denial does not signify approval of the lower court's decision. Indeed, there may be many reasons for a denial of certiorari besides triviality or political motives. Recall that appellate review of cases is limited to the factual record assembled in the trial court. It is very difficult to get new evidence into the record for appellate review. The Supreme Court may reject a case because it fears the trial process has not adequately elucidated all relevant factual considerations. The Court might simply wish to avoid making an important decision with national ramifications on the basis of faulty or partial information.

Similarly, the Court may consider timing important in granting or denying certiorari. The justices may choose to delay taking up a new issue, to allow lower courts to accumulate a body of experience in dealing with a particular problem. This would enable the Supreme Court to fashion a nationally binding precedent with the benefit of some empirical information concerning the operation of competing legal doctrines in real world situations. This kind of empiricism has long been deemed a strength in our jurisprudence. It also indicates that the Supreme Court is often only a coauthor of policies associated with it.

Rather than a reflection of the justices' approval of the disposition of the case by a lower court, a denial of certiorari is said to signify nothing more than a decision not to decide. Because a denial of certiorari has the immediate effect of leaving intact the decision of the last court to hear the case, it is certainly significant for the litigating parties. However, it has no value as a precedent or an indication of how the Court would decide a similar case in the future:[35] it is as if the Supreme Court had never been asked to look at the case in the first place.

For all that, however, the justices' view of the lower court's decision does not appear completely irrelevant to the certiorari decision. Among those cases accepted for Supreme Court review on certiorari, the Court overrules or vacates just over 60 percent.[36] Overruling is to render a decision favoring the party who lost in the previous court, while vacating is to erase the lower court's decision and order new hearings, sometimes including a new trial, in the previous forum, but to be conducted in a manner consistent with the Supreme Court's clarification of pertinent legal questions. So once a case is accepted on certiorari, chances are considerably better than even that the Court will not uphold the lower court's decision. This tendency to alter lower court decisions is so pronounced that it is impossible to ascribe to coincidence.

Perhaps the justices are more likely to perceive a case as significant if they also perceive it to have been wrongly decided. Chief Justice Taft aside, it seems the justices have not completely forsaken the role of correcting errors in law committed in the lower courts. Policy goals seem to play a role here as well, for we noted earlier the recent tendency of the Court to grant certiorari in civil liberties cases they want to reverse. We need to qualify this proposition, howerever, for the justices reveal a high level of unanimity in certiorari decisions, despite the presence of sharp ideological differences when they decide the merits of cases. Nor do the voting blocs revealed in case decisions reappear strongly in certiorari decisions. These observations suggest that the justices' perception of the institutional role of the Supreme Court—a perception that may partially transcend ideological categories—strongly qualifies their sympathy for the petitioner's claim when it comes to granting review.

We have spent a considerable amount of time on the certiorari process because it is important to our understanding of how the Court defines its own role in American politics. We should mention briefly the other ways cases may come before the Supreme Court, even though they are much less important than certiorari. A case might arise on "certification," which occurs when a U.S. court of appeals receives a case that is so novel and so perplexing that they do not know how to decide it. The judges may request intervention by the Supreme Court. This is rarely done, perhaps in part because appellate judges are loath to admit that they are stumped. For their part, Supreme Court justices would probably prefer to deal with the issue only after the lower court has finished it. Only three cases were decided on certification between 1946 and 1974.[37]

Until recently, a significant number of cases arrived before the Supreme Court on obligatory appeal. Statutory law required, in theory, that the Supreme Court review certain kinds of cases, especially those containing "a substantial federal question." While the statute established appeal to the Supreme Court as a litigant's right, in practice the Court avoided hearing most of these cases. If the justices dismissed the appeal "for want of a substantial federal question," there was no higher court to correct them, no matter how important the federal question seemed to the litigants. Thus, what the law deemed a right the Court rendered a privilege. Although cases once brought on statutory appeal were more likely to be accepted than those on certiorari, the difference between the two jurisdictions in later years became rather hard to find. To help the Court manage its caseload, Congress abolished the statutory appeal in 1988, extending the certiorari process to almost all cases.

Finally, the Supreme Court has a small original jurisdiction, defined by Article III to include suits involving ambassadors and foreign ministers and suits involving states. The former has never occurred. Ambassadors enjoy diplomatic immunity and cannot be sued in civil actions. It is traditional under international law not to prosecute the diplomatic representatives of a sovereign nation for criminal acts. Instead, an offending diplomat is simply expelled from the country. A small number of suits between states are accepted by the Court each year on original jurisdiction. Most of these, however, are relegated by justices to the district courts, perhaps to reappear on certiorari at some later date. Even when such a case is accepted on original jurisdiction, the justices do not hold a trial. Their practice is to appoint a federal judge as a special master, to hold a factual hearing on which the Supreme Court will later render its decision. Even when exercising its original jurisdiction, the Supreme Court acts much like an appellate court.

Oral Argument

Perhaps now it is time to move on to other things. How does the Supreme Court treat those cases it has decided to hear? Once a case has been put on the Court's docket, written briefs presenting the legal arguments of each side will be filed by a certain deadline, and oral arguments may be scheduled. Earlier in our history, when the business of the Court was much slower, the justices relied primarily on oral argument for their information about a case. Some lawyers, Daniel Webster for example, built distinguished careers on oral advocacy before the Court. Webster could argue important constitutional cases for days, and frequently did so. In an age that appreciated oratory, oral arguments were important social events, while briefs were exactly what the word implies: written summaries of the arguments the lawyer intended to present. Today the press of business is such that briefs have become more important, and considerably longer. Oral argument, in contrast, is usually restricted to one hour per case, each side being allotted one half-hour to make its presentation.

As with the lower courts, procedural shortcuts have had to be taken to enable the Supreme Court to dispose of the number of cases brought before it. For some cases, the Court dispenses with oral arguments altogether, deciding the appeal on the basis of written materials only. During the 1989–1990 term, only 146 cases received full oral argument before the Court; 80 were decided without oral argument.[38] When the Court chooses to hear oral arguments, the case will be scheduled for a hearing later in the session or during the next session.

The Supreme Court is in session from the first Monday of October until it is finished with cases accepted for oral argument that year, generally late June or early July. During two-week "sittings" from October until April, the Court will hear oral arguments Monday through Wednesday. The justices work in chambers on Thursday, and Fridays are reserved for judicial conferences. The first case will be argued at 10:00 in the morning, followed by another at 11:00. After a break for lunch, cases will be argued at 1:00 and at 2:00. Twelve cases per week is a heavy schedule, for during this time the justices continue to receive certiorari petitions, study briefs, and write opinions. After two weeks of oral arguments, the Court recesses for two weeks while the justices continue to work in private. This is followed by another two-week sitting.

The actual conduct of oral argument frequently is surprising informal, with considerable exchange between lawyers and justices. Chief Justice Warren, an avid baseball fan, used to announce scores of Washington Senators games from the bench—alas, the Senators were usually behind. Despite its informality, some lawyers find the Court intimidating. While a young government attorney making his first appearance before the Supreme Court, future Justice Stanley Reed approached the lawyer's podium, looked up at the assembled justices, and promptly fainted! The justices do not hesitate to interrupt an attorney's presentation to ask for clarification of an issue that troubles them. The Court does not like to be lectured to by attorneys. Rather, oral argument is used by the justices to probe those aspects of a case they may not fully comprehend, or which disturb them in some way. The proceedings often resemble a conversation, or at best a seminar, rather than the proceedings of the nation's highest judicial forum.

Oral argument can be riveting as well. Justices frequently fire questions from the bench to attorneys in mind-numbing succession. Often debate may erupt among the justices through the questions they ask. Lawyers find this disconcerting: they only have 30 minutes to make their case and most would prefer not to compete with the justices for scarce time. In addition, surely it is frustrating to have to keep up with nine very active minds, each going off in another direction on an issue that may be highly charged with national importance. After 20 minutes, a small white light on the lawyer's podium blinks on, informing him or her that there are 10 minutes remaining. This is so the attorney may summarize his or her main points, although with frequent interruptions from the bench, he or she might feel that he or she has not gotten to any of them yet. At the end of 30 minutes, a red light comes on and the lawyer stops. The petitioner, who argues first, has the option of reserving the last 10 minutes of their time for rebuttal after the respondent's argument. Come what may, after one hour, the oral arguments are over, for another case is in the wings awaiting the court's attention.

Deciding Cases

On Friday and late Wednesday afternoon during sittings, the justices hold conference in a secluded room adjacent to the chief justice's chambers. Conferences are held in the strictest confidentiality, with no one but the justices permitted in the room. Messengers are met at the door by the most junior justice. During his years as junior justice, John Paul Stevens referred to himself as the highest paid doorman in Washington. The Supreme Court is in some ways the most secretive of government bodies, in a city justly renowned for its cottage industry in press leaks and rumors.

Conference always begins with a round of handshakes, symbolic of the Court's unity of purpose, and no doubt an attempt to contain the conflicts everyone knows are only moments away. The Friday morning conference is usually given over to reviewing certiorari petitions. Wednesday afternoons are spent discussing cases argued the preceding Monday, and Friday afternoons are devoted to cases argued on Tuesday and Wednesday. The chief justice is the first to speak. While he or she is but the first among equals, each justice having one vote, the ability to speak first may provide an effective chief justice with additional influence among the justices: he or she gets to shape the issues in a case, while the other justices respond to his or her views. Not all chiefs have been very popular with their fellow justices, however, and how much a chief dominates a conference depends on many intangible and idiosyncratic factors, not the least of which is the willingness of the remaining eight justices to allow it.[39] The justices are permitted to speak in order of seniority, although evidence suggests that little conversation and debate occurs at this stage. A tentative vote is implicit in this discussion and will be noted by the chief justice.

Five or more votes will determine the winner of the case. Should the chief justice be on the winning side, he or she will assign to one member of the majority, perhaps himself or herself, the duty of writing an opinion of the Court, explaining and justifying the Court's decision. If the chief justice is a member of the minority, the member of the majority with the most seniority will make the assignment. Some theorize that a skillful chief may exert extra influence through the authority to assign the opinion writing. He may, perhaps, select the justice most likely to write an opinion consistent with the chief's views, or who would most likely be able to hold a majority behind the chief's preferred position on a closely divided Court, or to secure other goals.

It is said that when the Court first voted on the case of Roe v. Wade, the 1973 decision establishing the right to have an abortion, the vote was four to three (there were two vacancies on the Court) in support of a woman's right to have an abortion, with Chief Justice Burger in the minority.[40] Once Burger realized such a lineup would enable Justice William Douglas to make the opinion assignment, he apparently changed his vote. Douglas was known as a strong proponent of personal privacy rights, who in conference had taken an unequivocal position that the Constitution included a right of abortion and who would most likely have kept the opinion writing for himself. Wishing to avoid a strongly formulated right of abortion, Burger assigned the opinion to Justice Harry Blackmun. Burger and Blackmun had been boyhood chums in St. Paul, and during the early 1970s tended to vote together with such frequency that the press labeled them "the Minnesota Twins." In conference, Blackmun had again placed himself next to the Chief Justice, indicating a suspicion of the claim that the Constitution protects a right of abortion. It should be added, however, that Blackmun also had been for many years chief counsel for the Mayo Clinic, and had more experience in medical law than anyone else on the Court. It was experience Blackmun put to use in writing an opinion for the Court, ultimately staking out a very strong constitutional right to individual privacy, including the option of abortion. Blackmun's opinion pleased even Douglas, although it must have disappointed the chief justice. Burger concurred in the result, reluctantly favoring abortion only in limited circumstances and taking pains to point out that the Court had not created a right of "abortion on demand."[41]

Stories such as this are difficult to verify and should be entertained with a certain amount of caution. However, even if apocryphal, this story contains some important truths, for the way in which justices vote or write opinions will be determined by a variety of extralegal factors, including individual approaches to constitutional interpretation and ideological predilections. More than other courts, the United States Supreme Court is an institution involved in the making of political decisions. It was not hard in recent years to draw a sharp ideological line between Chief Justice Rehnquist and Justices Scalia, O'Connor, Kennedy, and White on one hand, and Justices Brennan and Marshall on the other. Only slightly more difficult to pigeonhole were Justices Blackmun and Stevens. During the 1991–1992 term, with Brennan and Marshall gone, Blackmun and Stevens graduated from "moderates" to "liberals" in the media's parlance, with Rehnquist, Scalia, White, and Thomas forming a recognizably conservative bloc and O'Connor, Souter, and Kennedy as an emerging bloc of "moderates" holding the balance. President Clinton's appointment of Ruth Bader Ginsberg, a federal appeals court judge with a record of moderate liberalism and judicial restraint, appeared to be an effort to build a bridge to this moderate bloc and reduce the influence of the conservatives. These labels are, of course, relative, and the blocs themselves are quite fluid, yet their presence illustrates how much politics is a part of the Supreme Court, even if manifested in peculiar ways.

The vote taken in conference is far from conclusive. Once an opinion is drafted, it is circulated among the other justices for comment. In addition, each individual justice retains the option to write an alternative opinion expressing his or her own views, either agreeing with the outcome chosen by the majority but for different reasons—called a concurring opinion—or registering disagreement with the reasoning and the result of the majority's opinion—a dissenting opinion. These are also circulated among the justices in draft form.

It is at this stage that the justices begin a process of debating and bargaining among themselves, each trying to secure as strong a bloc of supporters as possible behind his or her own position.[42] It is probably not too different from legislators lining up votes needed to enact a bill into law, except there is no evidence that justices actually trade votes, as legislators frequently do. Rather, they try to find common ground on which a number of justices can stand. The justice who has written for the majority would like to hold at least five votes in support of his or her opinion, but more would be better. This may require compromising some pet legal theories in the process, if other justices' objections might keep them from cosigning the opinion.

The threat of writing a side opinion is often an effective bargaining tool to convince a justice to soften or somehow alter an opinion he or she has written, but not so effective as the threat of switching votes! It sometimes happens that a recalcitrant justice will alienate other justices, or perhaps others will be persuaded to change their minds by a powerful dissenting opinion written by an erstwhile member of the minority.[43] With a switch of a few votes, the minority might become a majority, thus shifting the Court's judgment. Again, the process is thoroughly political, albeit dignified. Nothing is final until a decision is announced in open court, usually some months later.

When the process of intra-Court bargaining is finished and the Court is ready to announce its decision, the justice who has managed to hold a majority will read a summary of the Court's opinion. This opinion will explain who won the case, but, more important, must justify the decision. To be effective, the Court's justification for its decision should exhibit sufficient legal excellence to earn the respect, even if only grudging, of the public. We will defer to the last two chapters a brief examination of how this excellence may be exhibited. For now, it is sufficient to note that the need to develop a rationale for the Court's decision that is consistent

with written legal texts, be they statutes or the Constitution, with historical experience, judicial precedents, the moral values of the community, or whatever, considerably limits the scope of the Court's discretion. Whatever direction the members of the Court would like to take public policy, they can go only so far and must
be able to "sell" through their opinions. The Court depends on others, mainly the
executive branch, to enforce its decisions, so the Court's power may ultimately be
only its power to convince others of it correctness.

No doubt this is why some justices frequently go public with their side opinions, whether concurring or dissenting. These might be viewed as appeals to the
future, to soften, blunt, or even reverse the policy the Court has adopted.[44] Some
justices have become rather famous as dissenters who proved to be prophetic. For
example, in 1896, in the case of Plessy v. Ferguson, the Court held that racial segregation on railroad cars did not violate the Fourteenth Amendment's guarantee
that no state should "deny to any person within its jurisdiction the equal protection of the laws."[45] Justice Harlan, from Kentucky, the Court's only former slave
owner, dissented, arguing that the Fourteenth Amendment (as well as the Thir-
teenth) prohibited all vestiges of slavery, and rendered the Constitution "color-
blind." Not until the 1954 decision of Brown v. Board of Education declared that,
at least in the field of public education, the "separate but equal" doctrine of Plessy
had no place was Justice Harlan's dissent to be vindicated.[46] Later, Justice Oliver
Wendell Holmes would argue strongly against the Court's interpretation of the
Fourteenth Amendment to frustrate social welfare legislation, especially that
aimed at ameliorating the worst ravages of industrial capitalism.[47] After 1937,
Holmes's position became accepted constitutional doctrine and has been ever
since.[48] Justice Hugo Black made a career out of dissenting in a number of fields,
most notably freedom of speech and press and the application of the Bill of Rights
to restrain actions by state governments.[49] Today, we observe to a significant degree Justice Black's interpretation of the Constitution. The lesson of history is that
constitutional interpretation is not truly permanent but, like everything else in
politics, always in flux.

Often, in fact, a decision by the Court is the beginning of a round of political
decision making, often involving the coordinate branches of federal or state governments. Thus, a decision by the Supreme Court may represent only a new
phase in the policy-making process, not the end of the process.[50] Most decisions
by the Court receive scant attention beyond the narrow community of lawyers,
judges, some politicians, and perhaps a few professors. Others quickly attract considerable publicity, whether favorable or unfavorable, and alter considerably the
political landscape for other actors. Unfortunately, many decisions are the subject
of more controversy than understanding, for Supreme Court opinions tend to be
rather technical affairs that are not well represented in the nation's media. Indeed, the Court has to be the least understood branch of the national government.

For better or worse, decisions by the Supreme Court occasionally become political symbols around which, or against which, whole political movements may or-
ganize. Surely the Brown case was a significant boost to the nascent Civil Rights
Movement that would so redefine American politics in the late 1950s and 1960s.

By granting its imprimatur to a new set of expectations, the Court helped focus attention on one of our nation's most significant moral shortcomings. One wonders whether the New Right would have become a phenomenon of the 1980s were it not for a series of decisions by the Supreme Court, especially in the areas of abortion, race relations, and the separation of church and state. Would Richard Nixon have won the presidency in 1968 without the widespread public perception, however unsupported by empirical evidence, that defendants' rights decisions of the previous decade were responsible for undermining the criminal justice system? We can never know, of course, but the Supreme Court is frequently a convenient target for a politician in need of bogeymen. The Court can also crystallize public opinion concerning an issue, for it is not clear that a western lawyer named Abraham Lincoln would have achieved the presidency were it not for the controversy generated by the Court's infamous decision in Dred Scott v. Sanford, declaring Congress powerless to regulate the spread of slavery into the western territories.[51]

Powerful as the Supreme Court is, it bears reiteration that the lower courts are also significant political actors. One of the most striking features about the Supreme Court is the attenuated supervision it exercises over lower courts. Compare again the caseload figures represented in Tables 2.1–2.3. In terms of simple volume, we can see that the Supreme Court adjudicates only a small number of cases annually, when compared with the district courts. One important study of the flow of cases through a sample of U.S. courts of appeals conducted in the early 1970s found that only one in five decisions from the intermediate courts was appealed to the Supreme Court, and further that the Supreme Court granted certiorari to only 9.2 percent of these. In other words, the Supreme Court was found to interfere in only 1.9 percent of all cases in the sample studied (a figure more recently reduced to less than 1 percent). The Supreme Court upheld the intermediate court's decision in 0.5 percent of the entire sample of cases and altered the decision of the appellate courts in 1.4 percent of cases. The U.S. courts of appeals were the final court for 98.1 percent of cases they heard and made decisions that formally prevailed (i.e., were not changed on appeal) in 98.6 percent of cases.[52] The odds for any particular case ultimately being taken for argument before the Supreme Court are quite slim, almost akin to being struck by lightning. We know lightning strikes, but the chances of it striking any particular spot make for a poor bet.

Does this mean lower courts are largely unsupervised by the Supreme Court? The answer seems to be yes and no. Because so many cases never receive Supreme Court review, including apparently all cases in broad areas of law in which the Supreme Court has no interest, we cannot avoid the conclusion that the Supreme Court is not a participant in policy making much of the time. On the other hand, it is the Supreme Court that largely determines the areas in which it will be a key player and to some degree controls the depth of its intervention. By granting certiorari to more cases in a particular field, the Supreme Court can increase its own importance in policy making on some issues. We can predict, based on past observation, the fields in which the Supreme Court is likely to show the most interest—but then lightning strikes are not entirely random either.

In addition, the decisions rendered by the Supreme Court in cases it does accept become precedents that must be followed by all lower courts in similar cases.

Hence, if the Supreme Court selects a small number of cases, but selects carefully those cases presenting fundamental questions of policy, its influence will reach far beyond the few cases it actually decides. We will see in Chapter 6, however, that following precedents is not a mechanical process. Lower courts must interpret the scope and meaning of a precedent in applying it to a new case. All of this is to say that the Supreme Court, the courts of appeals, and the district courts share in the formulation of policy, although the precise ratios of influence may vary and are hard to calculate.

Sharing of power opens the door to conflict between the different courts. Often, lower courts respond to the local political culture of their particular region, which may put them at odds with the Supreme Court. On some issues, there may be considerable difference in outlook among these different levels of court. These conflicts recall the controversy between the antifederalists and the proponents of a unified national judiciary two centuries ago. We shall see in Chapter 3 why the appointment process for lower federal courts virtually guarantees this localism, building considerable decentralization into the federal bench. Chapter 4 will consider the appointment of Supreme Court justices. Throughout the next two chapters, the student should remain sensitive to the different roles performed by each layer of the federal judiciary, for these will influence the qualifications for those we might most want to see appointed to each.

NOTES

1. Thomas Jefferson, "Notes on the State of Virginia," in Merrill D. Peterson, The Portable Jefferson (Viking Press, New York, 1975) p. 164.
2. Ibid., p. 165.
3. Articles of Confederation, in Michael Kammen, ed., The Origins of the American Constitution (Penguin, New York, 1986) p. 10.
4. Alexander Hamilton, James Madison, John Jay, The Federalist (Random House, New York, 1937) p. 139.
5. Winton U. Solberg, ed., The Federal Convention and the Formation of the Union of the American States (Bobbs-Merrill, Indianapolis, Indiana, 1958) p. 78.
6. Ibid., pp. 77–78
7. Ibid., pp. 133–34.
8. Ibid., pp. 104–05. Also see Saul K. Padover, To Secure These Blessings (Washington Square Press, New York, 1962) p. 399.
9. Ibid., p. 105.
10. Ibid.
11. Letters of Brutus XI, in Herbert Storing and Murray Dry, The Anti-federalist (University of Chicago Press, Chicago, 1985) p. 165.
12. Ibid.
13. Solberg, op. cit., p. 336.
14. 14 U.S. 304 (1816).
15. Harry P. Stumpf and John H. Culver, The Politics of the State Courts (Longman, New York, 1992) pp. 2–3.

16. Ibid.
17. The Judicial Business of the United States Courts: Annual Report of the Director (preliminary draft) (U.S. GPO, Washington, D.C., 1992) p. 27.
18. Ibid., p. 27 and 299.
19. Unless otherwise noted, all data concerning personnel, caseload and so on are from the Annual Report of the Director of the Administrative Office of the United States Courts for 1985, 1988, and 1990. This annual publication is available from the U.S. GPO, Washington, D.C. Data after 1990 are from Judicial Business of the United States Courts: Annual Report of the Director, a preliminary draft of the former, also available from the U.S. GPO, Washington, D.C.
20. Richard A. Posner, The Federal Courts: Crisis and Reform (Harvard University Press, Cambridge, Massachusetts, 1985) pp. 63–64.
21. Marc Galanter, "Reading the Landscape of Disputes: What We Know and Don't Know (and Think We Know) about our Allegedly Contentious and Litigious Society," 31 UCLA Law Review 4 (1983), and Galanter, "The Day After the Litigation Explosion," 46 Maryland Law Review 3 (1986).
22. The distinction between criminal and civil law is a basic one, and although the general characteristics of a trial are similar, there are significant differences as well. We need only note that the rules of evidence are stricter and the prosecutor's burden of proof higher in criminal cases, making a successful prosecution harder to achieve than a favorable judgment in civil lawsuits. Criminal law includes all activities defined as offenses by legislation and for which punitive measures, such as a fine, incarceration, or, in a little over half the states, capital punishment, may be meted out. Civil law includes a broader category of activities and may serve to promote the protection of valued goods (the law of property) or to facilitate private arrangements (the law of contracts or trusts and estates). Some civil law (torts) regulates interpersonal relations, requiring us to behave in ways that do not unreasonably hurt others or subject them to unjustified risk, and may overlap with criminal law. Thus, an assault may be a crime and a tort.
23. J. Woodford Howard, "Litigation Flow in Three United States Courts of Appeals," 8 Law & Society Review 33 (1973).
24. Brown v. Board of Education, 347 U.S. 483 (1954). See Jack Bass, Unlikely Heroes (Simon & Schuster, New York, 1981).
25. H. W. Perry, Deciding to Decide: Agenda Setting in the United States Supreme Court (Harvard University Press, Cambridge, Massachusetts, 1991) pp. 23, 102, and Doris Marie Provine, Case Selection in the United States Supreme Court (University of Chicago Press, Chicago, 1980) pp. 9, 18.
26. Not everyone agrees with the usual assessment of efficiency in the cert pool; see Perry, op. cit., pp. 51–60.
27. John Paul Stevens, "Some Thoughts on Judicial Restraint," 66 Judicature 177, 179 (1982). See also Perry, op. cit., pp. 64–67.
28. Provine, op. cit., pp. 28–29.
29. Quoted in John R. Schmidhauser, Judges and Justices (Little, Brown, Boston, 1979) p. 123.
30. Perry, op. cit., has developed a complex model of certiorari decision making, incorporating a host of variables. See especially pp. 271–290. Also see Provine, op. cit., p. 7.
31. Virginia Armstrong and Charles A. Johnson, "Certiorari Decision Making by the Warren and Burger Courts: Is Cue Theory Time Bound?" 15 Polity 141, 150 (1982), and Gregory Caldeira and John R. Wright, "Organized Interests and Agenda Setting in the U.S. Supreme Court" 82 American Political Science Review 1109, 1116 (1988).

32. Rex E. Lee, "The Office of Solicitor General: Political Appointee, Advocate, and Officer of the Court," in D. Grier Stephenson, Jr., ed., An Essential Safeguard: Essays on the United States Supreme Court and its Justices (Greenwood Press, New York, 1991) p. 59. Perry's estimate is even higher, at 75–90 percent! See Perry, op. cit., p. 128.
33. Caldeira and Wright, op. cit., p. 1119.
34. Maryland v. Baltimore Radio Show, 338 U.S. 912, 917 (1950), memorandum of Justice Frankfurter.
35. But see Brown v. Allen, 344 U.S. 443, 542 (1953), for the suggestion that consistent rejection of certiorari in many similar cases may indicate approval of lower court policy. This was, however, the view of only three justices.
36. Provine, op. cit., p. 41.
37. Perry, op. cit., p. 25.
38. Annual Report of the Director of the Administrative Office of the United States Courts 1990 (U.S. GPO, Washington, D.C.) p. 103.
39. Walter F. Murphy, Elements of Judicial Strategy (University of Chicago Press, Chicago, 1964) pp. 82–89.
40. In conference, Burger was inclined to overturn the Texas abortion law on the grounds that it was too vague for a penal statute. However, he was then opposed to the notion that the Constitution included a right to abort a pregnancy. Blackmun initially agreed with this position, which would permit a state to proscribe abortion through a properly drafted statute. The internal maneuvering among the justices is described in greater detail by David O'Brien, Storm Center: The Supreme Court in American Politics, 4th ed. (W.W. Norton, New York, 1993) pp. 29–34.
41. 410 U.S. 113, 207 (1973).
42. The classic study of this intracourt bargaining is Murphy, op. cit.
43. Murphy, op. cit., pp. 54, 57.
44. Ibid., p. 60.
45. Plessy v. Ferguson, 163 U.S. 537 (1896).
46. Brown v. Board of Education, 347 U.S. 483 (1954).
47. Lochner v. New York, 198 U.S. 45, 74 (1905), Adkins v. Children's Hospital, 261 U.S. 525, 567 (1923).
48. West Coast Hotel v. Parrish, 300 U.S. 379 (1937), Ferguson v. Skrupa, 372 U.S. 726 (1963).
49. See, for example, Adamson v. California, 332 U.S. 46, 68 (1947), Dennis v. United States, 341 U.S. 494, 579 (1951).
50. See, generally, Stuart A. Scheingold, The Politics of Rights (Yale University Press, New Haven, Connecticut, 1974).
51. Dred Scott v. Sanford, 60 U.S. 393 (1857).
52. J. Woodford Howard, Jr., "Litigation Flow in Three United States Courts of Appeals," 8 Law & Society Review 33 (1973).

Chapter
3

Selection and Tenure on the Lower Federal Bench

The previous chapter explored the structure of the federal judiciary. Recall from our brief historical survey that the structure of our national courts evolved slowly, reflecting the concerns of various political interests in the community. We also saw that each of the three levels of the present-day judiciary has a significantly different role in the system. In this chapter we will examine the question of how federal judges are chosen for the U.S. district courts and courts of appeals. Appointments to the Supreme Court will be the topic of Chapter 4. We will also examine briefly the reasons for the unusually secure tenure enjoyed by federal judges after appointment and note the problems this poses on those occasions when disciplining of errant judges might be necessary.

The tenure of judges raises even more profound problems for democratic politics, for if courts make policy, their job security means they do so insulated from direct political accountability. The tenure and selection process for all federal judges reflects a balance struck between the competing values of democratic control and judicial independence, but it is a balance weighted heavily in favor of independence. Repudiation of Blackstone's formalism complicates this balance. We saw in Chapter 1 that modern jurisprudence views courts not as mere oracles of the law, but as discretionary policy makers. In Chapter 2 we saw that this discretion was implicitly recognized by political actors at the time of the adoption of the Constitution, despite the prevalence of rhetoric to the contrary. The existence of discretion in policy making has fueled debate over the judiciary ever since.

Were judicial decisions a matter of discovery, the selection of judges would turn solely on an evaluation of the technical skills needed to elucidate the law accurately. Such a judge could be recruited relatively free of political controversy.

But if judicial creativity is a normal part of adjudication, then we should expect greater demands for political accountability of the courts, especially in the process of appointing judges. We should not be surprised, then, to find contending interests in society who may be affected by judicial policies attempting to influence judicial recruitment. The trade-off between judicial independence and accountability is still a difficult one in American politics that has been further animated by the contemporary struggle to control some of the recent policies issuing from the courts.

APPOINTMENT POWER AND THE CONSTITUTION

Among the many sins attributed to King George III by the Declaration of Independence in 1776 were the twin charges "He has obstructed the Administration of Justice, by refusing his Assent to Laws for establishing Judiciary Powers," and "He has made judges dependent on his will alone, for the tenure of their offices, and the amount and payment of their salaries." In England, the creation of courts and the appointment of judges had been removed from the royal prerogative since the beginning of the eighteenth century to ensure the impartial application of the laws. This practice of judicial independence was viewed as a great advance in the preservation of liberty and justice. William Blackstone expressed the common view of the day in his *Commentaries on the Laws of England:*

> In this distinct and separate existence of the judicial power, in a peculiar body of men, nominated indeed, but not removable at pleasure, by the crown, consists one main preserve of the public liberty; which cannot subsist long in any state, unless the administration of common justice be in some way separated both from the legislative and also from the executive power. . . . For which reason . . . effectual care is taken to remove all judicial power out of the hands of the king's privy council; who, as then was evident from recent instances, might soon be inclined to pronounce that for law, which was most agreeable to the prince or his officers. Nothing therefore is more to be avoided, in a free constitution, than uniting the provinces of a judge and a minister of state.[1]

North Americans expected a similar administration of justice in the colonies. Instead, the king thoroughly controlled the colonial courts. He appointed and dismissed colonial judges according to his whim, without regard for their professional qualifications. He also raised or reduced their salaries while they served, thus compelling judgments heedless of the law. All the king required of his judges, it was generally believed, was their unquestioning subservience to his will, regardless of the legal merits of a litigant's claim. In the eyes of Americans, the result was the perversion of law and the corruption of justice. Judges were viewed as little more than royal henchmen, bent on carrying out the king's schemes of oppression of his heretofore loyal American subjects. Colonial sentiments were summed up by one writer who complained of the king's "sporting with our persons and estates by filling the highest seats of justice with bankrupts, bullies, and blockheads."[2]

After gaining independence, many of the 13 states undermined the principle of judicial independence by making judges equally dependent on the whim of the legislature. The results were predictable. If before the Revolution the interests of the king could always be expected to prevail, now it was the legislative majority, driven by the spirit of "faction," that seldom lost a lawsuit. Antifederalists, concerned for the protection of local interests, for popular accountability, and incidentally suspicious of aristocratic pretensions of the legal profession, were happy to leave things the way they were. Emerging federalist sentiment, however, sought a change to guarantee impartial administration of the laws for the protection of rights of all citizens, but especially for the protection of property rights of economic elites that legislatures seemed increasingly inclined to ignore.

The plan of government introduced by the Virginia delegation at the Constitutional Convention of 1787 would have given to the legislature authority to appoint personnel to both a judiciary and an executive branch. James Wilson, of Pennsylvania, objected to this provision, fearing it would encourage intrigue among vying legislative factions, who might be inclined to trade judicial appointments for partisan support.[3] He preferred an elected executive who would appoint judges. This would remove the selection of judicial officials from factious politics and focus responsibility for appointments in one person to ensure that judges would be of the highest caliber. Wilson's proposal divided the Convention between those seeking the enhancement of executive power and those who saw in such broad authority the foundations of monarchy. To some degree, this division reflected the controversy we discussed in Chapter 2, with those tending to prefer centralized national authority also tending to favor executive selection and those hoping to preserve greater state independence generally seeking legislative appointments.

It was Alexander Hamilton who first proposed that judges be nominated by the executive, subject to the approval of the upper house of the legislature. Initially, this suggestion gained little support. Several proposals were floated by other delegates, only to be sunk in controversy throughout the summer of 1787. It was not until nearly the end of the Convention that the Special Committee on Postponed Matters—the title is self-explanatory—revived Hamilton's suggestion. This time it was adopted, with some minor alterations, leading to the familiar language of Article II:

> [The president] shall nominate, and by and with the Advice and Consent of the Senate, shall appoint . . . judges of the Supreme Court, and all other Officers of the United States, whose Appointments are not herein otherwise provided for, and which shall be established by Law: but the Congress may by Law vest the Appointment of such inferior Officers, as they think proper, in the President alone, in the Courts of Law, or in the Heads of Departments.

This passage should be considered carefully. Notice that while the Constitution specifies a method for choosing members of the Supreme Court, it does not do so for lower federal courts. This should not be entirely surprising, since the very existence of lower courts was a question the Constitutional Convention had to put off for legislative determination. In fact, if lower courts were created, the

Constitution left open two possibilities for staffing. Judges on the lower federal courts might be deemed "other Officers of the United States," and be appointed through a process identical to that employed for the Supreme Court—nomination by the president, followed by approval by the Senate, in turn followed by final appointment by the president.

Alternatively, judges on lower federal courts might be viewed as "inferior Officers," whose mode of appointment might be determined by Congress. Under the latter view, Congress might authorize the president to appoint whosoever he or she wishes to the lower courts, without the required approval of the Senate. However, the magnification of executive power this would represent makes it an unlikely option. Perhaps Congress could authorize the chief justice to make appointments to the lower bench, but only at the cost of accountability to a representative legislative body. Decentralization of the judiciary might be achieved by vesting appointments of district court judges in the appellate courts of each circuit, or even in the senior judges of the districts. The Constitution gives us little detail concerning who are "Heads of Departments," but perhaps the attorney general could be given independent discretion for the selection of judges, or a nonpartisan merit commission might be established to make nominations, as has been done for the District Court for the District of Columbia. For all these alternatives, the historical fact is that all federal judges have been assumed from the beginning to be "other Officers of the United States," appointed in the same fashion as a justice on the Supreme Court. That this practice has not been seriously questioned since 1789 indicates that Hamilton's scheme, while slow to be adopted, quickly proved satisfactory to all parties.

The constitutional procedure for the appointment of all federal judges, then, is quite simple: the president nominates a candidate, the Senate gives or withholds its advice and consent, and if Senate action is favorable, the president may make the appointment. Approval of nominations was confined to the Senate as a concession to small states, who feared that their interests might be submerged in the popularly apportioned House of Representatives. Nomination and appointment are separate, so presumably were the president who nominated a candidate to change his or her mind, even after Senate approval, he or she could still decline to complete the appointment, nominating a second candidate instead. Perhaps a newly elected president could quash a nomination left uncompleted by his or her predecessor, as Thomas Jefferson attempted in 1801.

Another issue left unclear by the Constitution is the nature of the Senate's role. Does "advice and consent" mean the Senate should respond to presidential initiative, exercising only a veto on his or her choices? If so, should that veto be based solely on considerations of character and professional competence? Or should the political ideology of the nominee also be a topic for Senate exploration? Alternatively, should the Senate be more active in the earliest stages of the process, even in the selection of candidates from which a nominee will be chosen? By what criteria? Some presidents of recent memory have sought to emphasize "consent" and relegate the Senate to the more passive role. Senators have sometimes, although not as often as one would expect, placed more emphasis on "advice" and sought an expanded role in judicial appointments. We shall see that the practice has been to split the difference, with the president enjoying considerable latitude over appointments to the Supreme Court, but with Senators often controlling appointments to the lower courts in their home states. Here is our first hint that despite the assumed constitutional uniformity for all judicial appointments, the actual practice of judicial selection varies considerably, depending on the level of court.

The Constitution left the size of all federal courts, including the Supreme Court, to the discretion of Congress. However, the insulation of the judges from political intimidation after taking their seats on the bench was secured by Article III's protection of judicial tenure:

> The Judges, both of the supreme and inferior Courts, shall hold their Offices during good Behaviour, and shall, at stated Times, receive for their Services, a Compensation, which shall not be diminished during their Continuance in Office.

Judges were not to serve a fixed term of years, in which case their judgments might be influenced by inducements of reappointment, nor could they be intimidated by threats of removal from the bench at the will of any political office holder. Rather, judges would retain their positions so long as they exhibited "good Behaviour," a quality the Constitution left undefined. However, it must have occurred to participants in the Constitutional Convention that if the appointment procedure outlined in Article II worked well, "good Behaviour" might last a long time indeed! Some have suggested that Congress might define the terms of "good Behaviour" and establish provisions for the discipline of misbehaving judges, perhaps going so far as their removal from office. Legislation enacted in 1980 provided for some disciplining of lower court judges by their circuit colleagues, but it stopped short of authorizing removal from the bench. It has generally been assumed that judges are "Civil Officers of the United States" who can be forced off the bench only through the cumbersome and little understood process of impeachment.

A small number of lower court judges have been removed by impeachment, usually following indictment and conviction for criminal offenses. However, district judge Alcee Hastings was removed by impeachment even after his 1982 acquittal on charges of bribery. An unsuccessful attempt was made on the tenure of federalist Supreme Court Justice Samuel Chase in 1805, apparently in retaliation for Chase's partisan statements from the bench, which were highly critical of Jefferson administration policies. The senate's failure to remove Chase led Jefferson to despair that impeachment was a "mere scarecrow." The only other Supreme Court justice to face an impeachment charge was William O. Douglas, after he temporarily stayed the execution of convicted spies Julius and Ethel Rosenberg, and again in 1970. The motivation for the latter attempt was conservative displeasure with the Court's expansion of rights claimed by unpopular minorities. Douglas had taken especially strong positions on free expression and rights of criminal defendants, but became the conservative's target of choice in response to some of his off-the-bench writings and marital exploits. However, the effort to make an example of Douglas went nowhere. For all practical purposes, impeachment has not been much of a threat to federal judges. Tenure remains a matter between the judge and his or her Maker, for he or she retains a position on the bench for life, or until he or she chooses to retire. Most have remained in harness for many years.

Salaries may not be reduced as punishment, although they might be raised, a possibility the Virginia Plan would have prohibited. Some framers convinced the Convention to permit salary hikes to counteract the effects of inflation, indicating that they envisioned judges retaining their seats for a considerable period of time, transcending the vicissitudes of electoral politics. While judges are paid well when compared to most Americans, they are only modestly rewarded when compared to their earning potential in the private practice of law. Federal judges enjoy some of the most generous retirement benefits available to Americans in any profession. These benefits were intended to encourage retirement by superannuated judges, but with only partial success.

Here we see one of the paradoxes of American politics. The framers envisioned the House of Representatives as the popular branch of the government, with the Senate chosen by the states. The president was to be chosen by an electoral college, itself chosen by states. Both were expected to be sufficiently independent of popular opinion to check factious schemes that might be hatched in the democratic House of Representatives. The courts were even further removed from popular control, as judges were chosen by the president, subject to the advice and consent of only the Senate. Even as the first two institutions were subsequently democratized through the growth of political parties and the adoption of the seventeenth amendment in 1916, the courts have remained relatively distant from democratic politics. Secure tenure means that a federal judge need never answer to any other political actor, including voters, for his or her decisions. How does a democratic society tolerate such power in the hands of such an undemocratic institution? This question should be borne in mind as we survey the politics of judicial appointments.

APPOINTMENTS TO FEDERAL DISTRICT COURTS

We have seen that the Constitution requires the participation of the president and the Senate in the selection of all federal judges but that it is unclear regarding the precise role each should play in the process. The result is a virtual invitation to political struggle in the process of judicial recruitment. The precise dynamics of this struggle will vary, depending on the location of the court in which a vacancy has occurred, the party affiliation and interest of the senators from the pertinent states, and the power and tenacity of the president. We shall examine first the process of appointing judges to the district courts, where descendants of the antifederalist forces favoring decentralization of judicial authority may have won a substantial victory.

Executive Action

When an opening occurs on a district court, all appearances suggest that the first move is the president's. Appearances can be deceiving, however, for a simple reality the president faces in choosing a candidate is the need for advice. District courts are far removed from the concerns of most presidents, psychologically as well as geographically. The deeply ingrained custom of requiring a district court judge to be a resident of the state where the district is located means the president will need help in selecting a candidate from among persons he or she probably does not know. Being in need of advice places the president under the influence of those in a position to advise him or her. Of course, a president can seek advice from whatever quarter he or she wishes, but the most reliable advisors will tend to be persons familiar with and active in the local politics of the pertinent state. Presidents are usually most interested in hearing from local supporters in their own political party.

Presidents often delegate to the Department of Justice the responsibility of compiling lists of candidates who might be considered should openings occur in the future. Practice varies from administration to administration, but it has historically been the attorney general or the deputy attorney general who has kept files of potential nominees suggested by a variety of interested persons. These include governors and other political activists, prominent lawyers, law school professors and deans, judges, legislators, influential interest groups, and others in the state who have connections to the president's party or to the senators who represent the state. Connections to senators are particularly important, for senators wield enormous influence over who is likely to be considered. Justice officials will screen candidates according to criteria established by the White House, but also taking account of the expressed wishes of certain senators, and winnow the list of candidates down to a few who seem most promising. It has lately become practice to interview candidates and require that they fill out lengthy questionnaires concerning their education, professional background, financial interests, and, more controversially, compatibility with the president's political agenda or conception of the judicial function.

Candidates for all judicial openings are also screened by the Federal Bureau of Investigation to verify answers given in the questionnaires or interviews and to prevent the surfacing of embarrassing information concerning a candidate's past after the nomination has been announced. All of this is done behind closed doors, obviously, with the FBI's report available only to the Department of Justice, the White House, and, traditionally, the chair of the Senate Judiciary Committee. More recently, the FBI file has been available to all senators, increasing the risk that potentially damaging information might be leaked to the media to embarrass a candidate publicly.[4]

On the other hand, access to all relevant information enhances the Senate's ability to scrutinize candidates fully. Should the FBI turn up any matters of concern for which the candidate cannot supply an adequate explanation, or if the explanation will not sit well with the public, that individual's candidacy will likely proceed no further. However, it is not clear how thorough this FBI investigation is in practice. During the Carter administration, the FBI routinely interviewed 125 or more sources for each candidate.[5] During the Reagan administration, the FBI seems to have routinely interviewed considerably fewer sources, about 70 or 80.[6] It is difficult for political scientists to evaluate the role played by the FBI because of the secrecy of the investigation. We do not know how many candidacies are quashed as a result of FBI investigations.

Similarly, a short list of candidates under consideration will be circulated to the American Bar Association (ABA), to be screened and rated according to the ABA's murky criteria for professional acumen. The ABA is ostensibly nonpartisan and apolitical, dedicated only to improving the professionalism of the bench. Prior to 1989, its Standing Committee on Federal Judiciary rated candidates for lower court appointments as "exceptionally well qualified," "well qualified," "qualified," or "not qualified." As part of a political accommodation with the Bush administration, the ABA dropped the "exceptionally well qualified" designation.[7]

Review by the ABA has been one of the more controversial aspects of the appointment process, for the ABA is in reality nothing more than an interest group representing slightly less than half the lawyers in the country. Its membership is not even truly representative of the legal profession, tending instead to overrepresent the well-established, urban lawyer with a high-status practice in a medium to large firm, tending to be white, male, and conservative. It has shown a preference for candidates similar to its members: having prestigious educational backgrounds, high-prestige corporate practices, usually with over 10 years' experience, including trial experience for district courts or judicial experience for appellate court appointments, and a generally moderate to conservative political outlook. Although the ABA claims to employ only criteria of professional accomplishment, the committee has not always been able to separate these from considerations that at least appear ideological.[8]

In fact, the ideological component of ABA politics was revealed at its inception. Its interest in federal judicial appointments can be traced back to the 1930s, when in response to the Senate's rejection of Supreme Court nominee John J. Parker the ABA sought to lessen the influence of political parties and labor and civil rights groups. Some have complained that the ABA has remained unsympathetic to young, non-white, or female nominees, despite some recent efforts by the ABA at diversifying its membership.

In general, the ABA seems to have more influence during Republican administrations, with the exception of the Reagan and Bush administrations, when it came under the criticism of New Right activists. This should hardly be surprising, since the ABA membership tends to reflect closely the traditional cohorts of the Republican Party—economic and professional elites. Democratic presidents have tended to hold the ABA more at arm's length, also not surprising, since Democratic constituency groups are only weakly represented in the ABA. Nevertheless, it seems extraordinary that the ABA should exercise the influence it does, far exceeding that of any women's groups or the National Bar Association, which represents primarily African-American lawyers.

Even within the framework of a single administration, the actual influence of the ABA seems to vary and may generally be limited to eliminating from consideration only the weakest of candidates. An ABA rating of "not qualified" has not always stood in the way of a determined president, where senatorial support was present. Indeed, a few persons so honored have gone on to distinguished careers on the bench. It is difficult to evaluate the degree to which the ABA might deter early in the process the serious consideration of nominees who are weak in professional credentials. Probably a "not qualified" rating would only sharpen opposition that already existed in the Senate, but would seldom be enough by itself to defeat a candidacy. Even so, the possibility that the ABA may have considerable influence in some appointments is likely to remain a source of criticism.[9]

Senate Action

Once a nomination has been announced by the White House, it will be sent to the Senate and referred to the Senate Judiciary Committee. The committee's task is to evaluate the nominee and make a recommendation to the Senate, which must then grant or withhold its advice and consent. When a nomination is received, the chair of the committee sends out a "blue slip" to each of the senators from the state in which the district is located. These are letters printed on blue paper, soliciting the senator's personal "opinion and information concerning the nomination."[10] A senator may return the blue slip within a week indicating his or her glowing support of the candidate. Should the senator not return the blue slip, it is taken to mean that he or she finds the candidate "personally obnoxious."

Failure to return a blue slip probably never bodes well for a nomination, but failure to return a blue slip by a home-state senator who is also a member of the president's political party has traditionally constituted a veto of the nomination, for it is well understood that the Senate will not approve a nominee over such objections. This informal rule is known as *senatorial courtesy*, and is a unique product of the comity senators traditionally show each other. The effect of senatorial courtesy on district court appointments is a powerful one that must be explored in detail.

No one is sure exactly when senatorial courtesy became a practice. It seems to have become standardized by the 1840s, but a special role for home-state senators was invited, perhaps unintentionally, by the Judiciary Act of 1789. Congress established district boundaries that were coterminous with state boundaries, a practice that continues today insofar as districts do not cross state lines. This placing of districts wholly within a single state amplifies the proprietary interest of that state's senators over the district. Obviously, the home-state senators are more likely to know the candidate by local reputation, if not by personal association. It is highly likely that a judicial nominee will have been politically active and a member of the president's party. If the senator also shares the president's party affiliation, his or her association with the candidate will probably have been intimate. It is, therefore, quite logical for the Senate to consider carefully the views of the home-state senators.

For many years, a senator who wished to invoke courtesy simply announced his or her opposition on the Senate floor. No questions were asked, and the vote would always be negative. Since about the 1940s, the more confidential blue slip system has been practiced, which sidetracks a candidacy prior to floor action. The effect is the same: to a substantial degree, the views of a home-state senator who is a member of the president's party *is* the Senate's advice and consent for district court appointments. If no objection is registered by home-state senators, a perfunctory interview with a subcommittee of the Judiciary Committee will be held. A home-state senator will probably introduce the candidate in glowing terms. A few questions may be asked, but the whole enterprise is usually over in 5–10 minutes. Approval by the whole Senate is virtually assured, for few senators wish to do battle over an appointment outside their own state: the cost in comity is high and the rewards too few.

Senators who are not members of the president's party may also be asked for advice by the White House, and their views may also be given considerable weight by their Senate colleagues, especially if they are powerful and prestigious members with favors to trade. However, they will not have the same voice as a member of the president's party and will not be able to sidetrack a nomination single-handedly. Thus, the White House will have a stronger hand to play if an opening occurs in a state not represented by any senators from the president's party. If both senators are members of the president's party, they may have to reach some sort of accommodation between themselves, or watch a president play off one against the other. Occasionally, senators have agreed to take turns with their home-state colleague in exercising senatorial courtesy.

We can see that senatorial courtesy turns home-state senators who are members of the president's party into key players in appointment politics. Presidents will turn to such senators not only out of a need for advice, but also out of a recognition that these senators wield sufficient power to block an appointment they oppose. A powerful senator who wishes to play hardball over a nomination might inform the White House of his or her intention to oppose every nomination except one—his or her preference. The White House frequently relents, with the result that the senator, not the president, will have actually chosen the appointee.

Senators jealously guard the practice of senatorial courtesy. It is a prized source of personal patronage used to reward individuals who have in the past lent their support to the senator or the senator's party. Of course, a determined White House may still veto a senator's choice. The Reagan administration resisted senators' choices that did not conform to administration goals, but few presidents wish to expend their own scarce political resources in so futile a battle. At best, the appointment will be a compromise between the White House and the senator. It is probably fair to view the president and the senator as having practically exchanged constitutional roles: the senator nominates a district court judge, and if the White House has no strong objections the senator's candidate will get the job.

Senators usually have to maintain a strong commitment to local interests to preserve their careers on Capitol Hill. They are elected only by local voters and depend on local party organizations to facilitate their campaigns. Because of senatorial courtesy, district court judges will almost invariably be individuals with a strong record of political activism in local power structures. Recall that among the fears of antifederalists was the specter of national courts swallowing up state judiciaries, diminishing local autonomy. When Congress passed the Judiciary Act of 1789, creating lower federal courts, local interests suffered an apparent blow. The appointment process that has evolved, however, may represent something of an antifederalist victory, for it serves to soften the impact of national laws through the appointment of district court judges with strong local attachments and sentiments. This builds considerable localism into the federal bench and can sometimes place district courts at odds with national legal policy.[11] One example, admittedly extreme, will illustrate this.

In 1954, the United States Supreme Court decided the case of *Brown v. Board of Education.*[12] This celebrated case prohibited the practice of racial segregation in public education, the keystone to the system of racial exclusion that had dominated the southern half of the country since the end of the nineteenth century. Implicitly, the Court overruled its 1896 decision in *Plessy v. Ferguson,* which held that racial segregation did not violate the fourteenth amendment's prohibition of a state from "deny[ing] to any person within its jurisdiction the equal protection of the laws."[13] Half a century later, in *Brown,* the Court held that segregation of children solely on the basis of race stamped minority students with a badge of inferiority, creating a negative self-image that inhibited their academic success and denied them equal benefit of the state's educational system. The legal difference between *Plessy* and *Brown* was that only the latter considered the psychological impact of segregation. The *Brown* decision recognized the message implicitly sent to minority children concerning their own worth as members of the community. In reality, the two cases represent radically different political theories of equality and of membership in a political community.

White southerners valued racial segregation to preserve their own social status and their continued political and economic hegemony over black Americans. For the most part, they reacted to *Brown* with hostility. The critical question of implementation of the Court's new and unpopular policy had been delayed until 1955, when the Court decided to return the cases to the district courts from which they had originated. Cognizant of differences in local conditions and resources, the Supreme Court chose not to require a uniform policy of implementation. Instead, the judges of the federal district courts, themselves products of southern society and generally quite comfortable with segregation, were instructed to use their discretionary equity jurisdiction to figure out how to end racial segregation "with all deliberate speed."[14]

Viewed in the abstract, this course of action made considerable sense. From the standpoint of practical political reality, however, this deference to local considerations created opportunities for local evasion of the *Brown* decision, in many cases aided and abetted by district court judges, that was to delay for a decade the realization of desegregated education. In effect, the local culture of the South had been insulated against interference by the United States Supreme Court, by the very U.S. district courts charged with carrying out the *Brown* mandate. It was not until the already emerging Civil Rights Movement was able to shame Congress into action on behalf of racial equality that genuine progress in school desegregation was made.

The power of the Senate reaches its apogee in district court appointments. Once the candidate has been approved by the Judiciary Committee and home-state senators have raised no objection, approval by the whole Senate is assured. From there, appointment is virtually automatic. A brief swearing in ceremony at the district court will follow, and the new judge can get down to work. As we move up the judicial structure, however, the appointment process will begin to change. The power of the president will increase as we proceed to the higher courts.

APPOINTMENTS TO THE UNITED STATES COURTS OF APPEALS

We have seen that the recruitment of federal district judges is a process involving conflict and compromise among several powerful actors. These include the president (or, more likely, his or her designee, usually the attorney general or deputy attorney general), senators from the home state of the district court and of the president's party, to a lesser extent home-state senators not of the president's party and other key senators (especially those on the Judiciary Committee), the ABA, the local bar association, and other local interests having influence with the home-state senators. The politics of judicial selection for the U.S. courts of appeals is similar, with the main difference being the diminution or absence of senatorial courtesy, largely for geographic reasons. Circuits encompass several states, thus it is harder for individual senators to claim the same proprietary interest over circuit appointments. The effect is to strengthen the president's hand in selection to the appellate bench.

This is not to say that regional senators lack influence. The White House may still need advice or may wish to trade favors with key senators for support of the president's political agenda. However, senators are not likely to have the same power to veto appointments as they have for district courts. Certainly, with reduced bargaining power, senators are less likely to be able to muscle themselves into a position of designating judicial nominees for the president. The reality of reduced power in the hands of individual senators has led political scientist Henry R. Glick to speak of "senatorial clearance" for appellate courts, in lieu of senatorial courtesy.[15] Even this may be too strong a term for the Senate's role in many appellate court appointments. In some circuits, tradition requires candidates to be selected from the states in the circuit in rotation, or a seat may become the preserve of a single state in the circuit. Thus, if a judge from Alabama leaves the Court of Appeals for the Eleventh Circuit, there is at least a strong presumption in favor of filling the seat with another Alabama native. The strength of this custom varies from circuit to circuit, but it may provide an opportunity for a senator whose state may claim its turn to exert a certain amount of senatorial courtesy.

One example of a recent and controversial appointment to the appellate bench might illustrate the politics involved. In 1986, President Reagan announced his nomination of Daniel A. Manion to the United States Court of Appeals for the Seventh Circuit. Manion, a lawyer with almost no experience in federal court, was rated as "qualified" by the ABA. However, sample briefs Manion filed with the Senate Judiciary Committee revealed a rather pedestrian legal mind, as well as considerable difficulty with spelling and grammar. More damning was Manion's

New Right political background, including links to the John Birch Society, a right wing extremist organization hostile to most of the Supreme Court's policies of the past three decades. Some of Manion's behavior as an Indiana legislator also raised questions about his politics, including displays of racial insensitivity and his sponsorship of a bill to require the posting of the Ten Commandments in public school classrooms, despite the obvious unconstitutionality of the proposal. Dozens of labor unions, civil rights organizations, and liberal activists and the deans of some 40 law schools quickly organized in opposition to the nomination.

Spokespersons for the Reagan administration defended the nomination by asserting that Manion was fully qualified and that opponents were questioning his legal acumen only as a pretext for their political opposition. More controversially, President Reagan asserted that the Senate's role in the process of judicial appointments was limited to screening a nominee's character and professional fitness only, and should never include ideological considerations. We shall presently consider the merits of this argument, previously heard only in the context of Supreme Court nominations. As evidence of Manion's weak qualifications mounted, Reagan administration supporters were reduced to defending Manion as no worse than some other federal judges—something short of a ringing endorsement.

In 1986, the Senate was still controlled by a slender Republican majority, including Republican senators who gained their seats on Reagan's coattails in 1980. However, with the 1986 elections in sight, several moderate Republicans were seeking to distance themselves from the more extreme elements of the right wing and announced their opposition to the Manion candidacy. So long as Senate Republicans held a majority, the Judiciary Committee remained under the sympathetic chairmanship of conservative Senator Strom Thurmond. Even with Thurmond's support, the committee declined to support Manion on a nine to nine vote, an outcome that would ordinarily have been most unlikely, given the perfunctory nature of committee deliberations for lower court appointments. The administration's contention that opposition to Manion was motivated solely by ideological considerations was undermined by the fact that this was the first of Reagan's 262 judicial nominations not to be supported by the committee.[16] The committee sent Manion's nomination to the Senate floor without a recommendation. (A month later the Committee rejected outright the nomination of Jefferson B. Sessions for a district court seat in Alabama.)

The Senate vote was expected to be close, and Mr. Reagan and members of his administration lobbied hard for approval. Deals were cut with several key Republican opponents in exchange for their votes, notably with Senator Slade Gorton, of Washington. In exchange for his vote on Manion, Gorton was promised a White House nomination of his preferred candidate for the federal district court in his own state, one whom the administration had previously opposed. Democrats were apparently taken off-guard when the floor vote on Manion tied 47 to 47, reflecting a strong party alignment.

Senator Robert Byrd, the Senate Democratic minority leader, switched his vote at the last minute to render the final tally 48 to 46 to approve the nomination. Under Senate rules, this permitted Byrd to request a reconsideration of the vote, which occurred several weeks later. Since this second vote was to reconsider a nomination already approved, opponents now needed a clear majority to block the nomination. Instead, the vote was 49 to 49, which effectively allowed the previous vote in support of Manion to stand. For good measure, Vice President Bush exercised a seldom-used constitutional prerogative to cast a tie-breaking vote, as he would surely have done in the first tally had Byrd not changed his vote, to make it 50 to 49 in Manion's favor. Thus, Democrats, even with the aid of several dissident Republicans, failed to block one of the most controversial circuit appointments in recent years. The public was unimpressed with the Senate's performance. Slade Gorton was defeated in his bid for reelection, in considerable part because of hostile reaction to his sale of his vote on Manion. (Washington voters are quick to forgive, however, for they returned Gorton to the Senate in 1988.)

Several lessons can be drawn from this complicated narrative. First, although Manion seemed to be only marginally competent, the ABA was reluctant to rate him "unqualified." The ABA, which had previously been critical of nominations from the ranks of the New Right, was under increasing fire from the White House and from New Right activists and organizations during this period. Most notable was the filing of a lawsuit by the right-wing Washington Legal Foundation challenging the ABA's role in the selection process. In response to political pressure, the ABA appeared to relax its standards in a number of cases in which New Right nominees were rated "qualified."[17] The Manion nomination may have been just such a case.

Second, although Manion was opposed for reasons of competence, political ideology and partisan politics played a major, perhaps dominant, role for his supporters and opponents alike. This is revealed in the strong party alignment in the Senate votes. Questions of merit may have emboldened the opposition, but the coming election and its prospects for a restored Democratic majority certainly played a role as well. It must be remembered that American political parties are loosely organized coalitions, lacking in party discipline or strong ideological consensus. Thus, for some Republicans, the intrusion of electoral politics into the process provided a countervailing pressure that induced them to resist the blandishments of a Republican administration and oppose Manion. Slade Gorton's experience indicates that their political judgment was astute.

Finally, as we can also see from the behavior of Senator Gorton, the president has considerable bargaining power in the Senate through his or her ability to grant or withhold favors for individual senators in exchange for their support. In Gorton's case, district court patronage was traded for a vote, also indicating the value senators place on district court appointments. The White House was also strengthened in this episode by the absence of senatorial courtesy, since this was an appellate court appointment.

The experience of other Reagan nominations indicates that a more qualified or politically moderate candidate would most likely have generated less controversy. Yet, even with a marginal candidate such as Manion, the White House was able to dominate the selection process. Nor have we seen the fullest reach of presidential power in judicial selections, for we have not yet considered the Supreme Court. We shall turn to the highest tribunal in Chapter 4. We will conclude this chapter with a comparison of the lower court legacies of Presidents Carter,

Reagan, and Bush and a brief consideration of the opportunities that await President Clinton.

THE LOWER COURT LEGACIES OF CARTER, REAGAN, AND BUSH

Although President Jimmy Carter made no Supreme Court appointments, he left a substantial judicial legacy in the lower federal courts. Carter's influence may ultimately reach beyond the individuals he made judges, for he sought to alter the way in which lower court judges are recruited. While his reforms were abolished by his successor, they may be emulated by future presidents. President Reagan also made many appointments to the lower bench. Like Carter, he put his own distinct stamp on the recruitment process, creating a legacy largely continued by the Bush administration.

The political styles of Carter and Reagan differed as much as their ideologies, yet both presidents sought explicitly to shape the judiciary according to their views of the proper role of courts in society. These views reflected in part the demands of differing interest groups each president considered important to his own political success, and which they sought to represent in the recruitment of judges. To accomplish their respective goals, both sought to strengthen the influence of the White House in the appointment process, at the cost of senatorial power. They thus offer interesting case studies of judicial appointments, exhibiting considerable contrast as well as some important similarities.

Carter's Judges

The lower federal courts were profoundly shaped by President Carter's politics. During his single term, Carter appointed 202 federal district court judges and 56 appellate court judges. In all, Carter's 258 appointments accounted for 40 percent of the federal bench by the time he left office. This unprecedented record was, in large measure, the direct result of the adoption by Congress of the Omnibus Judgeship Act of 1978. In response to growing caseloads, 152 new judgeships were added to the trial and appellate bench. However, the partisan element revealed in the timing of this legislation should not be overlooked—a Democratic Congress authorized a Democratic president to appoint a sizable number of new judges. True to the patterns established by past presidents, 90 percent of Carter's appointees were Democrats.[18]

Campaigning in 1976, Carter promised to make merit, rather than patronage, the guiding factor in the appointment of judges. In addition, Carter sought to open up the selection process to women and nonwhites through the conscious use of affirmative action techniques. To accomplish these goals, he had to reduce the role of senatorial courtesy, a task that proved politically futile for the district courts. However, by an executive order early in 1977, Carter created the U.S. Circuit Court Nominating Commission, essentially a merit panel to propose nominees for the appellate courts. This merit commission was modeled in part after the so-called Missouri Plan of judicial recruitment used in a number of states, but with modifications to accommodate the rigid demands of Article III of the Constitution.[19]

The commission was subdivided into a single panel for each circuit, except for the Fifth and Ninth Circuits, each of which was given two panels because of their size. Members of the commission were appointed by the president and were to be nonpartisan and equally balanced between lawyers and members of the lay public. Despite these good intentions, 85 percent of the commission's members were active Democrats. A good balance of lawyers and nonlawyers was achieved, however, as well as a fairly representative cross-section of the American public, including women and nonwhites. This demographic balance ensured the inclusion of new voices in the selection process.

When a vacancy occurred in a given U.S. court of appeals, the panel for that circuit was authorized to give public notice of the opening and solicit applications. Members could also propose nominees, and the panel could screen suggestions from the White House, senators, or local officials. Panels were instructed to search for members of the bar in good standing, with solid reputations for character, demeanor, and integrity, in good health, and who had demonstrated outstanding legal ability and "a commitment to equal justice under law."[20]

Most of these criteria refer to professional attainments commonly denoted as "merit," although some, such as character, demeanor, or integrity, may acquire an ideological color in practice. However, the requirement of "commitment to equal justice under law" should be understood as reflecting Carter's political goals both of placing on the bench persons from previously underrepresented groups and of promoting, through appointments, greater judicial sensitivity to minority rights. This political goal seemed to be preeminent, for an important part of the Carter legacy was that he appointed a larger number of blacks, Hispanics and women to the federal bench than had been chosen by all of his predecessors combined.

A brief survey of the Carter judges illustrates the degree to which Carter achieved these goals. During the four years Carter was in office, he appointed 37 blacks to judicial posts (28 to district courts, including at least one in every state of the old Confederacy, save Mississippi and Virginia, and 9 to the appellate courts), elevating the representation of blacks on the federal bench from 4 percent to 9 percent. Forty appointments were women (29 on the district courts, 11 in the circuits), raising from 1 percent to 7 percent the representation of women. Sixteen of Carter's appointments were Hispanic and 1 was Asian.[21] These numbers exceed the total of minority appointments because some appointees appear in two demographic categories; for example, seven blacks appointed by Carter were also women, and so are counted twice.

Although it is doubtful that members of these demographic groups have exhibited judicial behavior that substantially differs from their white male colleagues on most issues, it is likely that they would be especially sensitive to the aspirations of socially disadvantaged groups. This is not to say that a judge's behavior is necessarily determined, in a simple and reflexive way, by group membership. At the same time, however, the influence of a judge's background and life experience cannot be ignored as contributing factors shaping the perceptions, values, and predilections he or she brings to the bench. To the extent that the American community remains sharply divided, imposing very distinct kinds of experiences on most members of certain demographic groups, we can expect their presence or absence on the bench to be a factor shaping judicial policy. Nor is there reason to believe that this demographic representation was purchased at the cost of quality. Indeed, while merit is a slippery concept to measure, Carter's appointments score rather high in terms of such traditional criteria as educational background and ABA ratings. For example, an unusual number of Carter's appeals court appointments were former law professors, some of considerable distinction.

The high proportion of women among Carter's judges did result in a lower-than-usual number of appeals court candidates with prior judicial experience. The women were further distinguished from their male colleagues in that they were less likely to have had a history of party activism.[22] Both of these characteristics might reflect the degree to which women were previously denied opportunities to develop such experience. This well illustrates the effectiveness of Carter's Circuit Court Nominating Commission in overcoming deeply institutionalized patterns of discrimination. Had the administration acted according to traditional practices, even without a conscious desire to discriminate, few women could have been considered. Most women lacked the usual indicators of qualification simply because of discrimination they had experienced elsewhere in society. The result would have been the continued exclusion of women, however unintentional or unjustified. It was only by making an affirmative effort to find female candidates (and the same is true for racial minorities) that fully qualified women could be adequately considered for appointment to the appellate bench. Carter's accomplishment, then, was the opening up of the process of judicial selection so that a broader field of candidates could be considered and a more diverse bench appointed.

Carter's strategy for imprinting his own political ideals onto the judiciary required the diminution of the power customarily wielded by senators. It quickly become apparent to the White House that the Senate was not about to part with its institutional prerogatives over district court appointments. However, Carter did encourage senators to establish their own merit commissions in their home states and to submit to the White House candidates chosen according to criteria similar to those promulgated by the White House for the circuits. Ultimately, panels were established in 30 states, including all with Democratic senators who could have claimed senatorial courtesy, save for West Virginia.[23]

Attorney General Griffin Bell strongly opposed questioning of candidates about their political views by the circuit panels (he also stopped the practice of the FBI reporting on the political affiliations of the candidates). Even so, the complaint was heard that some of these local panels probed into highly ideological issues, apparently seeking prior commitments to rule in preferred ways on controversial issues likely to come up in litigation.[24] Such behavior was also exhibited on the Senate Judiciary Committee by New Right Senators Strom Thurmond and Orrin Hatch, thus setting the stage for future controversies about the role of ideological screening in the recruitment of judges.

Generally, however, the performance of these nominating panels seemed to be of high quality. Not only were individuals who previously would not have been candidates able to gain consideration, but the overall quality of Carter's district court appointments remained quite high. The greater emphasis on proven professional acumen required by the panels resulted in a somewhat higher emphasis on prior judicial experience than had previously been common at the district court level.[25] There also appeared to be a higher emphasis on large firm practice and a deemphasis of former government employment in the nominees sent to the White House. The presence of these commissions considerably reduced the temptations of senators to use judicial appointments as patronage to reward political supporters.

Reagan's Judges

Even more than the Carter administration, President Reagan's team came into Washington with a clear agenda for the federal courts. Activists of the New Right had long identified the courts as the enemy of the social policies they hoped to establish. Essentially a "politics of resentment," New Right ideology sought to restore a perceived golden age of a hard-working, family-devoted American middle class, ensconced in ethnically and racially homogeneous neighborhoods from which sexually explicit literature, crime, and social strife were absent, and with neighborhood schools in which traditional religious and patriotic values were inculcated in the young.

Supporters of the New Right tended to perceive their former status in a traditional reward system favoring hard work, moral restraint, and individual responsibility to be threatened by court-ordered school desegregation, court-ordered banning of prayer in the public schools, and court-aided (if not -induced) enthusiasm for equality that had spread to demands by women to be valued for roles other than that of homemaker. Most distressing to New Right activists was the judicially created right of abortion, with its implications of female sexual freedom. Judicial solicitude for the rights of criminal defendants was blamed by the New Right for rising crime rates that threatened to make neighborhoods unsafe. To be sure, there was a thinly veiled element of racial antagonism here as well. Nonwhites are often blamed in the popular mind for rising crime rates, and talk about crime is frequently an encoded discussion of race. To the New Right, the federal courts in general, but the Supreme Court in particular, were representative of a perceived elite of the affluent, the educated, and the privileged who had gained dominance in Washington. This cabal, it was said, expected the forgotten lower middle class to pay an unfair share of the cost for the satisfaction of demands by the heretofore unworthy members of society.[26] A president elected with strong support from such a constituency could not afford to be indifferent to the courts.

The process of judicial selection was addressed by the Reagan administration almost immediately on inauguration. Successful completion of Reagan's plans for the courts required greater White House influence over the screening of potential nominees. Faithful adherence to Reagan's social policy agenda was to become a preeminent consideration for all nominations. This, of course, represented a continuation of the practice of past presidents, but the Reagan White House carried the ideological aspect of judicial nominating to new heights, raising controversy even among those ordinarily expected to be sympathetic to the administration's professed goals of securing a restrained judiciary. The charge was frequently heard that the administration was employing narrow issue "litmus tests" to exclude all who did not rigidly adhere to New Right formulas of acceptability. The result has been called "a more coherent and ambitious legal-policy agenda that has been more systematically, meticulously, and effectively imposed than that of any prior administration."[27] Whether or not this represented an excessive amount of politicization of the courts depends largely on the commentator's sympathy for New Right politics or the kinds of civil liberties policies the New Right finds anathema.

One of Reagan's first acts was to abolish Carter's Circuit Court Nominating Commission. Although the commission served to dilute the influence of senators in screening appellate court nominees, the panels themselves proved too independent for Reagan's taste. It was feared that they would favor moderate conservatives, not quite what the White House had in mind. Instead, the screening of candidates for potential nomination was moved more deeply into the White House than had previously been the case. The initial screening of candidates was done by the Office of Legal Policy, in the Justice Department, but the most thorough screening was moved to the newly created President's Committee on Federal Judicial Selection.[28] This committee was composed of some Justice Department officials, but primarily of high-ranking White House officials who sought to supplant the influence of career Justice Department personnel.

The National Bar Association, representing black lawyers, and the Federation of Woman Lawyers were both eliminated from all participation in the process, thus reversing another Carter innovation. In time, the ABA also came into disfavor among Reagan's advisors in response to its split ratings (qualified/not qualified) of some controversial nominees. This distancing of the ABA itself represented a new development for, generally speaking, the ABA enjoys an enhanced role in the process under Republican administrations. Rather than Carter's attempt to create an inclusive selection process, Reagan sought an exclusive process—one that would exclude from participation all who did not share the New Right's social agenda. This was to create considerable resentment among moderate Republican senators, who saw their choices for district court appointments blocked by a recalcitrant White House. Whatever party loyalty these senators felt for Mr. Reagan, this was an affront to the traditional institutional prerogative of senatorial courtesy.[29]

The rigid screening procedures implemented by the President's Committee on Federal Judicial Selection included completion of a lengthy questionnaire and, for the first time ever, routine interviews with all potential nominees that lasted for several days. Whereas previously personal interviews had been conducted only if investigation of a candidate's background indicated something potentially troubling, now all candidates were questioned in detail about their judicial and political philosophies. Some later charged that they were asked improper questions seeking to commit them to rule in certain ways on controversial issues that could be expected to come up in litigation. Such political "interference" with the independence of the judiciary was not wholly unprecedented but was sharply criticized, even by Republicans.[30] Traditional conservatives have tended to adhere to a neoformal view of judicial decision making, and this kind of politicization by one of their own was a bit hard for many to swallow.

Further innovations included computer-aided scanning of all published opinions, if the candidate had judicial experience, or other publications, speeches, and so on, to uncover any evidence of a lack of ideological enthusiasm. Issues of particular importance to the Reagan administration included abortion, the Equal Rights Amendment, religion in public schools, racial desegregation, affirmative action, gun control, business regulation, especially antitrust law, and criminal justice matters. With the exception of business regulation, a traditional Republican concern, this list seems to encompass most domestic matters important to the New Right. The effect was to eliminate from consideration a number of prominent conservatives who were viewed as ideologically unreliable, such as Philip Lacovara, a Justice Department official during the Nixon administration, and Andrew Frey, former deputy solicitor general, who apparently aroused suspicion by having made financial contributions to Planned Parenthood and the National Coalition to Ban Handguns.[31] Only after the Democrats regained control over the Senate after 1986 did the Reagan administration relax somewhat its ideological rigidity and accept moderate candidates.

During his two terms in office, Reagan appointed 47 percent of the federal bench. In addition to his four appointments to the Supreme Court, Reagan placed 78 judges on the intermediate courts of appeals and appointed 290 district court judges. The total number of candidates placed in the lower courts by Reagan came to 365 (slightly fewer than the total of the above, since several persons were appointed and then later elevated to a higher court).[32] The administration's concern for the ideological purity of its nominees tended to narrow the demographic range of Reagan's appointees, in sharp contrast to the record of his predecessor. Twenty-four of Reagan's district court appointments and four circuit appointments were women. Of course, the most visible appointment of a woman to the judiciary was that of Sandra Day O'Connor to the Supreme Court. Although Reagan appointed considerably fewer women to the lower bench than Carter, his record in this regard was exceeded only by Carter. This reflects official indifference and the relatively small pool of qualified female candidates prior to the mid-1970s. One of the most dramatic effects of feminism of the late 1960s and the 1970s was the enhanced presence achieved by women in the legal profession.[33] Thus, while Reagan may have experienced some difficulty finding women who supported his ideological program—the so-called "gender gap" has become a cause of considerable concern for Republicans—his record for appointing women surpassed that of Presidents Ford, Nixon, or Johnson by considerable measure.[34] It is likely that future presidents will have the opportunity to appoint women in large numbers as well as considerable encouragement to do so.

Reagan's record for appointing racial minorities is another story entirely. Since the 1930s, black voters have been rather distant from the Republican Party. During the 1980s this distance was exacerbated by Reagan's hostility to important civil rights measures, including the popular Voting Rights Act of 1965, rigorous enforcement of antidiscrimination laws, and, especially, affirmative action policies. Fiscal cutbacks in welfare programs also hit black Americans particularly hard. The result was a small field of black candidates who met the administration's ideological test. Finally, Reagan's abolition of Carter's Circuit Court Nominating Commission served to close off an effective conduit for minority candidates who were likely to be passed over by the traditional methods of judicial recruitment. The result was predictable: Reagan racked up the worst record for appointing black judges since President Eisenhower, with only six blacks appointed to the lower bench and only one to the appellate bench.

That this record may be for lack of trying is supported by Reagan's altogether healthier record of appointing Hispanics. Here again, Reagan is second only to Carter, with 14 Hispanic judges appointed to the district courts and 1 to the circuit courts. The Republicans courted the growing Hispanic vote with considerable persistence during the 1980s, which might help to explain the attention given to judicial appointments of persons with Spanish surnames. What the administration accomplished for Hispanic candidates it could have accomplished for black candidates, had Reagan and his associates had the will to do so. No Asian Americans were appointed. The Reagan record, then, shows a total of 29 women, 7 blacks, and 15 Hispanics appointed to the courts.

Another demographic trend characterizing the Reagan appointments—they are the youngest cohort of nominees in recent memory. A close student of Reagan's nominations, Professor Sheldon Goldman, has suggested that this reflects the relatively low pay scale for federal judges, at least in comparison with the income qualified candidates are likely to draw in private legal practice.[35] The suggestion is that young lawyers, not yet earning top salaries, may be easier to entice to the bench. This explanation seems inadequate, for judicial salaries have been low in comparison to the top incomes levels achieved in private practice for much of our history. Also, the young lawyer who leaves private practice forgoes the future prospect of earning top dollar, surely a disincentive to the fiscally ambitious.

The chief enticement to leave private practice for the federal bench has to be the prestige, not to mention the power, attached to the post. These benefits remain significant.[36] Further, many highly qualified lawyers already do not draw the salaries of partners in the top firms on Wall Street or K Street. Instead, they teach in law schools or enter public service in other capacities that also diminish their incomes. A more likely explanation, one conceded by Goldman and by Reagan supporters, was simply that the administration sought young nominees to ensure the continued influence of Reagan's politics well after his retirement from the White House. This illustrates another facet of the care given to judicial appointments by the Reagan administration.

Bush and Beyond

After taking over the White House in 1989, the Bush administration sought to continue Reagan policies regarding the federal courts. However, the new administration was often slow in selecting candidates for judicial openings, averaging a

13-month delay before sending nominations to the Senate.[37] For its part, the Senate Judiciary Committee delayed action on a number of nominations it received, due to a dispute with the administration over Senate staff access to the FBI reports on the candidates' background, an issue that came to a head in the wake of controversy surrounding Bush's nomination of Supreme Court Justice Clarence Thomas. Still later, personnel changes in the Justice Department slowed further the processing of judicial nominations. The result was a considerable backlog in judicial staffing, especially after Congress added 74 new judgeships to the district courts and 11 to the appellate courts, in 1990. This legislation provided Bush with an opportunity to deepen his impact on the bench in short order. It was an opportunity Bush lost, however, for as the election of 1992 approached, over a hundred judicial vacancies remained. By the time he left office, President Bush had appointed 148 judges to the district courts, but 85 district court seats remained open. Similarly, although he made 37 appointments to the U.S. courts of appeals, Bush failed to fill 15 more seats by the end of his term.[38] Thus, the Bush administration fell short of its potential for influencing the judiciary.

Unlike his two predecessors, Bush was not an innovator in the process of selecting judges. With only minor alterations in procedure, Bush kept in place the detailed screening process assembled by the Reagan administration. Candidates continued to be examined closely on matters of ideology and judicial philosophy in the Justice Department, although responsibility was transferred from the deputy attorney general to the attorney general's office. The President's Committee on Federal Judicial Selection continued to scrutinize potential candidates on political matters, ensuring close participation by White House staffers to ensure ideological purity. Resistance to senatorial prerogatives was softened only a little by the White House demand that senators submit three names they would like to see considered for an open spot on district courts. This left the White House to make the final selection, although the administration also permitted senators to indicate their preferred candidate. Bush's need to keep New Right conservatives in his corner induced him to emulate Reagan by nominating very conservative jurists, even over the wishes of moderate Republicans. However, conservative activists were also disappointed in the Bush administration's lack of forceful leadership in filling posts on the lower federal courts.

Bush nominations were well qualified in terms of merit, as imperfectly evinced by their relatively high ABA ratings.[39] A higher-than-usual proportion brought prior judicial experience to their new posts, on both district and appellate courts.[40] A large portion of Bush's nominees—more than those of any past president, including Carter—were women. However, the Reagan administration's poor record on appointing blacks was shared by Bush and was extended to Hispanics, a group the Reagan administration actively sought out.[41] Along with prior judicial experience and solid conservative credentials, Republican party activism seems to have been a major criterion for selection. Early empirical evidence suggests that Bush's goal of moving the courts in a more conservative direction are bearing at least some fruit, especially in civil rights and liberties issues.[42]

The election of Democrat Bill Clinton in 1992 promises to take the federal bench in a new direction. When Clinton entered office, Sheldon Goldman estimates, only one in five trial judges and only one in four appellate judges were appointed by Democrats, the sharpest partisan imbalance since 1952, when the election of Dwight Eisenhower ended 20 years of Democratic incumbency in the White House.[43] However, the large number of judgeships left unfilled presents President Clinton with an immediate opportunity to redress this partisan imbalance. With 15 seats on the courts of appeals and 85 seats on the district courts (plus a small number of other judicial posts) waiting to be filled, a determined Clinton administration could have made itself felt almost immediately. However, delays in appointing an attorney general and subordinate Justice Department personnel placed judicial nominations in a temporary holding pattern, leaving the courts considerably understaffed for another year.

The mechanics of how the new administration will select judges also remain unclear for now. A change in ideology, however, is quite distinctly on the horizon. The Clinton campaign espoused more tolerant views concerning the rights of homosexuals and campaigned on a pro-choice platform. Although he avoided making extravagant promises to racial minority groups, it is likely that Clinton will be more sympathetic to civil rights policies than the Reagan and Bush administrations were. Environmental and regulatory policy will certainly change. Perhaps most significantly, New Right partisans will lose their clout in judicial recruitment.

The political complexion of the courts will change, but slowly. Clinton faces the challenge of balancing his moderate neoliberal views with the demands likely to be made by more liberal interest groups in the Democratic party. Which wing of the party will dominate judicial selection remains to be seen. Further, the proportion of judges now sitting who were appointed by Presidents Reagan and Bush will diminish only slowly. Both administrations consciously sought relatively youthful judicial candidates to perpetuate their influence beyond the vicissitudes of electoral politics or the strictures of the Twenty-second Amendment. Finally, institutional restraints, to be discussed in Chapters 5 and 6, especially the commitment to precedent, mitigate considerably any pendulum swings the judiciary might take. Thus, the Clinton administration faces opportunities and challenges in shaping the federal judiciary, as did its 41 predecessors. The most visible impact of the Clinton administration, as for past presidents, may prove to be at the Supreme Court, to which we turn in the next chapter.

NOTES

1. William Blackstone, *Commentaries on the Laws of England*, vol. I (Robert H. Small, Philadelphia, 1825) pp. 259–260.
2. Quoted in Gordon Wood, *The Creation of the American Republic* (W.W. Norton, New York, 1972) p. 145.
3. Winton U. Solberg, ed., *The Federal Convention and the Formation of the Union of the American States* (Bobbs-Merrill, Indianapolis, 1958) pp. 77–78.
4. Griffin B. Bell, "Federal Judicial Selection: The Carter Years," in *Judicial Selection: Merit, Ideology, and Politics* (National Legal center for the Public Interest, Washington, D.C., 1990) p. 31. This possibility may have been realized during the confirmation process for Supreme Court nominee Clarence Thomas, when an unknown Senate

staffer leaked information concerning allegations of sexual harassment made by a former coworker of the nominee. Thomas supporters charged that the leak was intended to intimidate Thomas into quietly withdrawing his name from consideration.

5. Bell, op. cit., p. 28.

6. Stephen J. Markman, "Judicial Selection: the Reagan Years," in *Judicial Selection: Merit, Ideology, and Politics* (National Legal Center for the Public Interest, Washington, D.C., 1990) p. 41.

7. "Justice Department and ABA Settle their Differences," 47 *Congressional Quarterly Weekly Report* 1327 (June 7, 1989).

8. For a history of the ABA's efforts to improve the professionalism of the bar, and not co-incidentally to eliminate recent ethnic groups, racial minorities, and political reformers from influence in the legal system, see Jerold S. Auerback, *Unequal Justice: Lawyers and Social Change in America* (Oxford University Press, New York, 1976).

9. A thorough discussion of the ABA in the process of judicial selection can be found in David O'Brien, "Background Paper," in *Judicial Roulette: Report of the Twentieth Century Task Force on Judicial Selection* (Priority Press, New York, 1988) p. 81. See also Joel Grossman, *Lawyers and Judges: the ABA and the Politics of Judicial Selection* (Wiley, New York, 1965).

10. Quoted by O'Brien, op. cit., p. 71.

11. Walter F. Murphy, Elements of Judicial Strategy (University of Chicago Press, Chicago, 1964) pp. 92–93.

12. *Brown v. Board of Education*, 347 U.S. 483 (1954).

13. *Plessy v. Ferguson*, 163 U.S. 537 (1896).

14. *Brown v. Board of Education*, 349 U.S. 294 (1955).

15. Henry R. Glick, *Courts, Politics and Justice*, 2nd ed. (McGraw-Hill, New York, 1988) p. 108.

16. Harry P. Stumpf, *American Judicial Politics* (Harcourt Brace Jovanovich, New York, 1988) p. 207.

17. O'Brien, op. cit., p. 88.

18. O'Brien, op. cit., p. 37. A slightly higher estimate of 92 percent is offered by Stumpf, op. cit., p. 206.

19. Harry P. Stumpf and John H. Culver, *The Politics of the State Courts* (Longman, New York, 1992) p. 41.

20. Larry C. Berkson and Susan B. Carbon, *The United States Circuit Judge Nominating Commission: Its Members, Procedures, and Candidates* (American Judicature Society, Chicago, 1980) p. 24.

21. Sheldon Goldman, "Carter's Judicial Appointments: A Lasting Legacy," 64 *Judicature* 344, 349 (March 1981).

22. Goldman, op. cit., p. 352.

23. Griffin B. Bell, "Federal Judicial Selection: the Carter Years," in *Judicial Selection: Merit, Ideology, and Politics* (National Legal Center for the Public interest, Washington, D.C., 1990) p. 27.

24. Ibid., p. 26.

25. Goldman, op. cit., pp. 349, 351.

26. Kenneth M. Dolbeare and Linda J. Medcalf, *American Ideologies Today: From Neopolitics to New Ideas* (Random House, New York, 1988) pp. 165, 173–176.

27. O'Brien, op. cit., pp. 60.

28. Stephen J. Markman, "Judicial Selection: the Reagan Years," in *Judicial Selection: Merit, Ideology, and Politics* (National Legal Center for the Public Interest, Washington, D.C., 1990) pp. 38, 40.

29. "Congress, the President, and Judicial Selection: Lessons from the Reagan Years," written under the pseudonym "A Friend of the Constitution," by "a high ranking official in the Reagan Administration," in *Judicial Selection: Merit, Ideology, and Politics* (National Legal Center for the Public Interest, Washing ton, D.C., 1990) p. 54.

30. O'Brien, op. cit., p. 62. Questionnaires are also completed for the Senate Judiciary Committee.

31. O'Brien, op. cit., p. 63.

32. Sheldon Goldman, "Reagan's Judicial Legacy: Completing the Puzzle and Summing Up," 72 *Judicature* 318 (1989).

33. Paul Wice, *Judges & Lawyers: The Human Side of Justice* (HarperCollins, New York, 1991) p. 37.

34. Goldman, op. cit., pp. 322, 325.

35. Goldman, op. cit., p. 324.

36. Richard A. Posner, *The Federal Courts: Crisis and Reform* (Harvard U. Press, Cambridge, Mass., 1985) p. 36.

37. Victor Williams, "Solutions to Federal Judicial Gridlock," 76 *Judicature* 185, 192 (1993).

38. Sheldon Goldman, "Bush's Judicial Legacy: The Final Imprint," 76 *Judicature* 282, 286, 293, 297 (1993). Several judicial posts in specialized courts were also open.

39. Sheldon Goldman, "The Bush Imprint on the Judiciary: Carrying on a Tradition," 74 *Judicature* 294, 299 (1991), and "Bush's Judicial Legacy," op. cit., pp. 282, 286–287, 294.

40. Joan Biskupic, "Bush Treads Well-Worn Path in Building Federal Bench," 50 *Congressional Quarterly Weekly Report* 111 (January 18, 1992), Sheldon Goldman, "Bush's Judicial Legacy," op. cit., pp. 286–287, 294.

41. Goldman, "The Bush Imprint on the Judiciary," op. cit., p. 219, and Goldman, "Bush's Judicial Legacy," op. cit., pp. 290–291, 294.

42. Robert A. Carp, Donald Songer, C. K. Rowland, Ronald Stidham, and Lisa Richey-Tracy, "The Voting Behavior of Judges Appointed by President Bush," 76 *Judicature* 298 (1993).

43. Goldman, "Bush's Judicial Legacy" op. cit., p. 297.

Chapter
4

Appointments to the United States Supreme Court

It appears that Alexander Hamilton and several other framers of the Constitution intended the president to exercise the initiative in judicial selection, with the Senate occupying a more reactive role. This was in part an attempt to depoliticize the recruitment of judges and ensure selection solely on the basis of professional accomplishment. A significant legislative role, it was feared, would create temptations to trade approval of judicial nominations for political advantage, possibly reducing the quality of the bench. While states' rights proponents argued that only senators would know the caliber of persons in the locale of the court, federalists countered that only the president would be able to choose judges solely on the basis of their professional reputation.

Experience has proven both sides of this debate wrong. Selection involves a combination of factors, professional and political, that are inseparable in practice. Furthermore, despite federalist plans, individual senators often have the practical initiative for district court appointments, as we saw in Chapter 3. Power is more balanced between senators and the president in appellate court appointments. For appointments to the Supreme Court, it is clearly the president who is dominant, but this has certainly not purged the process of political considerations. To the contrary, an appointment to the Supreme Court is a highly visible and politically charged affair.

Several reasons might be cited for the weakening of the Senate's role in Supreme Court nominations. The Supreme Court is the only court with a nationwide jurisdiction. No senators can claim a proprietary interest in the Supreme Court based on regional considerations, eliminating senatorial courtesy. In addition, the visibility of Supreme Court appointments means a president can often use his or her popularity to generate public support for nominees. Finally, it is likely that the president's dominance in appointments to the highest court represents something of a historic bargain to preserve senators' highly prized access to patronage opportunities represented by district court appointments.

The same constitutional process described in Chapter 3 is followed: the president nominates a candidate, the Senate deliberates, and if advice and consent is granted, the president may appoint the new justice. The president is likely still to be in need of advice but has more freedom to choose his or her advisors. These may include cabinet secretaries or senators, although the influence of the latter will depend more on their own reputation or the degree of influence they wield over legislation key to the president's program, rather than on the state they represent. Frequently, presidents turn to staff advisors, party elders, or influential law school professors or deans in search of advice. Judges, even justices already on the Court, may be asked to make recommendations and are frequently willing to do so.[1] Or the president may simply ignore all advice and nominate one of his or her personal associates.

Generally, however, the attorney general or deputy attorney general will maintain a lengthy file of potential candidates in anticipation of the next Supreme Court opening. When an opening occurs, the president and those he or she trusts will consider names from this file. Once a short list has been selected, the FBI will conduct a background check and the ABA will probably be given a chance to conduct its own evaluation of the candidates. The ABA rates potential Supreme Court nominees as "highly qualified," "not opposed," and "not qualified." As in the case of lower court appointments, both the role of this interest group and the standards employed by the ABA to determine professional attainment are controversial.

The Senate Committee on the Judiciary will conduct hearings, but these will not be the perfunctory 10-minute affairs held before a subcommittee that are routine for lower court appointments. Committee hearings on a potential justice of the Supreme Court are highly visible proceedings at which various interested senators, legal scholars, interest groups, and others may request permission to appear. The candidate is likely to appear and perhaps testify about matters of concern to committee members. Harlan Fiske Stone, nominated in 1925, was the first candidate to make such an appearance, but the practice has become routine only since the mid-1950s.

This interview may provide an opportunity to learn more about the political orientation of the candidate, although it may also become an opportunity for senators to vent their anger against the Court for policies they disapprove or to embarrass the president politically. Testimony by the candidate may also be quite evasive. A candidate might justifiably fear that answering too specific a question will erode his or her appearance of impartiality once on the Court. In the highly charged atmosphere that has surrounded recent nominations, candidates might simply decide that avoiding controversy is the better part of wisdom. Deliberate obfuscation seems to have been the confirmation strategy of several recent candidates. Ultimately, the Senate usually grants its advice and consent, but this is by no means assured in every case. The president may dominate the appointment of a Supreme Court justice, but even his power has limits, as the defeat of President

Reagan's nomination of Robert Bork and the subsequent withdrawal of his nomination of Douglas Ginsburg both attest.

CRITERIA FOR SELECTION FOR THE HIGH COURT

It is useful to examine the criteria presidents consider when choosing a Supreme Court nominee. Every president is different, of course, but certain variables appear in nominees with such consistency that we may deem them criteria for a Supreme Court justice. In other words, if we examine the 107 persons who have thus far been appointed to the Court, certain characteristics they tend overwhelmingly to share would seem to be decisive in their having been chosen over others lacking those same characteristics. It is also interesting to examine how those criteria have changed over the past two centuries, for they reflect changes in the larger American political system.

Demographics

Criteria quite extrinsic to the attainments of the candidate are frequently important variables in Supreme Court appointments. Consider one that has decreased in its once considerable importance—geography. Since the Supreme Court is a national court, earlier presidents sought to give the Court a balanced representation of the nation's geographic regions. This was of critical importance in the initial periods of the nation's history, when local cultural and economic differences and resulting regional tensions were considerably sharper than they are today. Indeed, recall that the Judiciary Act of 1789 created circuit courts staffed originally by two justices and one district judge. Given the primitive state of eighteenth-century transportation, the division of the nation into three circuits in this fashion would almost require proportional representation of the north, south, and middle Atlantic regions among the circuit-riding Supreme Court justices.

Consider one early example of the political importance of geography, President George Washington's nomination of North Carolina lawyer James Iredell to the Court in 1790. Iredell was chosen because, in Washington's own words, "In addition to the reputation he sustains for abilities, legal knowledge, and respectability of character, he is of a state of some importance in the Union that has given no character to a federal office."[2] When the Constitution was first submitted to the states for ratification, North Carolina's Hillsboro Convention of 1788 had declined to approve it. Not until a year later, when a second convention ratified the Constitution, was North Carolina able to join the new nation. Hence, not only was the state late in giving a native son to any important federal office, but the very loyalty of North Carolina must have seemed in doubt. Washington chose to fill a vacant Supreme Court seat with a North Carolinian as a way of cementing that state more closely to the Union. It should be added, however, that Iredell had also gained popularity among federalists for his able defense of the proposed

Constitution at Hillsboro and for his published point-by-point refutation of one of the leading antifederalist tracts by George Mason.[3] Thus, ideology and ability were important considerations that were not sacrificed on the altar of regional representation.

It is worth noting that from Washington's appointment of John Rutledge, from South Carolina, in 1789, until the retirement of Lewis Powell, from Virginia, in 1987, there had always been at least one southerner on the Court, with only a brief interruption during Reconstruction. Californian Stephen Field was appointed in 1863 in part because the far western states had been as yet unrepresented. Willis Van Devanter, of Wyoming, was appointed in 1910 to restore a western presence on the Court that had been lost when Field departed in 1897. But the most striking geographic pattern was revealed in the implicit reservation of certain seats on the Court for nominations from a given region throughout the nineteenth and early twentieth centuries. Thus, until 1932, the third seat on the Court had been reserved for New Englanders. When the justice who hailed from New England retired, the expectation was that another Yankee would be chosen to replace him. This pattern was not broken until Benjamin Cardozo, a New Yorker, was chosen to replace the retiring Bostonian Oliver Wendell Holmes. Similarly, prior to the Civil War, the sixth seat was the reserved southern seat.[4] A vacancy here was always filled by another southerner.

With the increased integration of the nation in the modern period, the political salience of geography has declined. The abolition of circuit riding in 1891 no doubt contributed to this diminution of geographic considerations for Court nominees. Today, regional representation is all but irrelevant. During the 1950s, North Dakota's Senator Langer announced his intention to oppose all future nominees until a native of North Dakota was appointed to the Supreme Court. No one took Langer seriously, and there has still not been a justice from North Dakota. President Nixon argued in the late 1960s that the South needed representation, despite the presence of Justice Hugo L. Black, an Alabama native for whom Nixon had little regard on ideological grounds. The President's professed desire for a southerner was only a pretext for an appointment reflecting Nixon's ideological persuasion, especially concerning civil rights and criminal justice, and a thinly veiled appeal for electoral support from white southern voters unhappy with the Democrats. What was at issue was policy, not geography.

Geography has not stood in the way of nominations that would seem regionally redundant, such as the 1916 appointment of Boston attorney Louis D. Brandeis to a Court that already had Justice Holmes, or of New Yorker Benjamin Cardozo to a Court that in 1932 already had Harlan F. Stone and Charles Evans Hughes, or of Minnesota native Harry Blackmun to a Court that already included Warren Burger (both nominated by Nixon, further undermining the sincerity of his professions of finding a southerner), or of Sandra Day O'Connor to a Court that already included William Rehnquist, both coming from Arizona.

Representation of major religious denominations was for a time of considerable importance. Closely related is the representation of major ethnic groups in an increasingly heterogeneous society. In the early days of the Republic, our population was overwhelmingly Anglo-Saxon and Protestant. Without any thought being given to the matter, Supreme Court appointments naturally reflected this homogeneity. In fact, white male Protestant Anglo-Saxons continue to dominate the recent population of the Court, primarily a function of the privileged class background of most justices. With changed immigration patterns by the late nineteenth century, however, representing other groups on the Court was deemed useful, especially by Democratic presidents.

Thus, there has been at least one Catholic, and for much of the time only one, since Edward White was appointed in 1894 (although Joseph McKenna joined White four years later). Roger Brooke Taney, appointed in 1836, was Catholic but was of old English Catholic extraction by way of Maryland and was not drawn from what were in the nineteenth and early twentieth centuries the lower-status Catholic populations of Irish or Southern and Eastern European extraction. Similarly, from the appointment of Louis Brandeis in 1916 until the retirement of Abe Fortas in 1969, there had always been one Jew on the Court, except when Brandeis and Cardozo were there together. President Millard Fillmore had offered an appointment to Judah Benjamin as early as 1853, but Benjamin preferred to keep the Senate seat to which he had just been elected, delaying the appointment of the first Jewish justice for another 63 years. After Fortas's resignation, there were no Jews on the court until the appointment of Justice Ginsburg.

However, like geography, religious affiliation appears to be of declining significance as a divisive issue in the appointment process. Thus, there was only token pressure to replace Fortas with a Jewish appointee, and little notice was taken of religion during Douglas Ginsburg's aborted nomination in 1986, or when Ruth Bader Ginsburg was named to the court. Similarly, even with William Brennan satisfying the "Catholic seat" on the Court, little was made of the Catholic affiliations of Antonin Scalia (although some did note that he was the first Italian American on the Court) or Anthony Kennedy. President Bush's nomination of Clarence Thomas, an Episcopalian of Catholic background, generated no religious controversy, although he was only the second black justice nominated.

While religion and white ethnic affiliation are of declining significance, other demographic factors cannot be ignored. Only since the 1967 appointment of Thurgood Marshall has there been a black member of the Court. Despite President Bush's outspoken opposition to "racial quotas," it came as no surprise when he nominated a successor to Marshall who also happened to be black. Since the judiciary continues to be of considerable importance to black Americans for reasons to be explored later, Thomas's outspoken conservatism made him a nominee unwelcomed by major civil right groups, most notably the National Association for the Advancement of Colored People (NAACP), and one that left public opinion in the black community divided. Sandra Day O'Connor, appointed in 1981, is the first woman and has already been joined by another. With changing immigration patterns continuing to shape the demographic composition of the nation, we can expect in the near future the appointment of a Hispanic justice and probably an Asian justice, each carrying considerable symbolic significance.

It is commonplace to deplore resorting to such ascriptive criteria, ostensibly because they might replace merit in the selection of a justice. However, merit is as difficult to reject as it is to define. Past appeals to merit have frequently served to camouflage objections to candidates based on those very ascriptive criteria we claim to deplore.[5] Resorting to such group-based criteria also creates discomfort because it runs against the grain of American individualism, whereby each member of the community is to be evaluated for his or her own ability and character, and not for the group affiliations over which he or she has no control. The argument is well taken, for it is true that merit (if understood loosely as a combination of native ability, moral integrity, and professional attainment) is not an exclusive attribute of any race, gender, religion, or ethnic group. But then it must also be admitted that merit can be found among blacks, women, Hispanics, and members of any other demographic group. If this is true, then these ascriptive criteria need not compete with merit, and there should be no objection to looking for a black justice, a woman, an Asian, or a Hispanic, for merit need not be sacrificed in the process.

Indeed, since merit can still be found among black, female, Asian, or Hispanic nominees, there even seems to be good reason for ensuring that such persons are appointed to the Court. It must be understood that government plays a symbolic role in the community. It is a teacher, in that government, through its ceremonies and actions, continually articulates and recreates the standards of value that define the polity. The United States is committed to "equal justice under law," but we are a divided society with an unfortunate history of exclusion of certain ascriptive groups from full participation in politics. Given this legacy, it is valuable for a powerful policy-making institution that is also a prestigious symbol of justice to contain members of such disadvantaged groups. In an earlier day, it was important to remind ourselves that southerners, Catholics, and Jews were also part of the polity. It is equally important today to demonstrate to blacks, Hispanics, Asians, women, and others that they, too, are Americans. Reminding white Anglo-Saxon men of that fact on occasion may also have a salutary effect.

But more than symbolism is at stake. The divisions in society that create disadvantaged groups also create differences in historical experience, culture, and social perceptions. In other words, a black justice may be more likely to exhibit a sensitivity to issues of racial discrimination or socioeconomic class. Of course, he or she also may not, for a variety of reasons, but his or her experience will probably provide an understanding of the realities of American racial politics not so readily available to even a well-meaning white counterpart. Was anyone surprised that Justice Thurgood Marshall, who came from humble origins, was educated at Howard University, and served as chief counsel for the NAACP, displayed an eloquence unmatched by any other member of the Court in cases involving the status of minorities or the poor?

It is important to avoid crude notions of group determinism when discussing the merits of representation on the Court. Not all members of any ascriptive group will exhibit the same personal identification with group aspirations. Those who do may not share an identical understanding of the content of those aspirations nor of the best strategy for their realization. Not all women are feminists, nor are all feminists women. Not all blacks subscribe to the policy agenda of the NAACP. The nomination of Clarence Thomas drew criticism from a number of leading civil rights groups because of his stated policies inimical to their own, policies that had guided his tenure as director of the Equal Employment Opportunity Commission (EEOC). In fact, some charged the Bush administration with cynically exploiting Thomas's race to secure an appointment to fulfill a policy agenda of cutting back civil rights gains, including gains made when the Court was entirely white. One of those white justices most supportive of a strong civil rights policy was Hugo Black, a southerner and former member of the Ku Klux Klan. Human motivation is complex, and all that is being suggested here is that group membership is likely to provide experiences and insights that may offer a unique contribution to the making of a just policy.

Recall our earlier discussion of formalism and its rejection by legal realists and the Critical Legal Studies movement. If the law could be known by a court with near mathematical certainty, then perhaps the life experience of justices would not matter. A wealthy, white male Episcopalian recruited from a large urban corporate law firm would arrive at the same judgments as a poorer, black, Baptist, former legal aid attorney. But as we concede the political and the idiosyncratic aspects of judicial decision making, a commitment to democratic politics and equal justice seems to require efforts to represent disadvantaged groups, at least until they have overcome their subordinate status in society at large. The views espoused by the Critical Legal Studies group present an especially compelling reason for a judiciary in which many subcultures are represented. If law is a form of public discourse, democratic principles would require that no significant groups be excluded from the conversation, lest the discourse be limited to the perspectives of a single hegemonic community.[6] Our very understanding of political reality might be skewed as the experience and perceptions of marginalized groups are further delegitimatized and silenced. Until such divisions become irrelevant and unnoticed, we should not be afraid that merit must be overlooked to secure balance, for there is no evidence that this is so.

Experience suggests, in fact, that merit is much more threatened by considerations of political ideology than by ascriptive criteria, for ideology is clearly the highest White House priority. Senator Roman Hruska's defense of Nixon nominee G. Harold Carswell against the charge of mediocrity illustrates the point. In one of the strangest speeches offered on behalf of a nominee, Hruska told his Senate colleagues:

> Even if he were mediocre, there are a lot of mediocre judges and people and lawyers. They are entitled to a little representation, aren't they, and a little chance? We can't have all Brandeises, and Frankfurters, and Cardozos and stuff like that there.[7]

anti-Semitism

What Carswell offered was a conservative ideology that was so valuable to Hruska and to President Nixon that they were quite willing to appoint an acknowledged mediocrity to obtain it. On the other hand, the senator's examples of the overrepresented elite among the justices had each met opposition at the time of his appointment for being Jewish, most openly in the case of Brandeis. Affirmative action for the mediocre has since become something of a joke among scholars of judicial politics. If the mediocre are an underrepresented population on the Supreme Court, it is safe to say they have not been wholly excluded from consideration—nor are they absent from other forums of policy making. When viewed against the history of judicial appointments, charges that mediocrity will be the cost of efforts to include subordinated groups of the community on the Supreme Court ring hollow.

Experience

Prior judicial experience is valued by some presidents. Since the Supreme Court is the highest court in the land, from which there is no further appeal should it err, prior experience on a state supreme court or a lower federal bench would at first seem a logical prerequisite. Of the 107 justices appointed to date, 26 came directly from the lower federal courts and 21 came directly from state courts.[8] All told, about half of the justices had some sort of prior judicial experience. However, many of these had only a brief tenure as a lower court judge before ascending to the Supreme Court, so that only a minority of justices really had substantial experience on any bench. The others came directly from nonjudicial posts in the executive branch (21), the Senate (6), state office (3), or other nonjudicial posts (5).

Although the ABA values prior judicial service highly, political leaders tend to favor this experience mostly when the Court has, in their view, acted "politically." In other words, when the Court has charted a course of policy of which they do not approve, politicians see prior judicial experience as a means for securing judicial "objectivity," or formalism, and its promise of judicial restraint. Thus, in 1956, Senator Smathers, a Democrat from Florida, introduced a bill into Congress that would have required all Supreme Court nominees to have had a minimum of five years experience either on a lower federal court or on a state's highest bench. Smathers's bill appears to have been in retaliation for the Court's ruling in the school desegregation case, *Brown v. Board of Education.* Similarly, conservative presidents frequently favor prior experience out of pique with recent policies of the Court, notably on behalf of minority groups that conservatives tend to disfavor. Thus, President Eisenhower, angered over the participation of his recent appointee, Chief Justice Earl Warren, in the *Brown* decision, announced such a policy for his future nominations.

We must ask critically: Of what demonstrable relevance is prior judicial experience? The answer is at first surprising. Justice Felix Frankfurter, himself a former Harvard law professor with no prior judicial experience, criticized the Smathers proposal in 1957. Surveying the careers of 75 justices who had by then served on the Court (but omitting those still on the Court or in retirement), Frankfurter found that 28 had no prior judicial experience. The Smathers bill requiring five years of prior judicial experience would have eliminated from service more than 35 justices, including 7 of the 12 chief justices to date. Included in this list were many of the most distinguished justices in the Court's history. Furthermore, of the list of those who did have substantial prior judicial experience, a few of whom had become quite distinguished for their service on lower courts, many had turned in a rather disappointing performance on the Supreme Court. Indeed, several former judges complained, on elevation to the Supreme Court, that their prior experience had not equipped them very well for the demands made on them as justices. Frankfurter concluded that "apart from meaning that a man had sat on some court for some time, 'judicial service' tells nothing that is relevant about the qualifications for the functions exercised by the Supreme Court."[9] A more recent analysis confirms Frankfurter's findings. David O'Brien reports that of the 106 justices who had served to date (not including Ginsburg), a full 82 had less than 10 years' prior judicial experience, state or federal.[10]

Prior judicial experience is probably most valuable to presidents to document the candidate's judicial philosophy. Beyond these political concerns, prior judicial experience seems unimportant. The reason is that the Supreme Court does not concern itself with the kind of technical private law issues that are the nuts and bolts of lower court cases. Recall that the Supreme Court exercises discretion over its docket. It chooses only those cases that raise issues of national importance, leaving the kinds of cases for which professional legal technique would seem most pertinent to be settled by lower courts. Successful service on the Supreme Court would therefore call more for an astute political sensibility, rather than legal acumen.

Such political skills are developed more in the political process than in lower court litigation. Hence, it should be no surprise that all justices save one, George Shiras, appointed in 1892, have had a substantial amount of prior experience in politics, generally at the national level. Supreme Court appointments of the past decade have departed in a way from this pattern. President Reagan and, for his first appointment, President Bush each sought outsiders to national politics. Aside from his elevation of Justice Rehnquist to the chief justice's chair, Reagan's nominees include three law professors, a state judge, and one obscure federal judge. After appointing an unknown David Souter, Bush returned to traditional practice with his nomination of Clarence Thomas, who had served the Reagan administration in the Department of Education and later in the EEOC, prior to his very brief tenure on the United States Court of Appeals for the District of Columbia. How this reduced national political experience affects the acumen of the current Court is an interesting question, but one that does not yet lend itself to a precise answer.

Indeed, one is hard-pressed to understand why a justice even needs to be a lawyer. Every justice to date has been a lawyer, but Justices Hugo Black and William Douglas indicated that a nonlawyer could serve well on the Supreme Court. Presumably, many persons without law degrees have the breadth of political experience and sensitive judgment the Supreme Court requires. Justices also supervise a staff of law clerks who could supply technical advice as needed. No doubt some training in constitutional history and theory is useful for a justice, but law students typically take only a semester or two of constitutional law, and very few lawyers develop wide experience in constitutional issues from general practice. Lawyers would not seem to have a substantial advantage over those historians or political scientists who have made American constitutional theory and development their specialties. And few who have experienced it accuse the law school curriculum of providing students with a broad social vision. Of course, we would expect opposition to such an appointment from the ABA, but the ABA is only a

professional interest group with an agenda of protecting the status and prerogatives of lawyers and with a definition of professional competence that remains obscure. The nomination of a nonlawyer seems unlikely, however. Why would a
president invite the controversy such a nomination would probably inspire, especially in the Senate, which is also heavily populated with lawyers?

Party and Ideology

Clearly the most ubiquitous criteria for Supreme Court recruitment are ideology
and partisan service. Presidents are not famous for appointing persons who are
members of the opposite party. In fact, all but 13 appointments (and two of these
consisted of the elevation of a sitting associate justice to the position of chief justice) were drawn from members of the president's political party. This is consistent with lower judicial appointments. However, the most significant criterion a
president considers in nominating a new justice is political ideology. We have already seen Washington's concern to place on the Court reliable federalists—persons loyal to the new Constitution and the consolidation of national power it represented. It is safe to say that every president since Washington has to some
degree considered the ideology of every candidate prior to announcing his or her
nomination.

Most presidents have been satisfied if the candidate was in accord with their
broad philosophical orientations, but a few have been more explicit. Franklin
Roosevelt, after seeing most of the policy initiatives of his first term nullified by
the Supreme Court, was careful after 1937 to appoint Democrats sympathetic to
New Deal policies. Richard Nixon campaigned for the presidency in 1968 in part
on a platform that blamed the Supreme Court for a rising crime rate and
promised to appoint to the Court justices less sympathetic to defendants' rights.
Reagan's and Bush's Supreme Court nominees have reflected closely their conservative views—hostile to aggressive civil rights policies, abortion, and government regulation of economic activities. President Clinton's moderate liberalism
was reflected in his first appointment. Even those presidents willing to cross party
lines in selecting a nominee have resisted crossing ideological lines.

Subjecting judicial nominees to even a mild ideological test is disturbing to
some, for it seems to undermine judicial independence. Recall that the framers
sought to take appointments out of legislative politics to prevent partisanship and
ideology from becoming part of the appointment process. Their ideal was a depoliticized judiciary, one that could decide lawsuits according to technically derived principles of law, a goal they thought attainable only so long as political considerations did not interfere. Such a view depended on the acceptance of
formalism as an explanation of judicial decision making, a view long celebrated,
but, as we have seen, one presidents seem not to have trusted from the beginning.

Presidents have sought justices who shared at least a commitment to their
own broad political principles, believing such a commitment itself a necessary
prerequisite to justice. Among the more candid presidential statements concerning the role of ideology in Supreme Court nominees is a letter written by

President Theodore Roosevelt to Senator Henry Cabot Lodge, discussing the candidacy of Oliver Wendell Holmes:

> In the ordinary and low sense which we attach to the words "partisan" and "politician," a judge of the Supreme Court should be neither. But in the higher sense, in the proper sense, he is not in my judgment fitted for the position unless he is a party man, a constructive statesman, constantly keeping in mind his adherence to the principles and policies under which this nation has been built up and in accordance with which it must go on; and keeping in mind also his relations with his fellow statesmen who in other branches of government are striving in cooperation with him to advance the ends of government.[11]

It should be clear that disputes over "the principles and policies under which this nation has been built and in accordance with which it must go on" are the very substance of American politics. Roosevelt was a little more explicit in his definition of a "constructive statesman" in the same letter, when discussing Holmes's record on the Massachusetts Supreme Court

> The labor decisions which have been criticized by some of the big railroad men and other members of large corporations constitute to my mind a strong point in Judge Holmes' favor. The ablest lawyers and greatest judges are men whose past has naturally brought them into close relationships with the wealthiest and most powerful clients, and I am glad when I can find a judge who has been able to preserve his aloofness of mind so as to keep his broad humanity of feeling and his sympathy for the class from which he has not drawn his clients.[12]

What Roosevelt presents as a nonideological "aloofness" is, of course, a political sympathy for the objectives of the Roosevelt administration. But such presidential efforts to exert ideological influence over the Court through the appointment process are risky. After an appointment is completed, a president loses control over his or her candidate. Justices sometimes display surprising independence once they have donned their black robes. When Holmes disappointed Roosevelt with his vote in a major antitrust case, the president complained bitterly, "I could carve out of a banana a judge with more backbone than that."[13] Two years later, a chastened Roosevelt was still trying to establish his political agenda on the Court. Screening candidates for a subsequent nomination, Roosevelt wrote Lodge about Democrat Horace Lurton:

> He is right on the Negro question; he is right on the power of the federal government; he is right on the Insular business; he is right about corporations, he is right about labor. On every question that would come before the bench, he has so far shown himself to be in much closer touch with the policies in which you and I believe than even [Chief Justice] White because he has been right about corporations where White has been wrong.[14]

In the end, Roosevelt appointed to the Court William H. Moody, his attorney general, after Lodge convinced him that Moody had all the fine characteristics of

Lurton and the additional virtue of being a Republican. Lurton was to be the next Supreme Court appointee, after William Howard Taft succeeded Roosevelt in the White House.

If presidents consider ideology in choosing a nominee, so does the Senate frequently consider ideology before granting its advice and consent. Only a few candidates appear to have been denied appointment primarily due to incompetence or ethical deficiency. Often cited examples of such poor candidates include James Madison's nominee, political supporter Alexander Wolcott, and two of Nixon's nominees, Clement Haynsworth and G. Harold Carswell.[15] The most important criteria in Senate rejections of nominations have been political criteria. Thus did the Senate reject Washington's nomination of John Rutledge to become chief justice, even though he had already been serving some months as a recess appointment. Rutledge, a previously good federalist, had earned the wrath of the Senate by making speeches critical of the Jay Treaty with Great Britain. Most recently, the Senate's rejection of Reagan's nomination of Robert H. Bork was certainly motivated by strong antipathy to Bork's political ideology, especially his narrow constructions of individual liberties. Opposition to President Bush's nomination of Clarence Thomas solidified around charges of sexual harassment but were surely motivated by ideological suspicions as much as by ethical concerns.

The Senate may have been a greater obstacle to presidents wishing to place proponents of their own political goals on the Court in the past than it has been through most of the twentieth century, for until very recently the frequency of Senate rejections had been in decline. During the nineteenth century the Senate prevented 23 appointments to the Supreme Court, or about one in four. Eight nominees were rejected outright, 5 were withdrawn after intense opposition developed, and 10 nominations languished with no Senate action. In contrast, the twentieth century has seen the outright rejection only of John J. Parker in 1932, Clement Haynsworth and G. Harold Carswell in 1969 and 1970, and Robert H. Bork in 1987. President Johnson's elevation of Justice Abe Fortas to chief justice in 1968 failed because of Senate inaction, which rendered Johnson's nomination of Homer Thornberry to fill Fortas's seat as associate justice moot. Finally, Reagan's nomination of Douglas Ginsburg for the seat for which Bork had already been rejected was withdrawn after it was revealed that Ginsburg had used marijuana while a law professor at Harvard. In short, the twentieth century has thus far seen only four rejections, two nominations blocked or withdrawn, and one that never materialized because the expected opening on the Court did not occur. Excluding the latter, only 6 nominations of a Supreme Court justice were aborted due to a failure to receive advice and consent, out of 56 nominations over 93 years!

The approval of an evasive David Souter in 1990 and the narrow approval of Clarence Thomas in 1991 revealed most graphically the Senate's complaisance. Both seemed able individuals, but not of a caliber of experience that would make them obvious candidates for the high court. Furthermore, the Bush administration had an explicit agenda of seeking to overturn *Roe v. Wade*, the abortion decision, through its judicial appointments, a sentiment not shared by most senators. The former was to replace one of the most effective, and most liberal, members of the Court, William Brennan. Souter arrived before the Senate an unknown entity and left the same way, but with the Senate's advice and consent. Most recently, Souter has voted to weaken, but not to overturn, *Roe.*[16]

The next year saw the retirement of the last liberal, Thurgood Marshall. Clarence Thomas had built a reputation in the Reagan administration as a conservative partisan, espousing some highly controversial views on law and politics. During his confirmation hearing, he assured the Senate Judiciary Committee that his past statements had all been mere political speculation, often intended only to please his immediate audience, that would have no bearing on how he would decide cases. More specifically, he stated that his personal views on the question of abortion were irrelevant to how he would decide an abortion controversy. For good measure, he told the committee that he in fact had no personal views on the most divisive subject of the day and, although a Yale-educated lawyer in public service, had never even discussed *Roe* at any time during the previous 16 years. Subsequent allegations of sexual harassment by a former subordinate, while not conclusively proven, raised questions of personal integrity in an official charged with the enforcement of federal sexual harassment laws. And yet the Senate confirmed Thomas, albeit by the narrowest margin of any successful candidate in the twentieth century. During his first term on the Court, Thomas voted to overturn *Roe v. Wade.*[17] He has since proved a close ally of Justice Scalia, advocating a conservative activism.

It is difficult to say whether this reduced rate of rejections in the Senate, including the 36-year period without any rejections between 1932 and 1968, is the result of senatorial lassitude in the exercise of its advice and consent function. It may indicate greater presidential sensitivity to the views of senators when choosing a nominee initially, although the Souter and Thomas nominations seem to belie this. What is clear is that politics played a role in the rejections that did occur. It should also be noted that the rejections have tended to occur when the White House and the Senate were dominated by different political parties. Parker and Bork were rejected in response to pressure by interest groups and public opinion. Carswell was rejected due to questions of competence, while Fortas, Haynsworth, and Douglas Ginsburg ran into questions of ethics. However, it is safe to say that political objections to the activism of the Court during the 1960s in defense of minority interests, civil liberties, and defendants' rights, plus the good possibility of a Republican victory in the coming presidential election, really scuttled President Johnson's elevation of Fortas. Suspicion of Haynsworth, Carswell, and Douglas Ginsburg centered as much on the conservative politics of Presidents Nixon and Reagan, especially on civil rights issues, as on matters of ethics and ability.

Not surprisingly, presidents sometimes voice anger at the Senate's rejection of their nominations. The relative infrequency of rejections of recent nominations to the Court provided President Nixon with support for the view he expressed in a well-publicized letter to Senator William Saxbe in 1970, to the effect that the Senate's role in judicial appointments was limited to a consideration of competence and integrity only. The Senate, complained Nixon, had no right to reject his nominee on ideological grounds. Similar arguments were heard from the Reagan administration as opposition to the Bork nomination began to grow (also in support of the Manion nomination for the Court of Appeals for the Seventh Circuit, discussed previously). This view was obviated early in the Bork hearings when Bork, a constitutional scholar of considerable accomplishment, conceded that it was within the Senate's prerogative to consider a candidate's politics.

The argument that only the president may examine a candidate's ideology is constitutionally and politically disingenuous, and it is in reality this view that poses a threat to the independence of the judiciary. There is nothing in the text of the Constitution so limiting the Senate's examination of nominees, nor does the theory of the separation of powers support such a claim. Senators are frequently quite deferential to a president when considering his appointments to positions in the executive branch. After all, a cabinet secretary will work under the president's direction and will be expected to carry out the president's administrative agenda. Appointees to executive posts need to be individuals in whom the president has the utmost confidence and who will loyally serve the president's wishes.

However, this kind of deference is misplaced when appointments for the Supreme Court are being considered. The Court is emphatically not a part of the executive branch. To enable the president to place on the Court persons of whatever political persuasion he or she chooses, absent any check whatsoever, would render the Supreme Court a virtual extension of the White House and a tool for the advancement of the president's policy agenda. The framers of our Constitution, rejecting such a subservient role for the courts, wisely sought to restrain presidential power over the Supreme Court through the requirement of senatorial advice and consent. It may be that the framers hoped appointments could be made free of any ideological considerations, although in their hearts they seem to have known better. At the very least, if presidents are going to consider ideology in choosing their nominees, the Senate may rightfully resist a nomination on ideological grounds of its own choosing. To extend to the president the kind of deference Nixon claimed would amount to abdication of an important constitutional duty and would further augment already enormous executive powers.

Both the president and the Senate have a democratic responsibility to examine candidates for the nation's highest court on ideological grounds. Judicial independence is an important value, one that has often served the nation well. However, in the democratic society that the United States has become, judicial independence is not the only value at stake. We expect those making political decisions affecting our lives to be held accountable for those decisions. Ordinarily, this accountability is achieved through frequent elections, giving the public the opportunity to turn the author of unpopular policies out of office. We do not have the opportunity to vote for federal judges, nor can they be removed except through the cumbersome and rarely employed procedure of impeachment. This insulation of the judiciary ensures independence, but independence must be qualified to some extent by the opposing value of political accountability. Where accountability is absent, citizens will have lost control over a portion of the political process. The only useful opportunity for accountability afforded by the Constitution is at the moment of appointment.

We face here nothing less than the tension between constitutionalism and popular sovereignty, a complex issue in its own right that awaits us in Chapter 7.

Here we need only note that reconciliation of the values of accountability and judicial independence is never easy or complete. Rather, we face a tension that will continually haunt judicial politics and which must be addressed with every appointment. At best, political accountability can be only partially achieved through the careful screening of candidates by the president and the Senate equally. Judicial independence is threatened the moment screening occurs at only one end of Pennsylvania Avenue. Elected officials whose joint responsibility it is to staff the courts have a duty to ensure that the men and women who become judges for the remainder of their lives do not radically depart from the diverse currents of the community's political culture. This seems to be the best accommodation of independence and accountability possible in our imperfect world.

CONTRASTING LEGACIES: CARTER, REAGAN, AND BUSH

We will delay consideration of additional political controls over the judiciary for the last chapter. As we will see, this question raises difficult issues concerning the very nature of the American polity. We will instead conclude this chapter with a detailed examination of recent trends in Supreme Court recruitment, covering the last 15 years and the three presidencies prior to the Clinton Administration.

It was President Jimmy Carter's misfortune to become only the fourth president in U.S. history to make no appointments to the Supreme Court. In this dubious distinction he joins Presidents Andrew Johnson, Zachary Taylor, and William Henry Harrison. The novelty of Carter's experience is brought into sharper focus when one considers that the last two of these presidents died in office before completion of a single term. Johnson also served only a partial term and was prevented from making any appointments by a hostile Congress that reduced the size of the Court. Carter's unfortunate stroke of luck was in part the result of being a single-term president, but it also reflected a hiatus in the normal turnover of justices during the later 1970s, resulting in what one scholar described as "the greying of the Court."[18] Simply put, the aging justices in the late 1970s remained hale and healthy and were unwilling to retire from active service. Had Carter won reelection in 1980, his fortunes might have changed. As it happened, his defeat in the 1980 election heralded a distinct rightward shift in the political complexion of the Supreme Court during the next decade.

Although Reagan's influence on the district and appellate courts was profound, his most visible appointments were the three justices he placed on the Supreme Court. We noted previously the retirement of Justice Potter Stewart in 1981, which opened the way for the appointment of the first woman to the Court, Sandra Day O'Connor. Despite some opposition from New Right activists who found in the former Arizona legislator's voting record evidence of soft opposition to abortion, O'Connor's nomination was generally hailed as a good one, and she won easy confirmation in the Senate. Her voting record on the Court has revealed general fidelity to conservative principles, albeit somewhat more moderately than Reagan's other appointees, most visibly on gender-related issues.[19] Most recently, she lent some credence to New Right fears when she failed to join her conservative brethren explicitly to overturn *Roe v. Wade*.[20]

The resignation of Chief Justice Warren Burger in 1986 presented Reagan with the opportunity to reward Justice William Rehnquist for his faithful service to the conservative cause by placing him in the chief justice's chair and to appoint Antonin Scalia, a former law professor and federal appeals judge, to Rehnquist's former seat. Scalia has arguably been the justice with the most conservative voting record to date, although a justice of his ability cannot be expected to adhere blindly to any predetermined path. Considerable opposition developed in the Senate to Rehnquist's elevation, based on his alleged insensitivity to the interests of women and minorities, as well as some ethical questions, but his nomination was approved by a vote of 65 to 33, a very qualified endorsement of the president's choice by contemporary standards. Scalia's nomination, in contrast, passed by a unanimous vote, despite his ideological stance a bit to the right of Rehnquist. Here again, we see the Senate's reluctance to confront a president on Supreme Court appointments.

The return of a Democratic majority to the Senate after the 1986 election and the concomitant Democratic chairship of the critical Judiciary Committee, brought about a different political reality that the White House was slow to appreciate. Thus, when Lewis Powell announced his retirement in 1987, Reagan made his long anticipated nomination of former solicitor general, law professor, and circuit judge Robert H. Bork. The last chapter will elucidate some of the controversy surrounding Bork's judicial philosophy. Suffice it here to note that he became only the fourth nomination in the twentieth century to be rejected by an outright Senate vote. Part of Bork's difficulty lies in his very public record of severe—some would say intemperate—criticism of most of the Supreme Court's jurisprudence of the last 30 years. Especially in the areas of civil liberties—and most especially on the question of individual privacy, which includes the right of abortion—Bork's writings were sure to arouse suspicion of all but the truest believers in the conservative cause.

But another aspect of the Bork nomination deserves note—the highly public deliberation his candidacy generated. Never before had so may interest groups sought participation in a judicial nomination. Never before had so much money been spent lobbying in support or in opposition to a nomination for any court. And never before had such lengthy hearings—11 days, 5 of which were taken up by Bork's testimony—before the Senate Judiciary Committee received so much coverage in the media. This can be explained in part by the "swing" position occupied by departing Justice Powell on so many issues, including abortion.

For days the public watched the very unusual event of a detailed debate over such issues as the proper interpretation of constitutional provisions protecting the freedoms of speech and press, the equal protection clause, the putative rights of privacy, contraception, and abortion, and the sweep of executive power. It is doubtful that many understood very clearly the sometimes arcane constitutional theories being debated, and in fairness it must be said that television was a poor medium in which to present all of the complexities of Bork's point of view. But one thing was certain: as the public heard Bork deny that they had constitutionally protected rights against government interference in their most intimate activities, they did not approve. Mail was so heavy that even some conservative senators, Republicans and southern Democrats who would have ordinarily been expected to support the nomination, ultimately voted against Bork. Many of these, who had long championed views fully compatible with those of Bork, voted "nay," for a total of 58 negative votes. Only 42 votes were cast in support of Bork.

The response of the Reagan administration was, predictably, anger. Their solution was to find someone holding views similar to Bork's, but less notoriously. Douglas Ginsburg seemed to fill the bill. The former Harvard law professor and federal circuit judge was known to harbor vaguely conservative libertarian views, although his publications included absolutely nothing on constitutional issues. As it turned out, Ginsburg proved an unknown entity to the Reagan administration as well, when revelations of the nominee's marijuana use during his tenure on the Harvard law faculty provided grist for pundits and punsters alike, ultimately forcing Reagan to withdraw the nomination.

On the third try, Reagan succeeded in placing Anthony Kennedy on the Supreme Court. The latter also lacked a substantial public record, leading to fears he might be a "Bork without a paper trail." Nevertheless, he was confirmed by a wide margin by a Senate anxious to avoid further confrontation with an election approaching. Kennedy has since established his conservative bona fides on the Court. Although he joined the liberal wing to grant First Amendment protection to flag burning as "symbolic speech," he has also joined the most conservative of his colleagues to narrow the reach of important civil rights legislation and has indicated his willingness to narrow the abortion decision.[21]

It is not yet clear that Reagan's lower court judges, as a group, have behaved much differently on the bench than Republican judges generally.[22] The conservative cast they were expected to add to legal policy probably awaited more guidance from the Supreme Court, an initiative that appeared to commence only after the 1990 departure of Justice Brennan created a clear majority on the Court behind a conservative—and frequently activist—policy orientation. The election of George Bush to the White House, the first sitting vice president to be so elevated in more than a century and a half, preserved Republican dominance of the recruitment process, but with a firm Democratic majority in the Senate that seemed at first to induce a certain caution in the White House.

Bush's choice of David Souter to replace the retiring Brennan and of Clarence Thomas for the seat vacated by Thurgood Marshall are likely to alter the Supreme Court profoundly, beyond the switch of two votes. One of the most influential justices in the history of the Supreme Court, Brennan was long the intellectual leader of the faction of justices most sympathetic to individual rights, including the lightning rod issue of abortion. Marshall was for more than two decades Brennan's closest ally. Replacing both presented Bush with the opportunity to tip the balance on the Court more strongly in favor of a conservative agenda of retrenchment in the field of individual rights, to the near total exclusion of liberal voices.

In this politically charged context, the choice of Souter, a little-known former New Hampshire Supreme Court justice who has been appointed by Bush to the United States Court of Appeals for the First Circuit only two months previously, was astute. A conservative hand-picked by White House Chief of Staff John Sununu (not coincidentally, the former governor of New Hampshire), Souter had never written opinions or articles on abortion or other divisive national issues. Although highly regarded for his diligence, Souter had only a thin paper trail. Senate review of his nomination failed to turn up any skeletons in his closet, although it also failed to establish much about Souter's politics on judicial philosophy. Although Souter remained a largely unknown entity, the Senate approved the nomination. His first year on the Supreme Court was quiet, but his voting record is so far securely conservative, except for his reluctance to entirely overturn *Roe v. Wade.*

Although Bush has made much of his opposition to affirmative action, he ultimately chose not to incur the controversy that would greet a white replacement for Thurgood Marshall. In Clarence Thomas, Bush found a black man sympathetic to his administration's agenda. He had long been outspokenly critical of affirmative action programs in aid of minority groups, advocating instead a rigorous program of minority self-help. Similarly, he was on record as hostile to the abortion decision. Unlike Souter, Thomas had a long and well-documented public record of expressing his views, a record he sought to distance himself from at his confirmation hearings. Thus, if the first Bush nomination was designed to avert a confirmation fight by stealth, the Thomas nomination seemed almost designed to be a lightning rod for controversy, much as Bork had been five years earlier.

The political stakes appeared even higher after there surfaced some indication that Thomas was a proponent of natural law, a theory that posits the existence of binding moral principles standing above socially contrived law. A key question was whether Thomas considered such abstract law judicially enforceable. If so, then he would differ considerably from the judicial restraintist philosophies expressed by other Reagan and Bush nominees. Conservative activism has a longer history in American law than liberal activism, but Thomas was anxious to portray himself as a restraintist judge before the Senate Judiciary Committee. His first year on the Court, however, revealed him in a very different light. Thomas has voted most frequently with Justice Scalia, thus adding a voice for conservative activism on the Court.

The election of Democrat Bill Clinton to the White House in 1992 promises to moderate this rightward drift on the Court. When Byron White, the sole remaining Democrat on the Court, announced his retirement at the end of the 1992–1993 term, the new administration found in federal appeals court judge and former law professor Ruth Bader Ginsburg a combination of liberalism on social issues, tempered by a reputation for toughness on defendants' rights and with a preference for judicial restraint. While many conservatives were suspicious of her prior feminist activism and affiliation with the American Civil Liberties Union, Republican senators on the Judiciary Committee seemed almost relieved by her nomination. Orrin Hatch undoubtedly expressed the view of many, calling Ginsburg the best they could hope for from Democratic administration. Clearly, her nomination was intended to avoid controversy. The White House may have speculated that Republicans would be reluctant to harshly attack a woman nominee with the political fallout of the Thomas appointment still in the air. Ginsburg may have satisfied more long-range strategic planning as well, if her moderation serves to build a bridge to the swing bloc of O'Connor, Souter, and Kennedy, uniting them with Blackmun and Stevens more often than with Rehnquist, Scalia, and Thomas.

The retirement of Harry Blackmun at the conclusion of the 1993 term presents Clinton with an opportunity to make a second appointment. The nomination of federal appeals court judge Stephen Breyer seemed designed to avoid a confirmation fight and to further strengthen the Court's moderate bloc. Prior to his appointment to the U. S. Court of Appeals for the First Circuit, Breyer had been a law professor at Harvard University, and the chief counsel to the Senate Judiciary Committee. In this latter role, he earned the admiration of committee members across the ideological spectrum for his moderation, hard work, and legal skill. His nomination quickly gained the support of key committee members as diverse as Orrin Hatch and Ted Kennedy. The choice seemed to have been a difficult one for the White House, however, and came only after Senator George Mitchell removed himself from consideration, and after opposition from Republican and western senators dissuaded Clinton from nominating his secretary of the interior, Bruce Babbitt. Significantly, the ultimate choice of Breyer contradicted Clinton's repeatedly expressed desire to appoint a justice with broad political experience to balance the tendency of recent Republican administrations to elevate lower court judges.

It is impossible to predict how many appointments the new president will ultimately make, but even if he has the opportunity to appoint a significant number, it should be remembered that the Court tends to shift its policies only slowly. The next two chapters will explore some of the reasons why this is so. The result may be to perpetuate the influence of Presidents Reagan and Bush long into—maybe beyond—the Clinton years.

If the attention we have devoted to the issue of selection of federal judges seems at this point excessive, the next two chapters should vindicate our attention and convince the student that this has all been worthwhile. The question of who becomes a judge is politically relevant in direct proportion to the policy-making discretion judges bring to office. We explored this problem only briefly in Chapter 1. Now, with more information about judicial politics under our belt, we will return to this question, and consider for the next three chapters how judges go about judging. We will find that their policy-making discretion, while broad in some cases, is not unlimited. Its actual breadth is, as we shall see, hotly contested.

NOTES

1. Walter F. Murphy, *Elements of Judicial Strategy* (University of Chicago Press, Chicago, 1964) pp. 73–77.
2. Quoted in Fred L. Friedman and Leon Isreal, *The Justices of the United States Supreme Court: 1789–1969*, vol. I (Chelsea House, New York, 1969) p. 128.
3. James Iredell (under the pseudonym of Marcus), "Answers to Mr. Mason's Objections to the New Constitution, Recommended by the Late Convention," in Griffith J.

McRee, *Life and Correspondence of James Iredell,* vol. I (D. Appleton New York, 1857) p. 91.

4. David M. O'Brien, "Background Paper," in *Judicial Roulette: Report of the Twentieth Century Task Force on Judicial Selection* (Priority Press, New York, 1988) p. 44.

5. See Jerold S. Auerbach, *Unequal Justice: Lawyers and Social change in Modern America* (Oxford University Press, New York, 1976) pp. 71–72, for a sorry example of the distortion of merit in judicial selection, in the opposition to the nomination of Justice Brandeis. Religious opposition was kept further from the surface in discussion of subsequent nominations of Justices Cardozo and Frankfurter.

6. See generally, Alan Freeman, "Legitimizing Racial Discrimination Through Antidiscrimination Law: A Critical Review of Supreme Court Doctrine," in Allan C. Hutchinson, *Critical Legal Studies* (Rowman & Littlefield, Totowa, New Jersey, 1989) pp. 120–136, and Patricia J. Williams, *The Alchemy of Race and Rights* (Harvard University Press, Cambridge, Massachusetts, 1991) especially pp. 3–43.

7. Quoted in Harry P. Stumpf, *American Judicial Politics* (Harcourt Brace Jovanovich, New York, 1988) pp. 221–222.

8. O'Brien, op. cit., p. 39. Souter, Thomas, and Ginsburg have been added to O'Brien's list. Stephen Breyer, whose nomination is pending, would raise to 27 the number of federal judges elevated to the supreme court.

9. Felix Frankfurter, "The Supreme Court in the Mirror of Justices," 105 *University of Pennsylvania Law Review* 781, 785 (1957).

10. David O'Brien, *Storm Center: The Supreme Court in American Politics,* 3rd ed. (W.W. Norton, New York, 1993) pp. 67–68.

11. Quoted in Walter F. Murphy and C. Herman Pritchett, *Courts, Judges and Politics,* 4th ed. (Random House, New York, 1986) p. 150.

12. Ibid., pp. 149–150.

13. Quoted in Henry Abraham, *Justices and Presidents,* 2nd ed. (Oxford University Press, New York, 1985) p. 69. The Supreme Court decision in question was *Northern Securities v. United States,* 193 U.S. 197 (1904).

14. John R. Schmidhauser, *Judges and Justices: The Federal Appellate Judiciary* (Little, Brown, Boston, 1979) p. 90.

15. Schmidhauser op. cit., p. 91.

16. *Planned Parenthood of southeastern Pennsylvania v. Casey,* 112 S. Ct. 2791 (1992).

17. Ibid.

18. Laurence H. Tribe, *God Save This Honorable Court* (New American Library, New York, 1985) p. xvi.

19. Harold J. Spaeth, "Justice Sandra Day O'Connor: An Assessment," in D. Grier Stephenson, Jr., *An Essential Safeguard: Essays on the United States Supreme Court and Its Justices* (Greenwood Press, New York, 1991) p. 88.

20. *Webster v. Reproductive Health Services,* 492 U.S. 490 (1989) and, most recently, *Planned Parenthood of Pennsylvania v. Casey,* 112 S. Ct. 2791 (1992).

21. *Texas v. Johnson,* 491 U.S. 397 (1989), *Webster v. Reproductive Health Services,* 492 U.S. 490 (1989).

22. See Timothy B. Tomasi and Jess A. Volona, "All the President's Men?: A Study of Ronald Reagan's Appointments to the U.S. Courts of Appeals," 87 *Columbia Law Review* 766 (1987), Christopher E. Smith, "Polarization and Change in the Federal Courts: En Banc Decisions in the U.S. Courts of Appeals," 74 *Judicature* 133 (1990), and Bernard Schwartz, *The New Right and the Constitution: Turning Back the Legal Clock* (Northeastern University Press, Boston, 1990).

Chapter
5

From Dispute to Suit

Having examined the organization and staffing of the federal judiciary, we begin at last our study of the extent of the courts' power to affect public policy, focusing in this chapter on the question of how conflicts are brought before the courts for resolution. We will see that, compared to legislatures, courts play a narrow role in policy making. Only a fraction of the conflicts in the community represent potential litigation, and only a small fraction of these actually arrive in court. Recall that it is only in response to a lawsuit brought to their doorstep by a properly qualified litigant that courts can affect policy at all. Consequently, we will begin with a brief look at the behavior of potential litigants, for the decisions they make will profoundly affect the political role courts may play in the community.

We will also see that lawsuits are social constructs. They have no existence in and of themselves, but exist only as a set of social relations, according to rules courts ascribe to them. In formulating these rules, courts also shape to a considerable extent the role they will play in the political process. Further, in the process of becoming a lawsuit, a dispute may be transformed by these rules into something quite different from the original conflict, as it was understood by the disputing parties. The conflict ultimately resolved by a court may seem only tangentially related to the life experiences of the plaintiff and defendant, sometimes leaving both confused and dissatisfied.

Courts have traditionally been called on to resolve disputes between two discrete parties. These decisions might have a profound impact on the lives of the litigants. Repeated many times, these decisions would cumulatively affect public policy, but each suit by itself threatens only a minuscule impact on existing social arrangements. We might refer to such traditional suits as *individual dispute resolution*. In recent decades, we have witnessed the rise of *complex litigation*, distinguished by the number of parties affected, the nature of the questions raised, or the deep impact a single decision in such a case might make in our politics. Such lawsuits maintain the form of a dispute between two discrete parties, but with difficulty. In truth, they are attempts to use courts in lieu of legislatures to affect broad changes in public policy.

Frequently sponsored by interest groups, complex litigation may fundamentally alter the allocation of valued goods or opportunities for empowerment among contending constituencies or may profoundly alter the ways in which public agencies conduct their business. More controversially, complex litigation will involve judges in some distinctly nonjudicial roles, overlapping with those we normally attribute to executives or legislators. Such complex litigation will seriously strain the rules courts have developed to structure and manage litigation. Complex litigation frequently turns on issues of constitutional law, but we will discuss it here as a matter of convenience, addressing theories of constitutional interpretation in Chapter 7.

In Chapter 1 we borrowed Martin Shapiro's model of courts, which we Americanized, portraying them as: (1) essentially passive bodies (2) staffed by independent judges (3) applying previously existing legal norms (4) after adversary proceedings to reach (5) a dichotomous result. We then presented three views of the judicial decision: the formalist (which Shapiro's model reflects); the realist; and that of the Critical Legal Studies movement. The formalist view posited a radical separation between law and politics, a separation questioned in somewhat different ways by the latter two. When legal realism and Critical Legal Studies challenged the formalist notion of the judicial decision as a technical endeavor devoid of political considerations, they called Shapiro's model into question as well. It should be remembered that Shapiro offered his model only as a starting point for the analysis of courts and did not purport to be offering a complete picture. In these final chapters, we will add detail to the picture, ramifying the challenge to formalism presented in Chapter 1.

TO THE COURTHOUSE DOOR

The passivity of courts has been stressed many times: courts can do nothing until a suit is filed by others. The persons who can file a suit and what kinds of suit they might file are restricted in several important ways, also limiting the impact courts can have on society. Ordinarily, courts react only to injuries that have already occurred and are brought to their attention by the individual who has suffered the injury. We shall see presently that courts are frequently creative when defining judicially cognizable injuries, as their political will seems to dictate.

However, even as the courts employ a flexible concept of injury to grant or deny access to adjudication, their discretion lies only within the scope of choices previously made by potential plaintiffs. Courts can make passage over their threshold easy or difficult, but only an aggrieved individual can knock on the door in the first place. The initial decision to engage the judicial process, then, lies largely outside the control of judges. How individuals make the decision to seek judicial assistance is our first concern.

Dispute Formation

As we go about our daily lives, we are exposed to a host of potential conflicts, great and small. Most of these conflicts are resolved through a process of mutual accommodation among affected individuals. Some, however, result in one party injuring the physical, financial, or psychic interests of another in some way. Only a small fraction of these become lawsuits. We know little about the decisions people make to turn their conflicts into lawsuits, even though this is an important area of research. Investigation of this stage of the legal process by social scientists is hobbled by problems in data collection, but we do know a few things about dispute formation. The most suggestive study in this area is by Richard E. Miller and Austin Sarat, using survey data generated by telephone interviews with members of approximately 1000 randomly selected households in each of five federal districts.[1] Respondents were asked whether members of their household had in the past three years experienced one or more of a list of common legal problems involving a sum in excess of $1000. This threshold sum established a sample of what the authors called "middle-range" disputes, those that characterize the bulk of litigation in the United States.

The legal problems that became the basis for further inquiries were grouped into eight categories: torts, consumer problems, debt, discrimination, property disputes, problems with government agencies, postdivorce readjustments, and landlord-tenant relations. The data thus generated were used to determine the incidence of disputes in society that might result in litigation, to map the route followed from injury to suit, and to examine the attrition in potential cases on their way to court. Miller and Sarat's findings are useful for our purposes, but we must first enter a caveat: several of the legal categories studied are dealt with almost exclusively in state courts, while others, such as discrimination and problems with government agencies, could be litigated in state or federal courts. We are interested here solely in the pattern of dispute formation and offer the hypothesis that the journey to federal court is similar, a probability supported by the fact that Miller and Sarat found only slight deviation in pattern among the eight legal categories they included in their study.

The road from injury to suit was marked by several milestones: a *grievance* occurred if the respondent perceived himself or herself as injured in some way relevant to a potential suit, and a *claim* was made if the injured party sought a remedy from the person perceived as responsible for the injury. Notice that an injury not perceived as such by the victim could not be a grievance, and a perceived injury not acted on could not be a claim. The subjective perceptions and consequent behavior of putative plaintiffs, then, was an important component in the creation of litigation. Where redress was sought, the putative defendant could choose to concede his or her responsibility for the injury and make good on the claim. If redress was refused, however, the incident became a *dispute*. Thus, the behavior of defendants was equally vital to the creation of suits. Like dancing the tango, it takes two to litigate.

Extrapolating from their data, the researchers concluded that grievances and claims are a common part of an American's life. However, claims are frequently

Court filings	50
Lawyers	103
Disputes	449
Claims	718
Grievances	1000

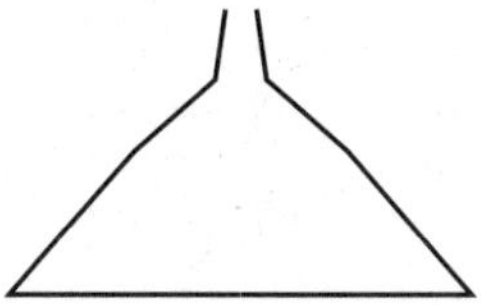

Figure 5.1 A dispute pyramid: the general pattern (number per 1000 grievances).
Source: Richard E. Miller and Austin Sarat, "Grievances, Claims, and Disputes: Assessing the Adversary Culture," *Law and Society Review* 15 (1981): 544. Reprinted by permission of the Law and Society Association.

rejected, in whole or in part, resulting in a high level of disputes. Most disputes were resolved by informal means, if at all. Only a strikingly small portion of the sample took the first step toward invoking judicial authority by consulting a lawyer, and a smaller portion of these actually filed a suit. Recall our observation in Chapter 2 that few filings actually go to trial; most are dismissed, withdrawn, or settled by negotiation between the parties. While case attrition occurs before and after filing, Miller and Sarat focused only on the decision to employ the courts in the first place. Adding what we already know, however, we get a clear sense that our litigation rate is but the tip of a vast iceberg of social conflict. Figure 5.1 illustrates the attrition of potential cases at each step up to filing a suit, per 1000 grievances.[2]

One frequently hears the complaint that Americans litigate to an excessive degree.[3] This alleged litigiousness is often lamented as a sign of communal decay, a drag on our economy, or a threat to socially beneficial innovation. Certainly, we saw in Chapter 2 that high caseloads are a problem in American courts. It is striking, then, that for all persons having grievances, only 10.3 percent consulted lawyers and only 5 percent filed suits. As burdened as our courts might be, the actual rate of litigation appears quite low when compared with the potential. Popular perceptions aside, as litigators, Americans appear to be underachievers. While most people sampled received some form of remedy, the great majority of perceived injuries never came to the attention of the courts. The picture drawn of American disputing by Miller and Sarat is of "a remedy system that minimizes formal conflict but uses the courts when necessary in those relatively rare cases in which conflict is unavoidable."[4]

When the sample was separated into the eight legal categories, the patterns of case attrition were generally similar. Three categories, however—torts, postdivorce readjustments, and discrimination—revealed the unique patterns illustrated in Figure 5.2. Torts tended to be settled early in the process, obviating the need to involve the courts. This was no doubt due to a well-institutionalized system of insurance, whose participants were anxious to avoid the cost and uncertainty of litigation. In contrast, postdivorce proceedings involved lawyers and courts more frequently, in large part because states require court intervention to alter the terms

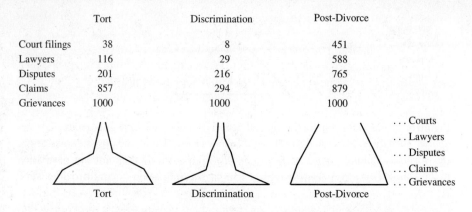

	Tort	Discrimination	Post-Divorce
Court filings	38	8	451
Lawyers	116	29	588
Disputes	201	216	765
Claims	857	294	879
Grievances	1000	1000	1000

. . . Courts
. . . Lawyers
. . . Disputes
. . . Claims
. . . Grievances

Tort   Discrimination   Post-Divorce

Figure 5.2 Dispute pyramids: three deviant patterns (number per 1000 grievances).
Source: Richard E. Miller and Austin Sarat, "Grievances, Claims, and Disputes: Assessing the Adversary Culture," *Law and Society Review* 15 (1981): 544. Reprinted by permission of the Law and Society Association.

of a divorce decree, and perhaps because parties to a divorce already had experience in using a lawyer for their conflict. Perhaps most distressing for public policy was the pattern found for discrimination, in part because of the corrosive effect discrimination has had on American society, but also because we have relied primarily on antidiscrimination laws to remedy the historic inequalities plaguing American society.

Miller and Sarat show that the great majority of individuals who perceive themselves to be victims of discrimination offer no protest—of every 1000 grievances, only 294 claims were made. This low level of claims may be due to the factual ambiguity of the incident in which discrimination is perceived. Few employers are foolish enough to make their bigotry explicit. Indeed, discrimination is frequently so subtle that the perpetrator may not be *consciously* aware of the motive for his or her own actions. Usually, discriminatory motives are mixed with others that appear sincere, leaving the victim uncertain as to whether race or gender was truly a factor in his or her failure to be hired, promoted, or find desirable housing. The victim's response to this uncertainty is often avoidance.

There are social disincentives to raising the issue as well. Where one hopes to preserve an ongoing relationship with others involved in the incident, as is typical in an employment situation, the putative claimant might fear being labeled a "trouble maker" or alienating coworkers and supervisors. The victim might reasonably fear future retribution for making the claim of discrimination or making himself or herself a very unattractive candidate to future employers. Another important disincentive has to be the high rate of resistance met by those who do raise the issue of discrimination. Notice that an unusually large portion of discrimination claims become disputes, the alleged perpetrator denying the charge or refusing relief. Difficulties in gathering evidence help to insulate such denials from legal inquiry.

It is also important to notice how infrequently lawyers are consulted or cases filed for discrimination—the lowest for all eight categories. American discrimination law is written in strong terms. Even with some recent judicial weakening, the laws promise the victim much, but they are actually able to deliver little if victims invoke them so infrequently. Put another way, whatever the content of discrimination law, the ability of such laws—or of the courts—to alter behavior in society is quite attenuated by the unwillingness of victims to pursue legal remedies. It should be understood that victims decline to pursue remedies not out of apathy, but because the social context within which discrimination occurs provides such powerful disincentives. We have placed considerable trust in the law and the courts to resolve racial inequities, but litigation has proven to be a most inefficient tool in practice. This inefficiency in resolving conflict arising from perceived incidents of discrimination must result in a high level of frustration and resentment throughout victimized communities.

It is important to reiterate the narrow scope of Miller and Sarat's study. While they paint a detailed picture of American dispute formation for the kinds of legal issues included in their study, to keep the study manageable they had to omit the innumerable smaller injuries suffered by many people in the course of their lives. Also omitted were the truly big questions occasionally resolved through lawsuits, such as constitutional rights or issues raised in complex litigation. These cases grab the attention of the mass media and have a profound impact on our political lives, yet there are so few of them that they have to be seen as exceptional instances of litigation. Note that even for the kinds of disputes that constitute the day-to-day business of the courts, actual litigation represents a fraction of the conflicts generated. Finally, plaintiffs should not bear the whole blame for the staggering amount of litigation we do have. Recalcitrant defendants contribute to American litigiousness as much as contentious plaintiffs.

The Law Office

The penultimate stage in dispute formation studied by Miller and Sarat, consultation with an attorney, deserves extended treatment. Law is a technical affair, and its practitioners are highly trained in its esoteric patterns of thought and elusive categories. Suffice it to say that it would be impossible for the untrained individual to adequately argue pro se—in their own cause—for any litigation beyond small claims court, or perhaps misdemeanor court.[5] Without the assistance of an attorney, individuals would be unable to activate courts to defend even those interests the law clearly protects. Lawyers therefore play the role of gatekeepers for the judiciary. Our interest is specifically how litigants take the step from law office to courthouse.

In this gatekeeping role, lawyers screen out many disputes before they arrive in court, thus serving to insulate the courts from excessive demands that might otherwise be made on their resources. Many disputes simply do not merit the attention of a judge or may be resolved in other ways. Lawyers also help structure those disputes that will be taken to court in a form that courts can understand and resolve. In so doing, they serve the interests of both court and client, although the client might not fully understand or appreciate the ways in which the dispute has been redefined. The lawyer ostensibly serves as an advocate on his or her client's behalf, placing the client in control of the litigation. Realistically, however, clients are in need of the attorney's expertise, contacts, and status to protect their interests in a rough world. This dependency must to some degree reverse the role of master and servant.

At the outset, we should dispel common stereotypes concerning the legal profession. Lawyers are not a homogeneous group. Although most lawyers, a little more than two-thirds, are in private practice, many are employed in industry, government, educational institutions, labor unions, and interest groups.[6] Those lawyers in private practice work in a variety of environments, ranging from huge urban law firms on Wall Street or K Street, serving primarily corporate clients, to solo practitioners on Main Street, who are more likely to serve the legal needs of ordinary individuals. In television, movies, and novels, we encounter lawyers involved in dramatic litigation, usually doing battle against the forces of evil and corruption. Portrayals of lawyers doing battle on *behalf* of the forces of evil and corruption have also been common, however, for public esteem for the profession is ambivalent. Indeed, rapacious lawyers have frequently been blamed for the allegedly excessive litigiousness of the American people.

It might come as a surprise, then, to find that litigation represents only a small part of the attorney's trade.[7] Many lawyers never litigate at all, and only a few do it with any regularity. One student of the profession has estimated that between 10 and 20 percent of the profession devotes a majority of their time to litigation, suggesting that litigation has indeed become a specialty among practitioners.[8] Much of a lawyer's time is spent counseling his or her clients, advising them on the best ways to handle a complex situation that may be rich with legal ramifications. A corporation might want to know whether a planned merger will run afoul of federal antitrust law, or an individual might want to know the tax implications of certain kinds of investments. Notice that what drives the client to the lawyer is the desire to avoid court. The lawyer is able to draw on his or her technical skill and experience to make a Holmsian prediction of how courts (and other legal officials, including regulators or prosecutors) would respond to the conduct under consideration. Thus, the lawyer is like a navigator, directing the client to a safe course and avoiding potential legal hazards.

Alternatively, a lawyer may spend much time engaged in securing a stable and predictable future for his or her clients through the drafting of legal documents that structure future relationships and events. An individual may desire to write a will disposing of his worldly effects after his or her departure from this world or may wish to set up a trust to finance his or her children's education. A flourishing business may seek advantages of incorporation or want a complex relationship formalized through a contract. Here, the goal is to create and preserve order in a chaotic world, so that the client might pattern a life confident that his or her intentions will continue to be respected. A predictable future is a valuable thing.

Notice that here again, the purpose of the lawyer's activity is defensive, in that he or she will employ legal skills to avoid future conflict regarding the client's purpose. A contract or a will that goes into litigation may represent a failure of an attorney to plan adequately for future contingencies and to express those plans clearly.

None of us is perfect, of course. Even the best counseling and drafting cannot guarantee a future entirely free of uncertainty and conflict, so lawyers may be called on for damage control as well. Recall that Miller and Sarat found that relatively few individuals embroiled in conflicts sought protection of the law. Most of those who consulted a lawyer were still unlikely to file suit. Perhaps for many such cases, the lawyer had to explain to the aggrieved individual that the law offered them no remedy for their pain. Perhaps a legal claim would be nearly impossible to substantiate factually due to problems in assembling evidence or the remedy available would come at such cost, in terms of time, effort, anxiety, and lost friendship, not to mention money, that it might be the better part of a client's wisdom to "lump it." The lawyer might simply attempt to diminish the intensity of the conflict to proportions the client can handle alone, perhaps by showing the client that the claim, while legally supportable, would be unreasonable when judged by some other standard of conduct.[9] Sometimes, lawyers find themselves in the role of therapist, helping to calm an angry client or to redefine a situation in a way that is more palatable to the client. All of these activities serve to divert conflict away from the courts.

A major function of lawyers engaged in situations of conflict is to negotiate a settlement between disputing parties. Litigants who value a future relationship may prefer to work out a compromise, rather than insist on an all-out victory at the cost of the relationship. Even without such an ongoing relationship, the client may prefer to settle for a portion of their claim to avoid the risk and trauma of a trial. The dubious prospect of facing a large, powerful institution in court may intimidate a client into compromise. Such an individual might call on a lawyer's professional distance, as well as expertise, to negotiate better treatment by a government bureaucracy or to induce a more generous payment by an insurance company. Going to court remains a possibility that weighs heavily on both parties, so we might characterize such negotiation as occurring in the shadow of the law. Law remains a variable affecting the outcome of the negotiation, since the bargaining strategies of both sides will be shaped in part by the predicted outcome, were the controversy to go to trial. Notice that for negotiation to work, trials must occur at least occasionally, to provide the parties with a basis for this important prediction.

Even criminal defense attorneys usually seek a lighter sentence for their clients in exchange for a guilty plea, employing personal contacts, cajolery, threats, and horse trading not usually thought of as legal skill.[10] Here again, bargaining is conditioned by a prediction of the likelihood of conviction and the likely sentence were a trial to be held. Successful bargaining, then, requires that both prosecutor and defender be aware of some kind of "going rate" for crimes similar to the one in question. Defense attorneys expend a good deal of effort helping defendants see the wisdom of accepting a plea bargain that avoids harsher punishment.

Slightly better than 9 out of 10 defendants ultimately plead guilty, and it is safe to say that our heavily burdened criminal dockets could never be cleared if all defendants insisted on a trial.

One study of how Wisconsin lawyers operate in the field of consumer protection found that most employed "people persuasion" skills having little to do with legal skills with the great majority of their clients. Indeed, most lawyers knew very little of consumer protection law, and even when clients had a legally solid claim their lawyers sought to avoid litigation, preferring nonadversarial techniques of conflict resolution.[11] Litigation for many such cases will cost more than a client is willing to pay. The lawyer might wish to avoid the investment in research and preparation a trial would entail, and so might find that negotiation better serves his or her interests as well. We must remember that a lawyer is also a businessperson, for whom litigation is seldom cost-efficient.

So we see that even lawyers who do represent clients in court spend much of their time trying to avoid the perils of a trial, for their client's sake as well as their own. Only when all else fails is litigation likely to be attempted. It is when litigation becomes the final option, however, that the problem of availability of legal assistance is most acute. Courtroom advocacy is a hazardous enterprise—costly, time-consuming, and risky—for which the prudent client wants the very best in representation. The United States relies primarily on free market mechanisms to allocate valued goods in the community, including legal representation. Although the free market provides an efficient allocation of many kinds of goods, imperfections in the market may be particularly troubling when the good in question happens to be access to justice. The simple fact is that legal representation does not come cheaply, and many deserving clients can afford it only with great difficulty, if at all. Those who cannot afford legal representation or who must compromise the quality of their representation will be hindered from employing courts to protect their legal interests.

In recognition of this problem, the federal courts have long required the appointment of counsel, at public expense, for the defense of indigents accused of federal crimes.[12] We have been slower to address the availability of legal assistance in the field of civil law. In the past, some cities supported charitable legal aid societies that provided representation to poor clients. Even today, some lawyers donate some of their time to meeting the needs of those who cannot pay, but such pro bono publico—for the public good—activity must compete with paying customers and is unlikely to be a high priority. In 1965, Congress created the Office of Economic Opportunity (OEO) as part of President Johnson's War on Poverty. The OEO disbursed grants to locally generated antipoverty projects, including legal assistance schemes in many cities. This public funding of legal aid was extended in 1974, when Congress created the Legal Services Corporation, a public corporation that disbursed grants to state and local law projects in much the same manner.

Although most of the work done under public sponsorship has been routine matters, such as divorce and child custody, landlord-tenant, consumer, and debtor cases, welfare rights, and the like, Legal Services lawyers have not always endeared themselves with local power structures. Businesspeople and local government officials, not coincidentally the persons Legal Services lawyers frequently named as defendants, have often been critical of Legal Services attorneys for excessive zeal on behalf of the lower classes. A Legal Services firm in California won an important welfare rights case against Governor Ronald Reagan that turned out to be fraught with political consequences. Reagan remained sharply critical of Legal Services lawyers, and as president attempted to eliminate the Legal Services Corporation from the federal budget. Although this effort proved unsuccessful, the Legal Services Corporation budget was seriously reduced during the 1980s. It has remained underfunded, at least when compared with previous levels, ever since. Many critics accused the Reagan administration of conducting a war on the poor. Whatever the motivation, the continued funding problems of the Legal Services Corporation must have the effect of contributing to the disempowerment of the lower classes.

But what of the middle classes, those who do not live at a poverty level but who may still find legal representation highly burdensome or prohibitively expensive? Legal clinics, legal insurance, and advertised flat rates for routine legal matters have made ordinary services such as wills, property transactions, and uncontested divorces available at a relatively modest cost. Some kinds of cases, notably personal injury suits, may be financed by contingency fee, in which the attorney receives a percentage of the final award as remuneration. Nevertheless, for anything but the most routine matters the cost of litigation must be a major disincentive to using courts. One study of litigation expenses, employing the same survey data as the Miller and Sarat study but focusing on disputes in which court filings were made, described lawyer fees as "modest" for the bulk of cases in their sample. However, cases in federal court tended to cost more than those taken to state judiciaries.[13] Specifically, the researchers found that 46 percent of disputes involved lawyers' fees of less than $1,000 and only 8 percent involved fees in excess of $10,000. Note, however, that this leaves another 46 percent of cases that cost between $1,000 and $10,000, not a sum the average American family can afford to expend frivolously.

Few of the cases studied went to trial, so the lawyers spent most of their time in negotiation rather than legal research and trial preparation. Surprisingly, the decision to go to trial did not add appreciably to the attorneys' billed hours, since most trials were finished quickly. Most cases involving hourly fees "paid" for the plaintiffs, in that they received an award equal to or greater than their legal expenses 78 percent of the time.[14] For those who filed suit, then, litigating proved economically cost-effective, assuming that the dispute could no longer be avoided and that alternatives to litigation were no longer viable. However, we must qualify this optimistic assessment with the realization that many disputes that did not result in court filings may have been abandoned precisely because they would not have paid. Probably most litigants, however, view their dispute as an unattractive and costly imposition on their lives that they would have preferred not to face at all.

Complex litigation presents unique issues. Litigation challenging the given allocation of resources in a society or the given way of conducting public business will likely be fought hard by both sides. Defendants in such suits will probably be government agencies or large economic entities such as corporations. As litigants, these organizations differ qualitatively from individuals. They possess many of the advantages in court that accrue to "repeat players," those who litigate fairly regularly. They have past experience in court, enjoy economies of scale, have access to specialized information, most notably highly specialized legal assistance, and have the ability to adopt long-run strategies to effect rules in their favor, even if it means compromising their interests in the immediate case.[15] These are advantages that individuals, who are likely to be "one-shot" litigators, cannot easily match.

Unequal economic resources also need to be considered. Public policy cases involve lengthy pretrial research, including *discovery*—the use of the court's compulsory processes to force one's adversary to divulge information needed to prepare one's case. This can be a very expensive proposition. The cost of each side will, to some degree, be driven by the activities of the other side, as the maneuvering of one must be met by the other, all of which adds to the attorney's billed hours. When litigants of greatly unequal resources face one another, it is sometimes possible for one to smother the other in an avalanche of pretrial motions that the poorer side simply cannot afford to respond to. When an individual of modest means takes on a government agency or a large corporation on an issue of major importance to the defendant, the suit may acquire some of the trappings of a kamikaze mission.

It is for this reason that complex litigation involving issues of public policy is most likely to be pursued by an interest group, which can mobilize resources exceeding those of the average individual. Research, expert witnesses, specialized attorneys, and relatively deep pockets needed to sustain protracted pretrial maneuvering, a trial, and multiple appeals can best be supplied by the collective advocacy interest group litigation represents. Unlike the ordinary individual, interest groups that litigate frequently have many of the advantages of repeat players. Few attorneys, for instance, can equal the NAACP's expertise in discrimination law. The ability to locate and pay expert witnesses, conduct extensive public policy research, even simply to wait out dilatory tactics or extended appeals, all contribute to the advantages interest groups bring to policy-oriented litigation.

There are dangers posed by interest groups as well. One of these involves the issue of control. Attorneys supplied by an interest group naturally serve the long-range goals of the group. The needs of the individual may become a subordinate consideration, should these depart from those of the group. Nevertheless, for appropriate cases, interest groups play an invaluable role in equalizing resources and permitting a thorough canvassing of issues brought before the courts.

Crossing the Threshold

The behavior of potential litigants is outside the control of law or the courts. However, the legal system itself also influences the volume of litigants passing over the court's doorstep. Consider the issue of *jurisdiction*, which refers to a court's legal authority to decide a lawsuit. Such authority might be limited according to the nature of the party who wishes to file suit, according to the nature of the suit he or she wishes to file, or according to the geographic location of the events in question. Thus, we saw in Chapter 2 that federal courts ordinarily exercise jurisdiction only over cases involving questions of federal law. The limited jurisdiction of Article III has been further narrowed by legislation. Alternatively, where a sufficient amount of money is at stake, certain persons might invoke the diversity of citizenship jurisdiction allowed by Article III—they gain access to the federal courts based on their identity as citizens of different states, even where the subject of their suit would ordinarily not be federal. Finally, federal district courts are limited to hearing disputes originating in their respective geographic districts, while the United States Court of Appeals for the Seventh Circuit, for example, is limited to suits coming from within the boundaries of its circuit, including only Illinois, Indiana, and Wisconsin. Even if neither party to a suit raises jurisdictional concerns, federal courts will frequently undertake their own investigation of jurisdictional questions; if they find jurisdiction lacking, they will dismiss the suit.

There is an additional set of limitations on judges under the concept of *standing*. We might understand jurisdiction as limiting the kinds of questions that can be brought before a particular court. Standing limits the persons qualified to bring a question within the court's jurisdiction. The rules of standing are of common law origin, although Article III is said to constitutionalize them to an uncertain degree when it extends judicial power to "cases" and "controversies." Since these terms are left undefined by the Constitution, the rules of standing remain, for practical purposes, self-imposed by the courts and are observed with such flexibility that their application often approaches the ad hoc.

Stated simply, a plaintiff must satisfy rules of standing by alleging that he or she has suffered a direct personal injury, that the injury is one recognized by some principle of law, and that courts have available an effective remedy for the injury alleged. It should be kept in mind that these rules do not address the merits of the plaintiff's case—the validity of the legal claims he or she intends to make. Standing is merely a threshold requirement that opens the courthouse doors. What happens to the case after the plaintiff enters the judicial forum is another matter. In practice, standing rules are seldom controversial for traditional lawsuits, but they become quite problematic in complex litigation.

Although the three requirements outlined above overlap in application, we will separate them for more detailed consideration. Our examples are drawn mainly from constitutional cases decided by the Supreme Court, because these are the most visible and because the cases discussed are found in many undergraduate texts and college libraries for the student to consult directly. However, the issues raised here are not specific to constitutional law, nor to the Supreme Court. Remember, the Supreme Court, through its decisions in a small number of cases, sends messages to lower federal courts about what kinds of injuries are recognized by which laws. Our examples are best understood as establishing guidelines that trial judges across the land will observe in future cases.

Direct Personal Injury   Because courts exist to remedy harms done to legally protected interests of individuals, only the harmed individual may initiate judicial inquiry. If Smith has injured Jones, Rodriquez may not raise the issue in litigation. Rodriguez's concern may arise from genuine compassion for Jones, but only Jones may speak for Jones in court, subject to a few exceptions that need not concern us at present. This seemingly innocuous rule has several important consequences. Obviously, limiting access to the injured party reduces the potential for frivolous litigation, not a minor consideration given the caseloads we saw in Chapter 2. Recall also the separation of powers consideration noted in Chapter 1, that courts remain reactive, unlike the proactive legislature. Limiting the court's response to injured parties ensures passivity by preventing courts from searching out injustices to remedy according to their own agenda. Litigants shape the courts' agenda, a factor that helps to distinguish functionally between courts and legislatures.

Finally, since courts are passive, rendering important decisions based solely on information brought to them in the course of an adversary confrontation, the direct personal injury is important to protecting the integrity of the fact-finding process. We assume that two parties locked in genuine combat will bring to the court all pertinent evidence and legal arguments that may win their case. Only if both parties do this can the court be confident that it has received a complete canvassing of the conflict. The assumption is that a third party who has not suffered a palpable injury may argue only half-heartedly. If only one side argues the case with diligence and zeal, the court may decide important legal questions based on a skewed account of the issues at stake.

Worse, consider the possibility of collusion between Smith and Rodriquez. If they share similar interests adverse to those of Jones, but feign a suit in which Rodriguez presents only imperfect evidence and weak arguments, the litigation will be a sham. We might borrow a term from boxing and say that Rodriguez has "taken a dive." The results could be a judicial decision favorable to Smith and Rodriguez, one harmful to Jones, but without Jones's interests ever really being heard by the court. Evidence of collusion between a plaintiff and a defendant will usually result in dismissal of the suit. Presumably, a party actually injured will not be in collusion with the party who inflicted the injury and so will be a reliable person to present zealously his or her side of the dispute.

Some examples will clarify these points. The state of Connecticut had since 1879 prohibited the use of contraceptive devices or the giving of advice about contraception. When legislative efforts to repeal this law proved unsuccessful, some individuals, aided by an interest group known as the Connecticut Planned Parenthood League, sought a ruling by the United States Supreme Court nullifying the statute as unconstitutional. The interest group, as an uninjured party, was barred from suit. It could litigate only through an individual who could claim injury and who sought judicial relief in the form of constitutional nullification of the statute. The problem, then, was to find an injured individual to "front" for the interest group. This person would need to share to a significant degree the goal of the Connecticut Planned Parenthood League of making birth control available in Connecticut and be willing to turn over to the group control of his or her litigation. In exchange, the group would finance the litigation and supply its own considerable expertise on the matter in question. If this exchange proved a good deal, and it often does, then the interest group would have found a way to enter court through the proxy of an injured individual. But who might constitute a person injured by this statute?

In 1943, the Court dismissed a suit filed by a physician in cooperation with the Connecticut Planned Parenthood League who claimed that the statute prevented him from giving birth control advice to three patients whose lives would be jeopardized by a pregnancy.[16] The Court reasoned that since the doctor was asserting no right of his own, but only the rights of his patients, he lacked standing to litigate in defense of rights the patients chose not to assert themselves. Perhaps the loss of privacy a lawsuit of this nature would require deterred the patients from going to court. It also seems likely that a physician would be a reliable party to defend the life interests of his patients, but the Court was inflexible on the matter, so avoiding having to rule on the merits of the contraception law.

In response to this initial rebuff, a subsequent suit was filed by a patient, again acting as a kind of proxy for the interest group.[17] Again, the allegation was that Connecticut had placed in jeopardy the lives of women who were prevented from obtaining reliable birth control information. Here, the threat of death or severe illness was faced directly by the plaintiff, but the suit was again dismissed for lack of standing. Notice that the alleged injury had not yet occurred. The plaintiffs in this and the previous case were seeking a *declaratory judgment,* an exceptional procedure allowing a court to declare the legal status of the litigants prior to the injury having been suffered. Trial advocacy is usually conducted in the past tense, but where the injury is imminent and irreparable after the fact, courts may choose to proceed to the merits of the case in advance of the injury. However, the Court declined the opportunity to intervene at so early a stage, dismissing the suit as not sufficiently ripe for adjudication, based on the observation that Connecticut had been less than thorough about enforcing the statute. Only a single prosecution was on record during the previous three-quarters of a century, although a birth control clinic had recently been closed by the state. Since birth control devices were sold in Connecticut openly, albeit illegally, the probability of the alleged injury actually being suffered seemed too hypothetical for the Court's liking. Courts prefer an injury that has already occurred, because the facts surrounding the controversy have solidified and can be debated without resort to speculation or clairvoyance. Here, it was not clear that an injury ever would occur.

This impasse was only broken four years later, when physicians in cooperation with Planned Parenthood secured their own arrest by opening a birth control clinic, arranging to meet patients and notifying the police in advance of their crime. The stigma of a conviction and a fine of $100 was sufficiently injurious to qualify the litigants as persons who could appropriately raise constitutional objections to Connecticut's ban on contraceptives.[18] Now, with the injured party before the Court and the injury no longer hypothetical, the Court agreed to review the merits of the case. The statute was found unconstitutional, violating an implied right of marital privacy, a holding that remains controversial to this day.

A criminal conviction is one of the more palpable injuries an individual might face, but note that this was a conviction invited by the plaintiff. Similarly, a fine of $100 seems a small injury when compared with the potential loss of life alleged by previous plaintiffs. It is difficult to avoid the suspicion that the difference between the latter case and the first two was in reality political. During 1949 to 1961, the Court tended to intrude into the political process only reluctantly. There were some notable exceptions, to be sure, but the Court clearly preferred to defer to the political decisions of the legislative process. One way to achieve this deference was to avoid confronting volatile issues through the rigorous application of standing rules. If litigants could not get through the courthouse door, controversial questions need not be addressed by the courts.

By the time the last case arrived at its threshold, the Court had adopted a significantly more activist demeanor, evident in its flexible observation of standing rules. The result was greater access for plaintiffs alleging violations of constitutional rights, to the chagrin of those groups who tended to win in legislative arenas. The departure of Justice Felix Frankfurter, a passionate advocate of judicial restraint, and his replacement by the liberal activist Arthur Goldberg may have been the decisive factor in allowing issues such as contraception into the judicial forum by 1965.

The flexibility of standing permits the Court to shrink or expand the role the judiciary will play in policy making. Since no two cases are really identical, it is hard to catch the justices red-handed, yet patterns emerge that bespeak a changed judicial attitude toward policy making. Through the 1960s, an activist Court loosened the barriers of standing to permit more access to the judicial forum by minority interests. More recently, a conservative Court less interested in the protection of rights claimed by such persons has again tightened the rules of standing.

Consider one singularly sharp contrast. In 1984, an increasingly conservative and putatively deferential Supreme Court denied standing to parents of black children who sought to sue the Internal Revenue Service (IRS).[19] Their allegation was that the IRS failed to enforce legislative policy denying tax-exempt status to private schools that practiced racial discrimination. As a result, a government-subsidized "white flight" into private "white academies" left behind a public school system that could no longer be desegregated. The Court found the injury to be neither specific enough to be judicially addressed nor sufficiently causally related to IRS conduct. Although blacks as a whole might be injured by IRS policy, it could not be shown that these parents suffered an injury particular to them that would be alleviated by a change in IRS conduct. In consequence, the behavior of the IRS remained immune from judicial surveillance.

Logical in itself, this ruling is difficult to square with the holding only a decade earlier that five law students calling themselves Students Challenging Regulatory Agency Procedures (SCRAP) were about to suffer sufficient injury to sue the Interstate Commerce Commission, challenging its failure to rescind a temporary surcharge on interstate railroad freight rates that threatened to discourage recycling of solid waste. The students alleged only an "economic, recreational and aesthetic harm" to their ability to enjoy the outdoors in the Washington, D.C. area, resulting from agency inaction.[20] We can all agree that the accumulation of garbage is an environmental problem, even an aesthetic injury, yet the injury hardly seems specific to these plaintiffs. The connection between agency policy and the aggregate behavior of individuals discarding trash also seems remote. It is difficult to consider these two cases side by side without coming to the conclusion that the Court's notion of a direct personal injury is so flexible as nearly to preclude useful generalization.

Legal Recognition of the Injury   Of the plethora of injuries we are exposed to in our lives, only a few create legally enforceable claims on the part of the victims. The jilted lover, for instance, has certainly suffered an injury, but it is one for which the law offers no remedy. Here, we are left to our own resources. In contrast, the party who reneges on a contract may well find himself or herself answering for his or her actions in court, where he or she may be ordered to perform the terms of the contract or pay a substantial sum of money in compensation for damages caused the plaintiff. Not too long ago, the victim of discrimination was left without a legal cause for action. Since enactment of the 1964 Civil Rights Act and many state laws and local ordinances, the law offers a remedy, even if an inefficient one, for those who suffer as a result of their membership in certain vulnerable racial, ethnic, or religious groups. For a court to take an interest in an individual's pain, the potential litigant must allege that a legal principle, whether of statutory or constitutional origin, already has taken cognizance of the injury and created a right to redress. In fact, each time Congress enacts legislation granting a right to relief for a new injury, such as a new consumer protection law, the potential result is an increase in litigation. In effect, a whole new class of individuals is offered the option of becoming plaintiffs, although it is an option only few will exercise.

Since laws are often unclear, it frequently happens that the breadth of this new class of potential litigants is uncertain, at least until courts have had their say. Again, when the courts are interested in pursuing a certain issue, they can encourage litigation through flexible interpretations of standing—or they can do just the opposite. Consider another sharp contrast that bespeaks changed political attitudes on the Supreme Court. In 1971, the Supreme Court agreed that damage to an individual's reputation and good name, essentially character defamation, by state officials acting under the authority of state law created a cause for legal action under the Fourteenth Amendment.[21] The state of Wisconsin, attempting to discourage alcoholism through the practice of "posting," authorized chiefs of local police departments to circulate an individual's name to local liquor stores and forbid the sale of alcoholic beverages to that person for one year. Posting rested solely on the chief's decision that some member of the community had met specified conditions to be considered a problem drinker. The victim was given no prior notice of his or her posting, nor an opportunity to refute the suspicion of alcohol abuse. On the caprice of a single individual, the victim was exposed to all the social obloquy the labels of "alcoholic" and "problem drinker" are likely to bring.

The Constitution says nothing explicitly about character defamation; in fact, it grants the states broad authority to regulate the sale of intoxicating liquors. The Fourteenth Amendment, however, provides that no state may deny a person "life, liberty or property, without due process of law." This general guarantee of fairness in legal proceedings is a fertile area for judicial interpretation and scholarly controversy. Could a person whose reputation has been unfairly tarnished by a state official argue for relief under this clause? Does the "liberty" protected against unfair abuse include one's standing in the community?

When a woman victimized by the practice filed a complaint in federal court, Wisconsin sought early dismissal of her suit, saying, in effect, "even if we did harm her in the way she has alleged, hers is not an injury the Fourteenth Amendment addresses, therefore we should not even have to discuss the facts she alleges." The Supreme Court disagreed, saying:

> Where a person's good name, reputation, honor, or integrity is at stake because of what the government is doing to him [sic], notice and an opportunity to be heard are essential. "Posting" under the Wisconsin Act may to some be merely the mark of illness, to others it is a stigma, an official branding of a person. The label is a degrading one.[22]

Two injuries might be present in this case. The critical one for the Court seemed to be damage to an individual's reputation and her consequent loss of standing in the community, peace of mind, personal self-esteem and possibly even career opportunities. The Court also noted, seemingly incidentally, that the victim could not purchase alcoholic beverages for a year as a result of the posting. Whenever a future litigant could at least arguably cite these harms and arguably trace them to the actions of state officials carrying out state policy, they now had standing to enter court and make a claim under the Fourteenth Amendment. One might still lose the case on the merits. Perhaps the state had provided prior notice and a right to refute the suspicion of alcoholism, or perhaps the reputation one sought to defend was a false one. But the Court conceded that officially sanctioned character defamation was an injury the Fourteenth Amendment recognized and protected against arbitrary abuse. As such, a new class of potential litigants was created, possibly a large one, were such character vilification a common practice of state officials.

Only five years later, the Court did an abrupt about-face. When police chiefs in Kentucky circulated a flyer containing names and mug shots of persons said to be "active shoplifters" to local merchants, they included the name of one Edward Davis. Mr. Davis had once been arrested on a charge of shoplifting, but after a plea of not guilty the charges had been dropped. Whether or not Davis had actually shoplifted, he was by law entitled to a presumption of innocence. The discretion of a single police chief, however, had the effect of imposing informal punishments on Davis in the form of public exposure and humiliation, absent any of the protections afforded defendants in a criminal trial. Imagine the greeting Davis would receive on entering a local shopping mall! Davis asserted a Fourteenth Amendment right against arbitrary character defamation by government officials. This time, however, a Court more squeamish about judicial supervision of police conduct held that damage to one's reputation alone by state officials was not an injury recognized by the Fourteenth Amendment.[23]

The astute student might wonder why the previous case was not followed as a precedent. Both cases seem to raise similar issues, but, as we shall soon see, precedents need to be interpreted before they can be applied to a new case. The Court's interpretation of the *Constantineau* case seemed rather odd, given the passage quoted above. Although the Court admitted that some of the language it had used in the previous case could leave one with the understanding that damage to reputation was a cognizable injury under the Fourteenth Amendment, it now claimed that it was in fact the right to purchase liquor that was being protected in that case. One defamed by police, in effect punished without trial, now had no standing to sue under the Constitution if only his or her reputation had been damaged. According to the Court, the Constitution protected the right to buy a beer, but not one's honor in the community.

The cases are not identical, but a change in judicial attitudes toward individual rights against the police seems unmistakable. The standing decisions of the Supreme Court open or close courthouse doors to future litigants whose problems may be as yet unforeseen. Again, we see how the Court might expand or contract the pool of potential litigation without a change in the text of a single law. Only the Court's interpretation of the kinds of activities to which a legal principle might apply has changed, but possibly with a profound effect throughout the community.

Available Judicial Remedy   There is one final question that must be addressed prior to litigation on the legal merits of a claim. Courts will hear a case only if a judgment agreeable to the plaintiff can be supported with an appropriate judicial remedy. Put simply, the question is: Should the direct and legally recognized injury alleged by the plaintiff be proven to have occurred as a result of the defendant's actions (or inactions), what can the court do about it? There is little sense in wasting court resources arguing about an injury that cannot somehow be fixed. Nor will the courts be anxious to squander their status as important decision makers by rendering judgments they cannot back up with remedial action. Consequently, the lack of available remedy a court can supply may be another basis for denying access to the judicial forum. The presence or absence of a remedy is not as clear as the uninitiated might have assumed.

In 1974, the Supreme Court dismissed a suit by a white man against the University of Washington Law School, alleging racial discrimination.[24] Marco DeFunis had been denied admission to the law school. However, under an affirmative action program, minority students had been admitted with grades and Law School Aptitude Test scores lower than DeFunis's. He filed suit in state court and won a mandatory injunction directing the law school to admit him. This decision was reversed by the Washington Supreme Court, but that court's order was stayed pending an appeal to the United States Supreme Court. In the meantime, DeFunis enrolled as a student in the law school.

It takes three years to complete a legal education. Coincidentally, it takes about three years to bring a case before the United States Supreme Court. During oral argument, the university conceded that DeFunis was near completion of his last quarter in law school. In response to a question from the bench, counsel for the university admitted that the law school had no intention at this late date of expelling DeFunis should it win a favorable judgment. The Supreme Court's response was to dismiss the appeal as *moot*, a controversy that has ceased to exist, in this instance simply because the Court was by then unable to affect the status of the litigating parties. Whether the Court found the university's affirmative action program to be racial discrimination or not, DeFunis was going to graduate with his class. Although neither party had argued for dismissal, the Court was able to avoid, at least for the time being, the difficult question of affirmative action under the Fourteenth Amendment. At the same time, the Court's evasion left the status of the law school's affirmative action program in doubt, clouding the admission possibilities for a considerable number of future applicants to professional schools across the country.

Only a year before, however, the Court had ignored the problem of mootness to hear argument on the constitutional status of abortion, in the case of *Roe v. Wade.*[25] The plaintiff began her case in a U.S. district court as a pregnant woman who wished to terminate her pregnancy but was prevented from doing so by Texas law. She brought suit seeking to enjoin enforcement of the statute, claiming it violated her right of personal privacy guaranteed under the Fourteenth Amendment. The normal human gestation of period of 266 days had lapsed well before the Supreme Court could hear her case. Roe had her baby, which was put up for adoption. When the state sought to avoid a Supreme Court ruling by arguing that the case was now moot, the Court disagreed. Since pregnancy is a continuing experience of women, and since the issue of abortion was not going to go away with the dismissal of one case, the Court concluded that public policy could best be served by waiving the mootness doctrine and ruling on the constitutional merits of Roe's claim, even in the absence of a remedy for Roe.[26] Scrupulous observance of the mootness doctrine would have effectively insulated the whole question of abortion from judicial review.

A similar argument would seem appropriate in *DeFunis* and was, in fact, made by the parties. Apparently, the Court was not yet ready to take up affirmative action, but considerations of social policy made abortion a different matter. A remedy does not become available in a case simply because the Court wishes it so, but again we see the Court exercising substantial discretion over its own admission standards, seeming to find a way around the remedy question when it wanted to hear a case. From this survey of standing issues, we can see that the values justices bring to the bench, especially regarding the role the judiciary should play in American life, will influence the availability of courts as a forum in which citizens may argue issues of public policy.

Traditional and Complex Litigation

The question of standing presents a good opportunity to examine in detail the distinction introduced at the outset of this chapter between traditional and complex litigation. We have discussed litigation so far as it typically occurs, as a process for resolving narrow disputes between two discrete individuals: Smith v. Jones. Because the interests involved are primarily those of two parties, we describe such litigation as *bipolar*. Of course, others may find their interests affected indirectly, for if Smith v. Jones appears to settle interests similar to ones that Green seeks to advance against Rodriguez, it may become a precedent for Green v. Rodriguez. However, only Smith and Jones have interests directly implicated in their suit, only they will be permitted to present arguments to the court, and only they will be bound by the court's judgment. Normally, litigation is a personal endeavor.

Also, most traditional litigation is *bounded* and *retrospective*. The evidence Smith and Jones offer will be about a relatively narrow set of events that occurred in the past. The parties may argue about the proper scope of inquiry into the events in question—how far back in a controverted chain of events judicial scrutiny should reach, or how many simultaneously occurring activities should be examined as part of this controversy. Every lawsuit is based on a simplified abstraction from the rich tapestry of events Smith and Jones have actually experienced. The parties may have different ideas about which strands are most relevant to their dispute, but it will be agreed in principle that there is a relatively precise set of past events relevant to the litigation and that all else can be ignored.

This focus on the particularities of Smith v. Jones is often expressed through a distinction made between *adjudicative facts,* the unique events shared by the parties in their narrowly defined dispute, and *legislative facts,* the repetitive social processes that form the context in which Smith and Jones met and interacted. The latter will be largely excluded from trial. Judicial inquiry will thus have fairly clear boundaries enforced through strict rules of evidence that direct the court's attention to the unique aspects of Smith v. Jones. As the name suggests, legislative facts are usually deemed more appropriate for legislative consideration.

Finally, should Smith win the suit, the remedy will be narrow in its reach, affecting only the litigating parties. It will compensate for past wrongs only, usually through a transfer of money from the defendant to the plaintiff. Once decreed, the remedy will end judicial involvement in Smith's and Jones's lives, although we might hope the future Joneses of the world would be deterred from committing similar injuries against future Smiths. We have previously called such litigation *individual dispute resolution.* We noted that several of the cases just discussed were actually the work of interest groups seeking a change in public policy. Thus, they already depart a bit from the individual dispute resolution model in their substance. However, their form adhered fairly closely to the traditional structure of litigation.

Now consider a case like *Wyatt v. Stickney,* decided by a United States District Court in Alabama, in 1971.[27] On the surface, this case stemmed from a suit by Ricky Wyatt against Dr. Stonewall B. Stickney, who happened to be the mental health commissioner for the state of Alabama. When a decline in revenue from the state cigarette tax caused budget shortfalls, Stickney sought to reduce expenditures in his department through a reduction in staff at Bryce Hospital, a state psychiatric hospital where Wyatt was confined as a patient. A number of discharged hospital employees and several patients filed suit to block employee discharges. Their allegation was in part that staff reduction would deny any possibility of delivering adequate treatment to the hospital's approximately 5000 patients, the majority of whom were, like Wyatt, involuntarily committed.

In pretrial conference, District Judge Frank Johnson was reluctant to intervene in a labor dispute he thought better argued in the state courts, but he expressed concern for the well-being of Bryce's patients. In response, the plaintiffs shifted their focus away from the labor aspects of the case, to sue explicitly for a right to adequate treatment under the protean due process clause of the Fourteenth Amendment. Their amended suit was certified as a *class action*, whereby the plaintiffs sue on behalf of themselves but also on behalf of all persons "similarly situated." In a sense, an entire population found to have similar legal interests to assert could sue as if they were a single party. This class now included all patients confined in Bryce Hospital, and all would be bound by whatever results the court decreed.

The conditions the trial proceedings exposed at Bryce Hospital were truly pathetic. The patient population was found to include about 1500 geriatric patients and about 1000 mental retardates, all of whom were in no need of psychiatric care and who were placed at Bryce simply because it was a convenient place to warehouse them. The remaining 2500 patients suffering from mental illness fared no better. This large and disparate population was cared for by a staff that included 17 physicians, only 3 of whom had some training in psychiatry and none of whom was a board-certified psychiatrist. A single person with a Ph.D. in clinical psychology and two social workers with an M.S.W. were among the 12 psychologists, 13 social workers, 21 nurses, and 850 psychiatric aids who rounded out the patient care staff.

Basic sanitary facilities were also lacking, and available recreational and therapeutic activities were found medically inadequate, failing to conform to any recognized minimum standards for the care of the mentally ill. In response, the court held as a matter of constitutional law that patients involuntarily held had a right to receive "adequate and effective treatment."[28] To hold patients against their will without providing them with appropriate medical care, Johnson held, was to transform the hospital into "a penitentiary where one could be held indefinitely for no convicted offense." Under Johnson's ruling, persons not convicted of any crime could be held against their will only to provide them with such care as might realistically offer the hope of improvement in their medical condition.

Further hearings were scheduled on the question of how to remedy the constitutional violations found at Bryce Hospital. At this point, the litigation began to change in character, in a number of important respects. First, it was expanded to include two other institutions operated by the state, Partlow State School and Hospital, a facility for the severely retarded, and Searcy Hospital, a psychiatric hospital similar to Bryce. The effect was greatly to expand the number and character of the class of plaintiffs affected by the litigation. Second, numerous interest groups sought the court's permission to intervene in future proceedings, each seeking status as an *amicus curiae*. The term means "friend of the court" and designates parties not directly involved in the litigation (neither plaintiffs nor defendants) who have significant interest in the outcome and so wish to present their own views to the court. Permission to appear as an amicus curiae is discretionary, as is the scope of participation the court will allow such third parties. In this case, such interest groups as the American Civil Liberties Union, the American Psychological Association, the American Orthopsychiatric Association, the National Association for Retarded Citizens, the National Association for Mental Health, and the American Association on Mental Deficiency were all accorded full participation rights, including the right to present and impeach evidence.

Discarding any pretense of passivity, Judge Johnson also invited the U.S. Department of Justice to appear as an amicus curiae. In addition, Johnson warned that insufficient funding would be found "legally insufficient" as a justification for failure to comply with whatever remedy the court might order.[29] In effect, the judge was adding the Alabama legislature to a list of defendants that included Stickney, Governor George Wallace, the Alabama Mental Health Board, and several hospital administrators. The parties to this litigation had expanded enormously, so that the suit could no longer be understood as a bipolar dispute between Wyatt and Stickney. It had become a sprawling affair involving numerous parties on each side, with potentially conflicting perceptions and interests.

Nor would the scope of facts deemed relevant to this litigation be confined to the narrow experience of Wyatt and Stickney. Indeed, it is doubtful that they had shared any mutual experiences or that they had ever met. Instead, state fiscal resources, the personnel and physical limitations of three large institutions, and various professional standards of minimum acceptable medical care for the mentally ill or retarded would be debated through expert testimony. Obviously, many of the parties involved had interests reaching far beyond those of Wyatt and Stickney and sought to appear not to achieve a fair resolution of a personal dispute so much as to shape public health policy in Alabama according to each group's political preferences. In this endeavor, the appearance of interest groups was akin to the routine lobbying in legislatures, raising some of the same problems, as the unorganized and underfunded interests might have been excluded from effective participation.

Some of the most significant differences between litigation like *Wyatt* and traditional lawsuits can be found in the remedy ordered by Judge Johnson.[30] Plaintiffs had urged the court to appoint a special master, a person who would administer the defendant institutions under court supervision and bring them up to constitutionally required standards. This the court declined to do, leaving the burden of compliance with the state administrative staffs. However, the final decree included a comprehensive and detailed statement of goals with which the defendants would have to comply, including such matters as guaranteeing to patients decent standards of privacy and dignity and placing patients in the least restrictive environment necessary to achieve the medical purposes of their confinement. The patients' environment was addressed in considerable detail, prescribing such items as minimum square footage for living quarters, day rooms, and dining facilities. Bedding, linen service, sanitary facilities, heating and air conditioning, record keeping, fire safety measures, even windows for light and ventilation were all specified in detail. Finally, the court mandated individualized treatment plans for each of the numerous patients confined in each institution.

To monitor compliance, the court appointed "human rights committees" for each institution, composed of laypersons active in mental health advocacy groups or the kin of patients living in the institutions. These committees were to be the eyes and ears of the court and were to be granted full access to all records, facilities, staff, and patients, with leave to report regularly to the court on matters affecting compliance with the decree's terms. Finally, and most significantly, the court retained jurisdiction of the case for the indefinite future, holding out the threat of sanctions or appointment of a special master should officials prove recalcitrant in meeting the court's requirements.

We see here a complex and multifaceted decree, one that was not confined to a declaration of the litigant's respective rights, nor which could be satisfied by a single transfer of cash from the defendant to the plaintiff. Instead, the court sought to compel certain standards of care in the future, in lieu of the legislative and administrative policies adopted by elected Alabama officials. The very detail of the court's order raised problems for separation of powers theory and federalism. Was the federal court merely guaranteeing constitutional right or usurping state legislative and executive functions? And what expertise does a politically unaccountable federal judge bring to the shaping of public health policy?

Through this brief survey of some very complicated litigation, we can highlight some of the distinguishing characteristics of complex litigation. First, the litigation was sprawling, both as to the number and nature of the parties involved and as to the scope of judicial inquiry into the parties' conduct. The designation *Wyatt v. Stickney* was quite misleading, for this case was in fact a contest between broad social groups, the state bureaucracy, the governor, the legislature, and the Justice Department. Second, although much of the testimony concerned decisions made in the past, the inquiry was directed toward uncovering ongoing practices involving a potentially limitless number of decisions by many people over an extended period of time. Third, the remedy offered was not intended solely to make the injured parties whole by compensating them for past wrongs. To the contrary, the intention of the decree was fundamentally to change the defendants' future behavior. If traditional litigation is backward-looking, complex litigation is often future-orientated. Fourth, the decision affected broad sectors of the public, well beyond those who entered court as parties to the suit. Much of Alabama's healthcare system was restructured, affecting a large number of present and future patients, with the cost felt by every taxpayer in Alabama. Finally, a simple declaration of the parties' rights did not end the court's involvement in the suit. Judge Johnson retained control over the case, with the ability to alter the terms of his decree as circumstances required, resembling in many important ways an executive official more than a judge.

It would be an exaggeration to say Johnson took over the administration of the three institutions in question, but only a slight one. Administrators would have to implement the court's priorities, not their own or those of the Alabama legislature. The court promised future monitoring of administrative performance, with the threat of deeper judicial involvement if its requirements were not met. We see here a double expansion of the judicial role. Judge Johnson's involvement reached more deeply into the pretrial stages of the litigation, helping to shape the issues that would be addressed and the evidence that would be marshalled in support of the court's final judgment. His involvement also extended further into posttrial developments in Alabama public health policy, as allocations of resources, even the adoption of a treatment philosophy, would now have to be cleared with him.

Such extensive judicial involvement in a case challenges our traditional understanding of the passivity and independence of the court, as well as the adversary nature of the proceedings.[31] One must wonder also about the preexistence of such detailed legal norms specifying the standards of psychiatric care, a field into which law had seldom entered previously. Finally, it is with difficulty that one characterizes Johnson's order as dichotomous. Instead, it apportioned responsibilities and benefits among a large number of actors. Such remedies are often the product of extensive negotiation among a diverse spectrum of parties, which may erode our perception that what is ultimately being applied is something we would recognize as law.

Not surprisingly, such *extended impact* or *institutional reform* litigation has drawn criticism. It should be emphasized that cases like *Wyatt v. Stickney* are few and far between. Even so, the fact that they occur at all indicates a significant shift in how we understand the judicial role in society. Critics question both the legitimacy of such judicial supervision of public policy and the institutional competence of courts to undertake such activities. They prefer that litigation adhere as closely to the Shapiro model as possible, tending to view adjudication as a special and unique form of social ordering that is appropriate only for certain kinds of narrow questions.[32] Within the strictures of that model, they question the ability of courts to uncover and process the large number of legislative facts, those broad social conditions that must be taken into account to decide the kinds of questions raised by *Wyatt*. Courts operate within the confines of an adversarial procedure, including strict evidentiary rules of relevance that focus judicial fact finding on the particular, unique aspects of the case at hand, divorced from their social context.[33] Critics wonder how representative of mental health policy generally are the arguments presented by advocates for Mr. Wyatt, and how representative of treatments afforded by Alabama are the conditions uncovered through the experiences of one patient.

A court would have difficulty discovering answers to such questions without substantially altering the nature of the adversary process. This was done in *Wyatt*, but at what cost? As the suit metamorphosed into a class action, as other hospitals were included, as a variety of interest groups joined the debate, a more representative population of interested parties could be expected to provide a more complete canvassing of legislative facts. But in the process, those very unique considerations pertaining to Mr. Wyatt might be overlooked. Worse, in the view of some, the very legitimacy of the judicial decision might be eroded as the adjudicatory process was contorted into something no longer adhering to the adjudicatory model.[34] Instead, the *Wyatt* decision looks to its critics like naked legislating from the bench, without an electoral mandate.

Defenders of complex litigation tend to argue that judicial legitimacy is not preserved by adherence to some ideal form of adjudication. Rather, they contend, the nature of adjudication has always been flexible, changing to satisfy the needs of the society that produced it. The old bipolar model of individual dispute resolution confined by strict evidentiary rules was adequate for a society that allocated values primarily through private ordering, relegating government to a narrow role of maintaining civil peace. For a society that has turned to government to supply a broad range of social services, and which leaves individuals like Wyatt at the mercy of impersonal state bureaucracies, changes in procedure must be made. The admission of interest groups to the proceedings will help the court to uncover broad legislative facts. Indeed, defenders of complex litigation often argue, judicial independence might even free judges to pursue questions the majoritarian legislatures would rather ignore. Surely, such occurred in *Wyatt,* when a level of human decency was finally secured for a population easily overlooked or abused in the legislature.

Finally, it is argued that judicial legitimacy is better derived from a sense that the courts deliver just results.[35] Since rights-enhancing decisions such as that in *Wyatt v. Stickney* are by definition countermajoritarian, this has to mean the courts will achieve legitimacy when they deliver results the majority will find proper one future day. Leaving courts to win over the public through accurate predictions of future popular sentiment is a risky enterprise, to say the least. At minimum, this creates problems for the short run, which may frustrate the court's ability to secure compliance at all. One detailed study of the *Wyatt* remedy's implementation at Partlow Hospital found that "substantial improvements have occurred in Partlow which have made it safer, more sanitary, and generally more habitable for the residents." However, the same study conceded that "a large disparity still exists between the existing institution and the standards contained in the decree."[36] To the extent that a court's decree may be frustrated in the short run, one wonders how it can ever gain acceptance in the long run.

Litigation as a form of public policy making is most cogently defended on the grounds that courts are able to respond to weak and unpopular minority groups who would be ignored or abused in the democratic process. Protecting minorities against the tyranny of the majority is one of the traditional goals of American politics. Perhaps only the minorities we have in mind have changed. It is significant that institutional reform litigation has tended to involve "total institutions," places of coercion and confinement—psychiatric hospitals, prisons, and public schools— where affected populations are completely dominated by decisions of state policy. Also, it should be clear that reform of psychiatric hospitals and prisons are causes that are unlikely to generate the kind broad public support needed to affect legislative response.

The latter half of the twentieth century has witnessed a burgeoning rise in interest group litigation on behalf of weaker and often unpopular groups in the community. As early as the 1930s, the NAACP (later through its offshoot, the Legal Defense and Education Fund) was pursuing an elaborate strategy of litigation to combat racial segregation and discrimination. The NAACP's battle plan involved targeting carefully chosen school districts, shopping for appropriate litigants, and carefully timing cases to best achieve its organizational goals.[37] Another such interest group is the American Civil Liberties Union (ACLU). Unlike the NAACP, the ACLU does not set out looking for lawsuits. However, when an aggrieved individual brings a dispute involving civil liberties issues to the ACLU, they will take over the case if it appears to be a good vehicle for the furtherance of the group's goals. The ACLU has thus been a litigator on behalf of criminal defendants, political and cultural dissidents, women, gay men and lesbians, mental patients, racial and ethnic minorities, and the poor. In the process, the ACLU has earned the ire of much of the American public, as evinced by the political capital

Republicans made of candidate Michael Dukakis's membership in the organization during the 1988 presidential elections. A host of similar groups sprung up as part of the social ferment of the 1960s and early 1970s as enthusiasm for "public interest law" grew, especially among ambitious young law students with a passion for social reform.

Their success, however, has produced a predictable reaction. First, we have already noted the judicial tightening of access to court through a more rigid approach to standing issues. This policy, largely the result of a more conservative Supreme Court after Richard Nixon's presidency, had an inhibiting effect on such litigation. The more conservative, and possibly more formalist, appointments of Presidents Reagan and Bush will no doubt continue this trend, discouraging litigation by such groups in the future. We can expect to see a similar diminution of institutional reform litigation, such as *Wyatt v. Stickney*.

A second and somewhat contradictory trend since the late 1970s has been the rise of conservative interest groups dedicated to litigation as a way of advancing their policy goals.[38] Such groups have relied heavily on addressing courts through the amicus curiae brief, mostly in cases involving government regulations of economic activities. More recently, they have shown an increased willingness to intervene directly as litigants in civil liberties cases, such as abortion, church and state relations, and discrimination suits, as well as litigation over environmental issues. The entrance of conservative interest groups to litigation may both reflect and contribute to a conservative shift in judicial policies. One thing is certain, however: the proliferation of conservative interest groups in court represents a recognition by many conservatives that courts are policy-making bodies in a sense similar to a legislature or an administrative agency.

We have spent considerable time examining the process by which disputes are transformed into lawsuits. We have seen that there are a number of steps in the process and that each is to some degree selective. Almost like a series of sieves, each of a finer mesh than the previous one, each step in the process of dispute formation filters out a certain amount of potential judicial business. Those issues that fail to make it through the sieve are left to the democratic institutions of society, especially the legislature, for resolution. One might wonder at this point how it is that courts do anything at all. In fact, they do a great deal, despite the highly selective sample of conflicts they ultimately hear. How they resolve the conflicts that make it across the courthouse threshold and the policy implications of their activities will be the topic of the next two chapters.

NOTES

1. Richard E. Miller and Austin Sarat, "Grievances, Claims, and Disputes: Assessing the Adversary Culture," 15 *Law & Society Review* 525 (1981).
2. Ibid., p. 544.
3. Jethro Lieberman, *The Litigious Society* (Basic Books, New York, 1981).
4. Miller and Sarat, op. cit., p. 545.

5. Even for misdemeanor trials, the desirability of counsel has been recognized by the Supreme Court. See *Argersinger v. Hamlin*, 407 U.S. 25 (1972), requiring appointment of counsel for indigent defendants as a condition of incarceration.

6. Barbara A. Curran, "American Lawyers in the 1980's: A Profession in Transition," 20 *Law & Society Review* 19, 25–37.

7. The classic study, from which our paradigm is drawn, is Martin Mayer, *The Lawyers* (Harper & Row, New York, 1967) especially p. 29ff.

8. Paul Wice, *Judges & Lawyers: The Human Side of Justice* (HarperCollins, New York, 1991) p. 101.

9. Stewart Macaulay, "Lawyers and Consumer Protection Laws," 14 *Law & Society Review* 115, 152 (1979).

10. Abraham S. Blumberg, "The Practice of Law as Confidence Game: Organizational Cooptation of a Profession," 1 *Law & Society Review* 15 (1967), Milton Heumann, *Plea Bargaining: The Experience of Prosecutors, Judges and Defense Attorneys* (University of Chicago Press, Chicago, 1977).

11. Macaulay, op. cit.

12. *Johnson v. Zerbst*, 304 U.S. 458 (1938). This requirement was extended to state trials in *Gideon v. Wainwright*, 372 U.S. 344 (1963).

13. David M. Trubek, Austin Sarat, William L. F. Felstiner, Herbert M. Kritzer, and Joel B. Grossman, "The Costs of Ordinary Litigation," 31 *University of California at Los Angeles Law Review* 73, 93 (1983).

14. Ibid., pp. 105, 112.

15. Marc Galanter, "Why the 'Haves' Come Out Ahead: Speculations of the Limits of Legal Change," 95 *Law & Society Review* 95, 98–99 (1974).

16. *Tileston v. Ullman*, 318 U.S. 44 (1943).

17. *Poe v. Ullman*, 367 U.S. 497 (1961).

18. *Griswold v. Connecticut*, 381 U.S. 479 (1965).

19. *Allen v. Wright*, 468 U.S. 737 (1984).

20. *United States v. Students Challenging Regulatory Agency Procedures (SCRAP)*, 412 U.S. 669, 675–676 (1973).

21. *Wisconsin v. Constantineau*, 400 U.S. 433 (1971).

22. Ibid., p. 437.

23. *Paul v. Davis*, 424 U.S. 693 (1976).

24. *DeFunis v. Odegaard*, 416 U.S. 312 (1974).

25. *Roe v. Wade*, 410 U.S. 113 (1973).

26. Ibid., p. 125.

27. *Wyatt v. Stickney*, 325 F. Supp. 781 (Middle District, Alabama, 1971).

28. Ibid., p. 785.

29. *Wyatt v. Stickney*, 344 F. Supp. 373, 392 (middle District, Alabama, 1972).

30. A detailed and cautiously optimistic assessment of the implementation of the court's remedy, focusing on Partlow State School and Hospital, can be found in "Note: The Wyatt Case: Implementation of a Judicial Decree Ordering Institutional Change," 84 *Yale Law Journal* 1338 (1975).

31. Judith Resnik, "Managerial Judges," 96 *Harvard Law Review* 347, 398–404 (1982).

32. Lon Fuller, "The Forms of Adjudication," 92 *Harvard Law Review* 353 (1978).

33. Donald L. Horowitz, *The Courts and Social Policy* (Brookings Institute, Washington, D.C., 1977) pp. 45–49.

34. Ibid., pp. 18–19.

35. Abram Chayes, "The Role of the Judge in Public Law Litigation," 89 *Harvard Law Review* 1281, 1285, 1316 (1976).

36. "Note: The Wyatt Case: Implementation of a Judicial Decree Ordering Institutional Change," op. cit., pp. 1338, 1378 (1975).
37. See generally, Richard Kluger, *Simple Justice* (Vintage, New York, 1977). The NAACP's style of public interest litigation was given First Amendment protection by the Supreme Court in *NAACP v. Button*, 317 U.S. 415 (1963).
38. Karen O'Connor and Lee Epstein, "The Rise of Conservative Interest Group Litigation," 45 *Journal of Politics* 479 (1983).

Chapter 6

Following Legal Norms

In this chapter and the next, we will turn our attention to the degree to which judicial decisions are determined by previously existing legal norms. In the United States, legal norms are derived from three sources: common law (mostly state), statutory law (both state and federal), and constitutions (both state and federal). Administrative regulations might be promulgated by an executive agency and might be binding on our conduct, but only under the authority of a statute enacted by the legislature delegating such authority to an administrative agency. A treaty might provide the source of some domestic law, but treaties are of limited consequence by themselves and usually require enabling legislation, again enacted by Congress. This chapter will consider decision making by courts based on statutes or common law.

Whatever the source of legal norms, we shall see that courts bring considerable discretion to the decision-making process. By discretion we mean all forms of choice exercised by judges that cannot be said to be determined—or absolutely required—by a previously existing legal norm. Thus, we are concerned with those aspects of the judicial process in which political, moral, or idiosyncratic factors have influenced or even supplanted the application of legal norms. A court's fidelity to previously existing legal norms is of crucial importance to political scientists. Were Blackstone's model of the judicial decision that we examined in Chapter 1 an accurate depiction, so that judges were the mere oracles of a law that could be known a priori, then we would not deem courts very powerful actors on the political stage. We would instead search for the origins of the legal norms the courts discovered and enforced, perhaps finding them in the legislature or at a constitutional convention. If, on the other hand, elements of discretion enter into the judicial decision, as claimed by legal realism and Critical Legal Studies, then political scientists should take a deeper interest in courts as the authors of many controversial policies. We should then want to know more about the political and the legal ideologies judges bring to the bench and the degree to which they shape judicial decisions. We might also seek a more discriminating theory about when a judge has exercised political judgment in a way that is beneficial to society, or when he or she has usurped legislative powers by making decisions on matters more properly left to democratic procedures in the legislature or executive agencies.

THE COMMON LAW

We assume today that it is the legislature that creates laws. However, prior to the twentieth century, American legislatures were relatively inactive. They convened annually, but their sessions were short and their activities consisted generally of appropriating funds to operate government for the coming fiscal year and the enactment of a few statutes dealing with matters of broad public concern. With only an occasional exception, the regulation of everyday life was left to the judicially created common law.

The term *common law* has multiple uses. It might refer to a substantive body of legal principles, including the terms of contracts, property, the family, torts, or the definitions of many crimes that owe their origin not to statutes but to a canon of judicially created doctrines. The common law in this sense is today almost entirely state law, although we will see that it has an influence on federal law as well. Alternatively, common law might refer to the legal system inherited from England that includes these principles as well as certain procedural norms for the conduct of trials, appeals, and the like and certain institutional arrangements that facilitate these procedures. In this sense of the term, we often contrast common law nations—Great Britain and generally those nations once colonized by the British—with European nations and their former colonies that have derived legal systems from ancient Roman law, called *civil law* nations. (Alas, legal terminology is not as neat as we would prefer: within the legal system of a common law nation, civil law denotes all laws regulating private conduct that are not backed by a criminal penalty, that is, contracts, torts, property, commercial law, and so on.) As used here, however, common law refers to a judicial technique of decision making, one that derives the solution to legal problems by looking to past decisions of courts faced with similar problems. The basic theory of common law is that what has worked to secure a just resolution for past controversies should work again. At the very least, there is good reason for making it work again.

To understand the technique of the common law, it might be helpful to journey briefly to Medieval England, an exceptionally decentralized nation that Norman conquerors found themselves in charge of after the Battle of Hastings. Justice was administered by local authorities, according to inconsistent local customs and predilections. While the Romans had previously set up shop for some years in England, they seem not to have left a very deep impression. Their elaborate legal codes remained confined to the Continent. Through the eleventh and twelfth centuries the Normans sought to establish a more centralized and efficient administration of government. To extend royal power over the realm, the Norman kings established courts dependent on royal will to administer justice in competition with local tribunals or the ecclesiastical courts that were enforcing the pervasive laws of the Church.

These king's courts were staffed with individuals who were politically reliable (and probably good with a battle-ax), whose charge was to enforce the law that was common to the realm, in contradistinction to the local laws prevalent in each village or shire. Whether any such common laws existed at the time is difficult to ascertain, but being practical men aware of what side their bread was buttered on, they set about adjudicating private disputes, as the king had ordered. As we should expect in a feudal society, these were primarily disputes over land titles, but not coincidentally also over the collection of rents—in modern terms, taxes. But how does a court enforce law that does not exist? The answer then, as now, was that they made it up as needed. They eventually began to publish reports of their decisions. At first these were merely cryptic accounts of the judgments issued in the cases they heard. Eventually, however, they became elaborate arguments intended to demonstrate the correctness of the decision as well.

One can easily imagine the problem of legitimacy presented by these king's courts. Why should their judgments be respected in lieu of the traditional local authorities? When possible, the king's court might write local custom into the law, but local customs were at best inconsistent and at worst were contrary to the designs of the king. Justice might be administered in the king's name, but in the short term, at least, the battle-ax probably helped secure compliance. In the long run, ruling in the king's name meant ruling consistently throughout the realm and securing some level of voluntary compliance.

In the process of combining local custom, royal fiat, and practical wisdom to decide disputes, judges began to employ the technique of *stare decisis*. Usually translated as "let the past decision stand," stare decisis is the basis for the common law technique of deciding cases by adherence to precedent or following what has been decided previously in similar cases. As the practice became more deeply ingrained in English law, judges could legitimatize their decisions by saying, in effect, "This is how we have always decided such cases, and absent a good reason for doing otherwise, this is how we must decide today's case as well." The judge who can make such an argument successfully demonstrates that the result is not the product of his or her own caprice or predilections—any other right-thinking judge would have ruled the same way. Litigants, especially losing litigants, are more likely to accept such a ruling as proper and therefore entitled to their respectful compliance.

Adherence to precedent offers several benefits in addition to legitimation. Stare decisis imparts consistency to the law, both temporal and spatial, so that the law means the same thing in Dorchester as it means in Lancaster and that it applies to Mr. Smith in the same fashion as it applies to Ms. Jones, thus satisfying the first requirement of fairness—that similarly situated persons be treated similarly. Notice also that stare decisis lends predictability to the law by guaranteeing that it will mean the same thing next week that it meant last year. This enables Mr. Smith and Ms. Jones to pattern their conduct, perhaps after receiving reliable advice from their attorneys, in such a way as to avoid unpleasant legal consequences. Mr. Smith might refrain from committing fraud against Ms. Jones, or Ms. Jones might take additional care not to injure Mr. Smith. If Mr. Smith and Ms. Jones wish to enter a joint enterprise, set up a business partnership perhaps, they will know how to do it because their attorney can predict future court behavior based on an assessment of past court behavior.

A commercial society such as ours could not long function without stable and knowable laws of contract, tort, and property. It should also be noted that adherence to precedent, to some degree, conserves court resources by making decisions easier to reach. If a judge does not have to rethink all legal premises, in effect to reinvent the wheel for each case, arrival at a successful conclusion will be facilitated and more cases can be processed in a given period of time. Since case backlogs seem to be an endemic fact of court life, this benefit should not be viewed lightly. Indeed, greater predictability in law results in fewer cases filed, since disputants who already know the legal consequences of their controversy with some certainty will more likely avoid litigation by settling their dispute out of court.

More important for our present consideration is the degree to which adherence to precedent confines the discretion of willful judges. Blackstone's formalist argument was that a conscientious judge studied the law as it was already articulated in published court opinions and codified in a few treatises such as his own, and by applying correct canons of judicial technique, "discovered" the single correct answer. Remember that for Blackstone, even the rare overruling of a previous judgment was not the creation of new law, but only the correction of the previous court's misrepresentation of what the law required. It was rather like a mathematics teacher correcting the student's erroneous solution to an algebraic equation. Today, even among those who view stare decisis as rigidly confining judicial discretion, this depiction of the role of precedent in law is generally deemed inadequate. All admit, as they must, that stare decisis is a flexible doctrine that permits some degree of judicial innovation.

Formalism holds that courts do not exist to make determinations of broad social policies, but only to resolve individual disputes. Of course, they do both in practice, but the way in which judges define the institutional role of courts shapes their behavior. If courts identify their role as the resolution of disputes, then it follows that they should not pronounce on issues broader than the ones actually presented by the disputants. In other words, the rule of law purportedly announced in a case is validly determined only within the factual context of that case. It is, after all, only within the scope of those facts that lawyers have argued the case and informed the judge through an adversary confrontation. If the judge chooses to pontificate on possible applications of the rule to additional facts, exceptions to its application not present in the case, or another rule that would be superior to this rule were it only available in the case, these extraneous comments are all relegated to the status of *dicta*, or, more properly, *obiter dicta*—"words dropped by the wayside."

These extraneous comments by the judge are not binding as precedent, but if dicta does not declare law, we cannot know what a prior decision means until we separate the law from the dicta. Lawyers are by training a contentious lot, and one of the things they frequently disagree on when looking at a previous case is the precise line between the binding rule of law that serves as a precedent for the case under consideration and the dicta, which may be persuasive but which may also be ignored.[1] Simply put, the legal meaning of past decisions requires interpretation. Where there is interpretation, there is discretion, at least within a limited compass.

Suppose, however, that all agreed on the meaning of a previous ruling. All would then have to agree further that the rule of law announced in that case would be applied to all future cases presenting the same set of facts. The truth is that, strictly speaking, no two cases ever present an identical set of facts. At the very least, the litigants will be different personalities, bringing with them different characteristics. History never repeats itself, really, so that in practice every new case will also present new facts that may have a bearing on whether or not the rule of the previous case should be followed. One lawyer will argue that the facts of today's case are materially similar to last year's case, so that the same rule of law must apply.[2] The other lawyer will argue that some fact present today but not last year (or vice versa) makes this case so different from the previous one that a different rule should be followed. The question is always: How important are the differences or the similarities in facts between the old case and the new one? This requires reasoning by analogy, which again imparts creativity—hence politics—to the judicial decision.[3] There may be good reasons of policy for extending the old precedent to include this new fact, hence broadening the scope of the legal rule. Alternatively, the new fact may be of such an exceptional nature that the old rule should not apply, hence limiting the scope of the precedent. Either decision will have consequences for social policy.

Where there is only one precedent, it is not uncommon to find lawyers arguing over whether or not it should govern a new case. In practice, there will likely be numerous precedents, each a little different from the others, that may or may not determine today's case. Mr. Smith might contend that his dispute with Ms. Jones resembles cases A, B, C, and D and should be decided (in his favor, of course) in accordance with a rule encompassing all of those cases. Ms. Jones might argue that this case is nothing like A, B, or C at all. Rather, it is much more like precedents D, E, F, and G (and Mr. Smith misunderstood the meaning of D). These cases require the court to rule in her favor. The point of law over which Mr. Smith and Ms. Jones disagree may be obscure, but in the course of many cases, each nudging the law one step this way or that, incremental changes in law can result in significant alterations of policy benefiting or burdening large classes of persons in situations resembling those of Mr. Smith or Ms. Jones.

Our presentation of the use of stare decisis is admittedly abstract. A more concrete illustration will await the next section, but we can see here that the court must choose which side has the more persuasive arguments. An inevitable side effect will be that the judge will reinterpret and, it is hoped, clarify (but this is by no means certain) the meaning of some small piece of the common law. We see that even in this most traditional of roles, courts cannot avoid creative choice. Nor should we be surprised to find that a nation with a common law heritage would also have a tradition of judicial involvement in the shaping of public policy. It is important to observe that today's choice will itself be cited as a precedent in future disputes that are similar to, but also different from, today's case. Thus, in deciding today's case, the judge cannot escape responsibility to the future and necessarily adds to the meaning of the law. To interpret existing law is to make new law.

With this in mind, we may now consider the role of stare decisis that is probably of greatest interest to political scientists. United States district courts are to apply the law to individual disputes in a fair and unbiased manner, but since even the most conscientious trial judge might err, the U.S. courts of appeals are available to rectify misapplications of federal laws by the district courts. The primary role of both courts is to guarantee a just resolution for individual disputants.

In contrast, the United States Supreme Court is given, through its certiorari jurisdiction, a more explicit policy-making role. Rather than deliver just resolutions to individual disputants, the Supreme Court is charged with the task of selecting the most important cases to use as vehicles for clarifying legal ambiguities, resolving conflicting interpretations of law among the circuits, or creating new legal norms. To do this, the Supreme Court chooses only a small portion of the cases brought to its attention, less than 1 percent of the federal cases litigated in any year. With precious few cases actually decided by the Supreme Court, its role in the judicial system would be small indeed were its decisions not binding as precedents in all lower courts. Lacking any direct control over lower court cases not appealed to them, stare decisis is the only way appellate courts supervise the decisions of lower courts.

Courts are in many ways like any other bureaucracy. The challenge for those at the top of a bureaucracy—and it is a big challenge in the best of circumstances—is to control the activities of those in the lower echelons. Whether the bureaucracy in question is the state department of motor vehicles, a financial corporation, a small liberal arts college in New England, or the federal court system, those at the top of the structure, those in the middle, and those at the bottom may have different problems, diverging perceptions, and conflicting agendas that may at times lead them to work at cross-purposes. To the extent that policies originating at the top of the structure are vague, ambiguous, or otherwise indecisive, interpretive discretion is increased for those at the bottom of the structure.[4] Thus, the lower courts, even when they sincerely want to comply with Supreme Court precedents, may have considerable flexibility in deciding how to do so.

Now recall that there is considerable localism built into the federal courts at the district level, a product of senatorial courtesy that increases the likelihood that lower courts will not always share the policy goals of the Supreme Court. We can see that creativity in following stare decisis may turn lower federal courts into one of the most troublesome obstacles to policies of the Supreme Court. Power to make policy, it must be understood, is shared jointly by the Supreme Court and the lower federal courts, as well as state judiciaries. A good example of this was noted in Chapter 3, where we saw the compliance with the school desegregation decision, *Brown v. Board of Education,* frustrated by federal district courts in the South.

We noted that much of the common law has today been supplanted by statutory law. Further, since 1938, the Supreme Court has renounced an independent federal common law for suits between citizens of differing states, leaving such "diversity of citizenship" cases to be determined by federal courts under state law.[5] The practical effect of this decision was to eliminate the largest part of the federal common law. Perhaps the most significant remaining field in which a federal common law exists is admiralty law. However, under statutory authorization, federal courts have created a kind of common law for antitrust and for collective bargaining, both of which have a profound impact on the economic well-being of many Americans. Remaining federal common law fields are quite narrow.[6] The technique of the common law, however—the reasoning by analogy from old cases to new ones—remains a staple of litigation. It is this technique of the common law that today influences the interpretation of statutes and even, to a lesser extent, the Constitution. We shall turn next to the question of statutory interpretation, where we shall illustrate the creativity given courts by stare decisis.

STATUTORY LAW

The twentieth century is the age of regulatory government. This has brought with it an immense growth in statutory law, so that most suits today involve the application of one or more statutes. The presence of statutes would seem to eliminate judicial creativity by requiring the faithful application of the law as written. This expectation, derived from separation of powers theory, would be all the stronger in a democratic system, where the sovereignty of the majority in policy making should lead logically to a theory of legislative supremacy. For the most part, judges agree that courts should defer to the legislature's political choices articulated in the statute. Indeed, judges frequently pay homage to their role of carrying out "the intent of the legislature." But knowing exactly what the legislature intends can be a tricky enterprise. Merely reading the statutory text is seldom sufficient.

The lay public's understanding of law is that it is a highly detailed, internally consistent, comprehensive body of rules that need only be consulted for a clear answer to every legal question that might arise. In fact, nothing could be further from the truth. Statutes are sometimes written in excruciating detail, and they are frequently of considerable length. To the best of their imperfect ability, legislators try to anticipate all possible conflicts and supply reasonable accommodations when drafting statutes, but the quest for the perfect statute is elusive. Often, statutes supply only the broad outlines of policy, leaving administrators, and ultimately courts, with considerable discretion when supplying the specific details called for by individual cases. This process of filling in the details of a broad legal principle should be understood as "interstitial legislating." Rule making is a function shared by all three branches of the federal government, although we might still posit legislative supremacy for reasons that will presently become clear.

There are a number of reasons why statutes do not supply precisely detailed rules for society. We might begin by noting what law professor Zechariah Chafee termed the "disorderly conduct of words."[7] Language is an imprecise medium for the conveyance of thought. When an author chooses a word that best approximates the thought he or she wishes to convey, this choice is based on his or her own uniquely individual experiences, which are shared in their entirety by no other individual. The reader necessarily interprets the author's words in light of his or her own equally unique background. A dictionary might supply some guidance in determining the meaning of words, but only by referring to some set of experiences commonly shared by members of a community. A heterogeneous society may not exhibit enough commonalty of experience for a word to mean the same thing in all its subcultures. The word *bad,* to cite a simple example, might mean very different things coming from white and black Americans. These two Americans are also likely to understand words like *discrimination* or *racism* in very different terms,which might generate different expectations from civil rights legislation.[8]

Even if we assume that statutes are written in the language of the dominant group's culture (itself a politically contentious issue), the fact remains that words acquire meaning only in a specific context. What is true for a single word is similarly true for a sentence. Professor Lief Carter offers a fine example in suggesting a sign on an outdoor escalator that says, "Dogs Must Be Carried."[9] Would one incur a penalty for riding the escalator without carrying a dog? Must a pedestrian, before riding up this escalator, capture some hapless dog to carry? Probably not, but one can't know this merely from reading the text. Instead, one has to place the words in context, supplied by asking oneself what problem the sign was probably intended to address. The prospect of frightened dogs running amok on a crowded escalator seems a more likely explanation for the regulation than any imagined threat posed by pedestrians not carrying dogs. We would reasonably conclude that one need carry a dog only if one happened to have Fido in tow prior to boarding the escalator. Our conclusion would based on an examination of the text only in light of our past experiences with dogs, pedestrians, and escalators, not from the text alone.

Relating statutory words to factual experience understood by some relevant community is a major task of litigation. In the Tariff Act of 1883, Congress imposed a 10 percent duty on imported "vegetables in their natural state." However, fruits, whether "green, ripe, or dried," were allowed to enter the country duty-free. When customs officials in New York sought to impose a duty on imported tomatoes, the importers litigated all the way to the Supreme Court, claiming that tomatoes were not a vegetable at all, but a fruit. Wrote Justice Horace Gray for a unanimous Court:

> Botanically speaking tomatoes are the fruit of the vine, just as are cucumbers, squashes, beans and peas. But in the common language of the people, whether sellers or consumers of provisions, all these are vegetables which are grown in kitchen gardens, and which, whether eaten cooked or raw, are, like potatoes, carrots, parsnips, turnips, beets, cauliflower, celery and lettuce, usually served at dinner in, with, or after soup, fish, or meats which constitute the principle part of the repast, and are not, like fruits generally, as dessert.[10]

When the Court chose to understand this statute through the medium of everyday speech, reflecting American culinary habits, instead of scientific speech, reflecting the tomato's reproductive function, they were not merely reading the statute and literally applying its terms. Rather, the Court was exercising discretion informed by a political calculation as to the intended audience of the statute—importers serving the consumer, not botanists—and reading into the statute the functional definitions of fruit and vegetable employed by that community. Without specific guidance from Congress, the Court made public policy requiring the duty to be paid. The cost of imported tomatoes and tomato products, from soups, to catsup, to spaghetti sauce, to chili, all increased in price. No doubt, domestic tomato farmers were a happy lot. The Court could have chosen otherwise within the terms of the statute. Perhaps only a minor change in late nineteenth century American dietary practices or the presence of several botanists on the Supreme Court, would have brought about a different decision.

To linguistic ambiguity we must add a further consideration. Legislation is prospective, or forward-looking. It is meant to define events that might take place in the uncertain future and to compel certain legal consequences when and if such events occur. Legislators might be well informed when they draft a statute, but they are not clairvoyant. Of course, they might not be very informed, either, responding as politicians often do to nothing more than inchoate public sentiment demanding the appearance that something is being done about a problem. But even assuming the best scenario, we still face the problem of how legislators can find language that comprehensively encompasses the unforeseeable myriad of future events.

The easiest way to achieve comprehensiveness is to employ vague language that is capable of future expansion into new situations. Legislators now face another dilemma. They must write with enough specificity to adequately distinguish the conduct they have in mind as needing regulation yet comprehensively enough to include all possible variations on such conduct. Statutes often enumerate specific facts to which they apply but then summarize with vague catchall clauses capable of expansion to include related, unforeseen facts. Recall the Interstate Vehicular Theft Act of 1919, discussed in Chapter 1. Congress sought to proscribe the transportation of stolen "vehicles" across a state line. "Vehicles" were specifically defined to include automobiles, automobile trucks, automobile buses, automobile wagons, and motorcycles. Trains were specifically excluded from the statute. Yet Congress felt compelled to include "any other self-propelled vehicle not designed for running on rails." It was this clause that proved problematic when one McBoyle stole an airplane and would be problematic again were an equally creative thief to steal and transport into another state a moped, a golf cart, a helicopter, or a zeppelin. The use of such open-ended language by a legislature constitutes an invitation to courts to use their own best judgment, on a case-by-case basis, to determine what sorts of future conduct ought to be included in the statutory prohibition. Obviously, legislators feared that future technology would provide many more opportunities for vehicular theft than they could ever foresee in 1919, and in this Congress proved prescient.

We will consider another example of this kind of judicial classification and introduce the role of stare decisis in statutory interpretation. This example is old, but it presents issues very much in evidence in contemporary statutory interpretation. In 1910, Congress enacted the Mann Act, also known, according to its own terms, as the White Slave Traffic Act. This title may be perplexing. The term *white slavery* arose out of a rumored practice long ago of abducting teenage girls throughout Western Europe to populate the harems and seraglios of the Middle East. Ever since, white slavery has described any coercion of women of any race or color into prostitution. The title can be misleading in another way, however, for the statutory text did not require duress. The willing participation of the woman in question provided no defense. The relevant portion of this act specified that:

> Any person who shall knowingly transport, or cause to be transported . . . in interstate or foreign commerce . . . any woman or girl for the purpose of prostitution or debauchery, or for any other immoral purpose . . . shall be deemed guilty of a felony.

Here, Congress evinced a clear intent to proscribe, within its limited constitutional authority, acts that facilitate prostitution. Assume that the act of prostitution is clearly understood as the offering of sex for financial gain. "Debauchery" is more problematic, as it may refer to a variety of kinds of excess. Assume it, too, is confined to certain forms of sexual degradation. Now consider the catchall phrase "other immoral purposes." The reach of this clause is potentially limitless. Could one be charged with violation of the Mann Act for driving one's mother into the next state to gamble at bingo?[11] Lawyers would tend to understand the context supplied by the rest of the quoted text as also limiting "other immoral purposes" to sexual immorality. But even with that clue, we will have problems knowing the precise boundary between criminal behavior and acceptable commerce. Immoral people, including the sexually profligate, cross state boundaries all the time. Are all of them guilty of violating the Mann Act for every trip they make? Or just some of them? If the latter, which ones?

In 1913, F. Drew Caminetti was convicted of transporting a willing woman from Sacramento, California, to Reno, Nevada, so that she might live with him outside the bonds of matrimony. On appeal before the Supreme Court, Caminetti argued that the terms of the Mann Act did not include his behavior, but instead proscribed only "commercialized vice," or the exchange of sex for financial gain.[12] The phrase "other immoral purposes" was intended to encompass only various forms of mercenary sex. To support this argument, he claimed to discern the intent of Congress from the legislative history of the act, including statements made on the floor of the House of Representatives by the bill's sponsor explaining its meaning to other legislators. This is a common, though not foolproof, technique for interpreting ambiguous statutory language. However, the Supreme Court rejected Caminetti's understanding of the Mann Act, a decision that could be predicted on the very first page of the majority's opinion, when Mr. Caminetti's companion was described as his "concubine," a word laden with unflattering connotations.

Did the historically contingent moral predilections of the Court color the meaning of the statute? The Court agreed that "prostitution" denotes sex offered for commercial gain, but pointed out that the deliberate inclusion of words like "debauchery" or "other immoral purposes" indicated a broader intent on the part of Congress. To the common understanding, at least as it was discerned by the Supreme Court, such words would include the behavior of Caminetti. Dismissing

Caminetti's construction of legislative intent, the Court wrote, "when words are free from doubt they must be taken as the final expression of the legislative intent . . .," and not the nebulous inferences drawn from legislative history. All that is controversial about this proposition is the Court's facile claim that the meaning of "other immoral purposes" was free from doubt. It seems, in fact, unlikely that a contemporary court would describe Caminetti's living arrangement as so inherently immoral as to be comprehended by the Mann Act free of any doubt.

Fearing the apparently limitless sweep of the Court's interpretation, three justices dissented. For them, the title and legislative history of the Mann Act indicated that Congress had not legislated in response to every form of sexual immorality. The general regulation of sexuality could be left to the perfectly able state legislatures. The federal offense consisted only in using the channels of interstate commerce for the promotion of commercialized sex. Caminetti's behavior revealed no such commercial purpose and so did not violate federal law. Had these three justices convinced two more, not only would Caminetti's conviction have been overturned, but, as we shall see, subsequent interpretation of the Mann Act would likely have been altered.

There are problems with the dissenters' appeal to committee reports and statements made in the course of congressional debate as evidence of legislative intent. The technique assumes that the legislature acted from a single intent that can be discerned from statements by individual partisans in the heat of debate. Students of legislative politics regard this as naive. There may, in fact, be as many intents as there are legislators, and the final product of the legislative process will likely represent a compromise among a number of factions pursuing very different agendas. Legislators, realizing that courts might turn to floor debate as an indication of legislative intent, will frequently place in the debate their own, often contradictory, views about the meaning of a bill. Judges are then presented with a confusing smorgasbord of legislative intents from which they might pick and choose, according to their policy predilections. Finally, critics of legislative history often point out that it is the words of the bill that legislators vote on and which the president signs into law, not the disparate statements of various committees or individuals.

Yet, the dissenting opinion does seem more satisfying than the majority position. In contrast with the majority's pretense of formalism, the dissenters faced up to their discretion honestly and openly appealed to policy considerations of federalism, as well as the common law practice of construing penal statutes narrowly. Even more overtly political was the dissenters' reluctance to extend the Mann Act as much as the majority seemed inclined to do, based on a fear that doing so would create opportunities for blackmailers. We might still criticize the wisdom of the dissenters' position, but only after we have taken the majority to task for its hollow claim to have "discovered" a clear legislative purpose in unambiguous language.

We are now able to predict that future applications of the Mann Act will not be confined to acts of sexual immorality for mercenary gain, but we still have no indication of how much conduct is included in "other immoral purposes." In 1940, Hans and Lorraine Mortensen, operators of a Nebraska brothel (legal in Nebraska at the time), decided to close down their business for two weeks to take a drive to Salt Lake City, stopping off briefly at Yellowstone National Park. They generously agreed to take two of their employees, admitted prostitutes, along for the ride. The Mortensens expected that their employees would return to work in two weeks, but no prostitution or immoral acts were contemplated or engaged in during the trip. It was simply a vacation, and presumably a fine time was had by all.

Nevertheless, an ambitious federal prosecutor theorized that however innocent of criminal intent the trip west had been, the return trip could be treated separately for purposes of the Mann Act. In transporting known prostitutes home to Nebraska with the assumption that their trade would resume, had the Mortensens run afoul of federal law? Notice that under the prosecutor's interpretation, the difference between a legal and an illegal trip consisted solely of the Mortensens' intentions. The words of the statute do require that the defendant "knowingly" transport women in interstate commerce for the purpose of "prostitution, debauchery or other immoral acts." We often assume that people intend the foreseeable consequences of acts they knowingly perform. Could the Mortensens have predicted that returning home from their vacation would be a federal offense? Neither the words of the statute nor any prior judicial interpretations support the prosecutor's bifurcation of the trip, although the *Caminetti* decision might encourage a permissive view of the Mann Act's terms. On appeal from their convictions, however, the Mortensens won a Supreme Court reversal of their convictions.[13]

This time, the Supreme Court was inclined to give the Mann Act a narrower interpretation. Before there was a violation of the statute, the trip had to be undertaken for the express purpose of bringing about an act of prostitution or whatever other conduct the act might include. Such conduct must be the dominant motive of the trip. The mere occurrence of immoral conduct incidental to the trip's conclusion was not sufficient to infect the journey with criminality. Since the sole purpose of the Mortensens' trip, from beginning to end, was recreational, there was no evidence of criminal intent on which a jury could have found them guilty of violating the Mann Act.

There are sound policy reasons, well recognized in the common law tradition, for the strict interpretation of criminal statutes. For one thing, we want to ensure that the citizen has a fair opportunity to recognize a clear line drawn between legal and illegal conduct, so that he or she might fashion his or her conduct in such a way as to avoid punishment. The purpose of criminal law is to deter wrongdoing, not to ensnare and punish for its own sake, and the deterrence value of a statute is undermined if the citizen cannot recognize the proscribed conduct. Another reason for the narrow construction of criminal laws, well illustrated by this case, is to confine administrative discretion and ensure that only the conduct the legislature specifically identified as criminal is punished. A society that values liberty would resolve ambiguity in favor of the individual, not the repressive machinery of the state. Such considerations, clearly political in nature, seem to have been far from the Court's thinking in *Caminetti*, but informed *Mortensen* directly.

Since the facts of the *Mortensen* case are substantially different from *Caminetti*, the prior case remained a valid precedent but perhaps now confined to a narrower set of facts. The Court was clear in expressing its unhappiness with previous interpretations that took the Mann Act into areas of conduct not contemplated by Congress. There is little doubt that policy considerations militated against adding another chapter of statutory construction that would further justify the fear that the act's broad provisions "are liable to furnish boundless opportunity to up and blackmail and make unnecessary trouble, without any corresponding benefits to society."[14]

Three dissenters were unhappy with such explicit policy making. They wrote:

> Courts have no more concern with the policy and wisdom of the Mann Act . . . or any other which Congress may constitutionally adopt. Those are matters for Congress to determine, not the courts.[15]

This disclaimer of policy making is typical of many that still issue from the courts, proving that the rhetoric of separation of powers formalism remains alive and well on the bench. But rhetoric in this case is not reality. The dissenters would have upheld the Mortensens' convictions, thus writing into the Mann Act the prosecutor's ingenious bifurcation of their trip. This would also have created policy beyond that explicitly made by the legislature. One can certainly debate the relative wisdom of the Court's policy or that of the dissenters. In both opinions, however, judges are adding rules to fill in the interstices of the Mann Act. Functionally, this is legislating. Better, then, to legislate wisely, which requires courts to consider carefully and explicitly the policy ramifications of what they decide.

Students by now should understand that legislating is a shared function. When the Congress enacts statutes having broad terms such as "other immoral purposes" into law, the practical effect is a delegation of rule-making authority to courts. Even so, it should be clear that the discretion exercised by courts is narrower than, and subordinate to, that of the legislature. Courts act in response to legislative action. Further, courts cannot ignore the text of a statute. It is inconceivable, for example, that one who drove a known prostitute to another state so that she might turn a few particularly well-paying tricks would not be found to have violated the Mann Act, regardless of any judge's views concerning the wisdom of Congress's policies. The scope of judicial discretion to make policy is directly a function of the ambiguity of the statutory language Congress enacts, but such ambiguity has its limits.

Moreover, had Congress been sufficiently annoyed by the judicial interpretation of the Mann Act, it retained complete power to revise the statute. If Congress felt that a man and a woman who lived together in a stable relationship, but without the sanction of a marriage license, were not a threat to society's morals, they could so amend the Mann Act. Congress could not erase the conviction of Caminetti (although the president could, through a pardon), but they could prevent any future prosecutions similar to Caminetti's by the passage of a new law permitting such persons to travel in interstate commerce.

Similarly, if Congress wanted people like the Mortensens punished, they could not reverse their acquittal (no one can), but legislators could specifically write the prosecutor's bifurcation of the trip into law for future application. If it is policy making when Congress does this, is it any less so when the courts do it? Democratic control over policy is restored, at least to some degree, by the possibility of legislative reversal of judicial policy, as well as by judicial caution. The latter brings us back to the values of stare decisis: legitimacy, fairness, predictability, and confinement of judicial discretion, all of which are as valuable in statutory interpretation as in common law.

We have one more Mann Act case to consider. If Congress has not seen fit to enact new legislation on the subject of prostitution after *Caminetti* and *Mortensen,* how might an attorney advise a polygamous member of a religious sect considering relocating with his numerous wives to another state? Heber Kimbal Cleveland, a member of a sect of the Mormon religion who cling to the doctrine that plural marriages are required by holy scripture, was convicted under the Mann Act when he undertook such a journey with his several wives. *Caminetti* supports a generous definition of the conduct proscribed by the act, one not requiring a profit motive. *Mortensen* reflects a more cautious approach to avoid the dangers of statutory vagueness, requiring the interstate trip to be taken for the specific purpose of engaging in prohibited conduct. Yet neither case compels a decision one way or another for Mr. Cleveland's circumstances. His conviction was upheld by a divided Supreme Court, on which the majority was willing to equate religiously sanctioned polygamy with "debauchery and other immoral purposes" not having a commercial motive.[16]

Cleveland had argued that the Mann Act was aimed primarily at prostitution and similar immoral behavior, and that his relationship with his traveling companions was one of marriage, with no commercial purpose. Nor, he claimed, could a stable family arrangement sanctioned by religion, no matter how unorthodox, constitute "debauchery or other immoral acts" within the meaning of the statute. The majority noted, however, that polygamy was widely condemned by American law and was at the time of the Mann Act an even more pervasive presence in society than the "casual, isolated transgressions" revealed in *Caminetti.* Thus, to conclude that polygamy was not prohibited by the Mann Act would first require that the statutory terms be limited to commercialized sex. In other words, in the majority's view, reversal of Cleveland's conviction would require the Court to overturn the *Caminetti* precedent. This they declined to do.

Citing the *Mortensen* case, Cleveland had also argued that since he was already participating in a plural marriage before relocating to another state, he did not undertake the trip for the specific purpose of polygamy. The majority rejected this defense, claiming that since Cleveland intended to cohabitate with his several wives after arriving at his destination, sufficient intent to promote immoral purposes within the scope of the act was present. Thus, the majority built on the *Caminetti* precedent to broaden the scope of the Mann Act further to proscribe sexual activity deemed immoral, even in the absence of a profit motive, now including the new situation of polygamous marriage required by religious tenets. At the same time, they seem to have adopted a more flexible interpretation of the state of mind requirements than had been used in *Mortensen,* possibly indicating a narrowing of that precedent.

That this decision was not clearly compelled by statutory text, legislative history, or judicial precedent is revealed by the fact that three justices dissented. Two thought *Caminetti* to have been wrongly decided in the first place, and while unwilling to overturn it they were also reluctant to broaden its rule as the majority was doing.[17] In a more elaborately argued opinion, the third dissenter argued that polygamy, as a form of marriage, should not be placed by the Court "in the same genus" of immoral activity as prostitution or debauchery.[18]

We can see here an example of judicial discretion to construe the application of law to the facts of a case in different ways, according to the moral values brought by the judge into the process. All members of the Court agreed that "other immoral purposes," as used in the act, was restricted to sexual immorality related to "prostitution" and "debauchery." All agreed that polygamous marriage was generally deplored by American society and was not the moral equivalent of a monogamous marriage in the eyes of the American community. At least one member of the Court however, thought polygamous relationships were a form of marriage, based on deeply held religious and moral belief, and should not be equated with prostitution. He showed a greater sensitivity for the value of cultural pluralism than the majority of the Court and certainly greater respect for individual liberty to make intimate choices about one's own life than had been revealed in the Court's decision in *Caminetti*. Thus, political values, and not just legal rules, led one justice to declare openly a desire to overrule *Caminetti* and confine the Mann Act to immoral acts related to commercialized sex.

It should be clear from our brief survey of Mann Act cases that courts are frequently, and necessarily, participants in the policy-making process and that the values judges take to the bench are important factors determining the policies they will make. When the meaning of legislation is vague, ambiguous, or incomplete, courts must add details to resolve disputes brought before them. The skeptic might ask if such statutory vagueness does not represent an abdication of legislative responsibility. "Congress," one might say, "not the courts, is charged under the separation of powers with the rule-making function. Besides, legislators, unlike judges, are elected and so can claim democratic authority to make policy." Such complaints are frequently heard in high places in American politics, even from members of Congress. Implicit in the statement is the question, "Why does Congress not draft more specific statutes?" The answer is found in the nature of the legislative process itself.

Cynics are fond of repeating that there are two things the public should never see being made—laws and sausages. One need not be a cynic, however, to understand that laws are products of compromise. In the process of building a legislative consensus, many points of view need to be reconciled, or at least pacified. The more specific a legislative proposal is, the harder it may become to hold together a coalition of interests needed to secure passage. But in addition to such practical considerations, there may be prudent reasons for statutory ambiguity that might be revealed by the Mann Act cases we have just reviewed. Society is dynamic, constantly in a state of change. New technology produces new desires, new needs, and new threats. Social mores, the commonly accepted limits of what is moral or permissible conduct, change constantly, if sometimes imperceptibly. As dynamic as society is, appropriate alterations in public policy are often difficult to achieve and at best require the expenditure of considerable attention, political resources, and good will. At some cost in predictability, the legislature might wisely purchase flexibility in the laws by choosing ambiguous language to accommodate future change.

Consider the behavior at issue in *Caminetti*. A man crosses a state line accompanied by a woman with whom he lives, but without a legally sanctioned marriage. Such behavior is today much more commonplace than in 1913. It seems unlikely that today's courts, if writing on a clean slate, would construe it as "concubinage" and equate it morally with prostitution. Perhaps the Supreme Court would even be willing at last to overrule *Caminetti* were an appropriate case to be presented, a decision that seems already to have been made by federal prosecutors, who have not brought such a case to court despite ample opportunity to do so. Statutory vagueness permits the Court to accommodate the conventions of both 1913 and 1994. This is not to say that a precedent as long-established and reaffirmed as *Caminetti* would or should be discarded frivolously, but litigation permits a new generation to make its case that simple cohabitation has become respectable, even while we continue to proscribe interstate trafficking in prostitution or polygamy.[19] Flexibility entails risk, of course, but so does all politics, including the politics of legal ossification.

We have seen in this section the intersection of law and politics, of judicial technique and moral values, supporting the view of litigation associated with legal realism. But there may be even more at stake here. One of the most fascinating insights of the Critical Legal Studies movement, discussed briefly in Chapter 1, is that litigation is a form of political conversation, albeit a highly rarified one. In conversation, whether in the legislature, in the media, on the street corner, or in the local pub, we exchange insights into our mutual experiences and seek reconciliation of our differences and validation of our values. This is a process involving at any one time literally thousands of conversations, some great and some small, not all of which attract much attention beyond the actual participants. On a continual basis, society creates and recreates its own image of itself through the ideology these conversations create. It is a diffused but important part of social life. In law, a similar phenomenon occurs, described by Robert Gordon as follows:

> Legal norms are primary expressions of and means for reproducing the "shared values" that function as the integrating glue of liberal societies, orientating everyone's highly differentiated tasks towards a set of common social purposes.[20]

Critical Legal theory offers several versions of this insight. Of of interest here is the notion that the power of law and of courts as law-interpreting institutions is not confined to their capacity to coerce recalcitrant citizens into conformity with society's norms. Power is also exerted through the law's "capacity to persuade people that the world described in its images and categories is the only attainable world in which a sane person would want to live."[21] That law has an educative function in society is not a new insight. When government proscribes conduct, there is a moral lesson included. Powerful signals are being sent that may reaffirm or alter community norms and expectations. Some might continue to defy those norms, but at considerable risk of censure as well as prosecution.

Critical Legal Studies scholars suggest that litigation, as a highly structured conversation, also helps to condition the ways in which we perceive our world, and that this further opens up or closes off opportunities to envision a world different from that which we already know. In this way, legal processes shape our expectations of politics and our willingness to accept the status quo as legitimate, beneficial, or at least inevitable. We might also be led to reject a rival vision as illegitimate, unfounded, unworkable, or simply crazy. Law then must be seen as influencing our understanding and thought, not just our behavior. This is a new contribution to our understanding of the way society is governed.

A social scientist looking at judicial interpretation of the Mann Act would want to document the presence of policy-making discretion. Looking further, one might evaluate the wisdom and legitimacy of broadening or narrowing the act to proscribe specific forms of conduct. A social scientist, however, might peer more deeply into how the Supreme Court's interpretation of the Mann Act has helped to shape social consciousness on a broad range of issues. A complete discussion of the symbolic aspects of litigation would require a book in itself, so our discussion will be only suggestive. Consider, for example, sexual politics, the relations between men and women in society, and the relative power these two groups bring to bear on the process of shaping those relations. Part of that power consists of the ability to impose on such relations a definition of social reality. "Reality" consists of differing experiences of men and women, experiences on which men and women might initially have very different perspectives.[22]

The Mann Act vests punishment on men who use the channels of interstate commerce to violate women. In this sense it is legislation protective of women. But neither the Mann Act nor the cases applying it protects women by addressing the social conditions that help produce prostitutes and their customers, including the social conditions of female disempowerment and sexual exploitation.[23] It is true that public policy might of necessity address issues piecemeal, and it is true that there are other conversations occurring in other forums throughout society that might correct for some of the deficiencies of the Mann Act and its interpretive cases. In fact, the Mann Act was part of a broader agenda of the progressive movement, which included minimum wage legislation and other protections of women in the workplace.

But notice that the litigation we have discussed has been essentially a conversation among men and primarily about men. It has taken place within what might be termed a "male metaphysic," or a definition of reality centered on the male experience. Despite its protective goals, the Mann Act and its interpretive cases reaffirm the male experience when they portray men as potent transactors and women as passive articles of trade—sexual commodities in a market activated by men. Certainly the decisions in *Caminetti* and *Cleveland* have viewed the women involved as objectified, voiceless beings incapable of shaping their own lives by making their own choices concerning their intimate relations. It is also possible to portray the legal structure of marriage as an economic relationship that is not so sharply distinguished from prostitution as lawmakers have assumed.[24] Perhaps what the Mann Act cases we have surveyed have accomplished has been to define some women as contraband articles of trade, while leaving some other forms of exchange in women not only legally protected but also ideologically legitimated.

Litigation might, in fact, be only part of a vast network of conversations, including a broad array of social transactions occurring throughout society operating on similar premises. Some of these conversations, including legislative debates, appeals from criminal convictions, and administrative decisions, occur in forums we traditionally define as "public." Others, including dating patterns or family arrangements, occur in what we are accustomed to calling a "private" realm. But each reinforces the other, and taken together they create a social climate that defines roles, perceptions, and even aspirations for men and women alike.

Viewed against this background, the law making we have seen here, while ostensibly designed to protect women, may at a deeper level perpetuate women's ideological subjugation to the male metaphysic. When this metaphysic dominates the process of litigation, it may receive an especially prestigious and persuasive stamp of legitimacy, coming as it does from the official forum established by the state to dispense justice. Perhaps those who would question the male metaphysic are excluded from the forums of official conversation about law and policy and are instead relegated to the background, placed on the defensive, and implicitly labeled as quacks and malcontents.[25]

Students should consider whether this statement by Catharine MacKinnon, a feminist scholar associated with Critical Legal Studies, accurately describes the cases we have discussed:

> I propose that the state is male in the feminist sense. The law sees and treats women the way men see and treat women. The liberal state coercively and authoritatively constitutes the social order in the interests of men as a gender, through its legitimizing norms, relation to society, and substantive policies. It achieves this through embodying and ensuring male control over women's sexuality at every level, occasionally cushioning, qualifying, or de jure prohibiting its excesses when necessary to its normalization. Substantively, the way the male point of view frames an experience is the way it is framed by state policy.[26]

The degree to which legal discussion is premised on a male-centered definition of reality may be difficult to grasp since we have so assimilated its intellectual categories that to some they seem obvious and natural. Men may be resistant to considering MacKinnon's critique as it may seem to threaten their privileged status. But if the arguments of Critical Legal Studies scholars prove correct, if legal categories help to shape ideological consciousness, we should not be surprised also to find women reluctant to challenge received wisdom, even a received wisdom that disadvantages them. Exposure of just such hidden hierarchies constitutes much of the Critical Legal Studies agenda. While the claims of Critical Legal Studies should be treated as tentative, they do open up new territory for social scientific exploration for this proposed role of litigation in the creation of consciousness raises questions that still need to be explored empirically.

RESPONSE BY THE POLITICAL PROCESS

Our discussion of the Mann Act cases might leave the impression that the legislature's ability to shape policy is at the mercy of unelected courts. It seems as if Congress enacts statutes that fix only the outer boundaries of judicial discretion but that the significant details of public policy are made piecemeal, out of sight, and without a democratic accounting. Were such a picture accurate, we would be raising serious questions about the degree to which the American people form a self-governing community. Given that courts supply much of the detail to statutory policy in the course of resolving lawsuits, they clearly do stand as intermediaries between individuals and legislative policy. Are they, therefore, negating popular control over government?

The truth is that public policy, while it does not represent a simple reflection of public sentiment, is also not the product of a secretive judicial cabal. In fact, public policy results from complex interactions between the legislature, the executive, and the courts. The specific roles played by each are considerably richer than those limited to rule making, rule implementing, and adjudication that figure in some introductory texts and that dominate the popular imagination. In fact, the three branches of the government share power over policy, including limited power to correct each other's mistakes. We have already alluded to Congress's authority to enact new legislation that may alter a court's interpretation of a statute. We have noted that if Congress refrains from doing so, it is often taken as an indication of legislative approval of judicial policy. On the other hand, the enactment of new legislation that prospectively reverses a judicial decision is often seen as the democratic process replying to a judicial error. Both of these views are a bit oversimplified and so merit a closer look.

Consider the case of *General Electric Co. v. Gilbert*.[27] A major corporation offered to its employees, as part of their employment compensation, an extensive health insurance package that included comprehensive disability benefits for a wide array of conditions affecting employment. Not included, however, was compensation for the loss of income incurred during a normal pregnancy. Gilbert brought suit, charging sex discrimination in violation of Title VII of the Civil Rights Act of 1964. Her claim was that by excluding coverage for a normal pregnancy, a condition experienced only by women, the corporation was denying its female employees equal compensation. Male employees were protected from loss of income arising from virtually all conceivable medical conditions they might experience, including elective surgery. Women, in contrast, were forced to endure a significant loss of income for a medical condition that most of them will face at some time during their work lives.

Title VII of the 1964 Civil Rights Act prohibited discrimination "against any individual with respect to his compensation, terms, conditions, or privileges of employment, because of such individual's race, color, religion, sex, or national origin."[28] The motivation of Congress, when the legislation was enacted, was to outlaw discrimination based on race. The banning of sex discrimination was virtually inadvertent. Congressmen opposed to federal legislation against race discrimination sought to defeat the proposed bill by loading it with "killer amendments"—a multiplicity of amendments attached to a bill in the hope that each will alienate some group of supporters, until the bill as a whole can no longer pass the legislature. The effort failed, but one of these killer amendments, proscribing sex discrimination, did slip into the bill and survived to become part of the final version of the Civil Rights Act. A consequence of this odd history is that Congress prohibited sex discrimination in employment virtually without consideration or debate, and some years before there was strong organized pressure to do so. Hence, no legislative intent regarding the status of pregnancy could be discerned. In all probability, there was none.

The case is complicated by the fact that while nearly all women experience a pregnancy at some time, only a small fraction of the female work force is pregnant at any particular time. The question presented to the Court was whether the exclusion of disability compensation for pregnancy effected discrimination against a protected class—women—or against a smaller class not protected by the statute—pregnant persons. While the latter class included only women, its boundaries were considerably narrower than the class specifically protected by Title VII.

The Supreme Court rejected Gilbert's claim, relying in part on one of its own recent precedents, *Geduldig v. Aiello*, which had denied a similar claim made by a government employee under the Fourteenth Amendment to the Constitution.[29] The Court was fragmented, however, and a strong dissent argued that the majority had neglected to consider how the selection of pregnancy for exclusion from an otherwise comprehensive benefits package worked to disadvantage women as a class, when each member's total compensation was considered over the period of her entire work life. Congress was also not impressed with the majority's performance and amended Title VII two years later to prohibit employment discrimination on the basis of pregnancy.[30]

We see here a quick override of judicial policy by the democratic process. Such legislative overrides do not change the judgment for a case already decided, but they do prevent the Court's decision from defining future relations among similarly affected parties. In contrast, Congress was less inclined to react to an even more sharply divided Court's resolution of *American Tobacco Co. v. Patterson,* in which the Court found no racial discrimination in a seniority system negotiated between a company and its unionized employees after the enactment of Title VII, despite its demonstrably adverse impact on black employees.[31] The Court here reasoned that Title VII required a demonstration of an intent to disadvantage a racial group. Lacking prejudice as a motivation, the mere effect of disadvantaging a racially defined group of employees did not create legally actionable conduct by an employer. This time, Congress did not even consider an override, which one scholar of statutory construction has attributed to differences in political clout of the groups affected.[32] *General Electric* was hailed by employers and insurance companies. But the decision also earned the ire of powerful women's groups that had come into being in the years since enactment of Title VII, labor unions, and the Equal Employment Opportunity Commission, a division of the Justice Department that investigates discrimination complaints. The White House was also supportive of an override. Faced with a powerful coalition of interests, Congress acted quickly. On the other hand, when *American Tobacco* was decided, after the 1980 election, the politics of the Justice Department and the White House had changed dramatically. Less supportive of civil rights laws generally, the Reagan administration was hostile to any theory of discrimination based on adverse impact, absent a clear showing of an intent to discriminate on the part of an employer. Congress had also taken a conservative, pro-business turn, while labor unions that often had supported civil rights groups in the past now tended to support seniority, protecting their white members. Bereft of powerful allies, black laborers were simply unable to muster the support needed to effect a legislative override.

Consideration of these cases reminds us that courts do not exist in a political vacuum. The configuration of interest groups in support of the winners or losers, the policies of the bureaucracies, and the sentiments of the president, relevant congressional committees, and their parent chambers will all determine the longevity of judicial policies. In fact, the likelihood of legislative overrides has increased dramatically since the late 1970s, especially for ideologically contentious issues in which the losing side has been supported by government agencies, women's groups, environmentalists, or organized labor.[33] It has increasingly become a practice of losing parties or the interest groups that support them to turn Congress into a kind of final court of appeals to reverse judicial policies that adversely affect them. In this way, the activities of interest groups aid Congress in monitoring judicial policy making and provide support for a legislative response.

However, interest groups reacting to litigation in this way introduce a new element into the political balance—or, rather, they reintroduce it. Even to the extent that judicial decisions can still be said to turn on principle, it should now be apparent that their ability to survive legislative scrutiny will in no small measure be a function of power. The main problem with interest group politics is that interest groups do not form evenly throughout the community. Generally speaking, the smaller and more cohesive, well-financed, and previously organized groups will be most effective in the legislative arena.[34] The larger and more diffuse, underfunded, and unorganized groups will be more vulnerable. At the same time, the truly small and unpopular minority groups lacking in political resources will be unable to muster sufficient support to defend the judicial victories they may have achieved. Ironically, the latter are the very interest groups that depend most on courts for protection for the very reason of their powerlessness in the legislature. Obviously, the possibility of a legislative override must hang like a Sword of Damocles over the Court when it is asked to defend the rights of weak or unpopular minorities. Just as clearly, such minority groups cannot rely solely on the courts for protection but must also cultivate the proper connections in the legislative arena if they are to protect their political interests.

This picture is complicated further by the dispersal of power within Congress since the mid-1970s. Efforts at congressional reform in the wake of the Vietnam War and the Watergate scandal had the unintended consequence of producing a proliferation of subcommittees. These small centers of power provide many more points of access to the legislative process for small groups. However, critics charge that they are also highly susceptible to capture by interest groups and may function quite independently of their parent chambers or of the leadership of the majority party.[35] Such subcommittees may not be able to impose their policy preferences on the rest of Congress, but they have a notorious ability to veto policies inimical to their client groups' interests. Thus, winners in court who are minorities in Congress may still be able to protect their victory by blocking an override measure if they have the right connections. In such circumstances, legislative silence may not signal democratic approval of judicial policies so much as it reflects legislative gridlock.

Failure of Congress to override a statutory policy may also reflect pressures from the White House. A credible threat by the president to veto override legislation puts proponents on notice that they will need majorities exceeding two-thirds in both houses to succeed. Presidents, of course, also communicate their desires directly to the Court, through amicus curiae briefs if the United States is not a party to the suit. Consider one more sex discrimination case. In *Grove City College v. Bell,* the Court was asked to consider the breadth of remedy offered by another civil rights statute, Title IX of the Education Amendments of 1972.[36] This statute prohibited sex discrimination in any educational program receiving federal funds, on penalty of the termination of financial support. The question before the Court was whether funds were to be cut from the entire educational institution or merely from the specific program in which sex discrimination was found to have occurred. The former was obviously the more significant penalty, one likely to be a stronger deterrent against discrimination in educational settings. While Congress had indicated through a nonbinding resolution its preference for this broader remedy, the Reagan administration announced its support for the narrower termination of federal funds. The Court adopted the administration's position over the dissents of Justices Brennan and Marshall, who protested the Court's shifting of policy according to the administration's weather vane.[37] Within months, the Democratic House of Representatives voted to amend Title IX, in effect to override the Court's policy. However, the Republican-dominated Senate refused to go along. Only after the Democrats regained control of the Senate, and in the final months of the Reagan administration, did Congress finally enact legislation overriding the policy of *Grove City College,* overcoming at last the veto of a politically weakened president.

The foregoing indicates that statutory interpretation by the Supreme Court or by lower courts will not always be the final word on an issue. To the contrary, statutory cases often become the occasion for renewed political struggle between all three branches of the national government, as well as between the various contending interest groups in the community. Litigation is sometimes a useful tool to focus attention on a grievance that the legislature seems unwilling or unable to address. However, an important factor influencing courts' ability to shape public policy will be the strength and commitment of organized interests in the community that might seek to override or preserve judicial policies.

Before we turn our attention to issues of constitutional interpretation, we need to note a special problem. On occasion, the interpretation of statutes occurs in the shadow of the Constitution, where the difference between statutory and constitutional law can become quite nebulous. This happens where a statute might be interpreted one way that would be consistent with the Constitution, while an alternate interpretation would run afoul of the Constitution's requirements. The courts will generally assume that the legislature would never intend to violate the Constitution and will give the statute the *saving construction* that preserves as much of the policy sought by the legislature as the Constitution will allow. The potential for legislative reversal of the Court's interpretation is considerably narrowed in such cases, for the new legislation risks nullification on constitutional grounds.

These saving interpretations of statutes become most controversial when they seem to run contrary to what the legislature evidently did intend. Consider *United States v. Seeger*, a case involving the scope of the exemption from conscription given to religiously motivated pacifists by the Selective Training and Service Act of 1948.[38] The statute granted an exemption for one who objected to warfare on the basis of sincere religious belief, defined as "an individual's belief in a relation to a Supreme Being involving duties superior to those arising from any human relation, but [not including] essentially political, sociological or philosophical views, or a merely personal moral code." Although not an atheist, Seeger was unable sincerely to avow a belief in a supreme being as understood by western monotheistic religions. He admitted only a "belief in the existence of a god or gods; belief in superhuman powers or spiritual agencies in one or many gods," a belief that appeared sincere. Denied conscientious objector status, Seeger filed suit, claiming that the statute, as written, violated the First Amendment's prohibition that "Congress shall make no law respecting an establishment of religion, nor prohibiting the free exercise thereof. . . ." In a nutshell, his argument was that the statute violated the Constitution by selectively granting conscientious objector status only to pacifists who subscribed to standard western religious beliefs.

The Court, however, interpreted the question before it as whether the term "Supreme Being" as used in the statute was limited to the Judeo-Christian God, or whether it comprehended less orthodox understandings of a transcendent power "to which all else is subordinate or upon which all else is ultimately dependent." The Court noted that the former interpretation would exclude from consideration adherents to a number of well-established religions, including Buddhism and Hindu. In a religiously heterodox community, a narrow interpretation of the statutory language would effect discrimination against sects that do not subscribe to western monotheism, and so ran afoul of the First Amendment. Thus, the Court interpreted Congress's use of "Supreme Being" as including any "sincere and meaningful belief which occupies in the life of its possessor a place parallel to that fulfilled by the God of those admittedly qualifying for the definition."[39] In this way, constitutionally troubling distinctions on religious grounds were avoided, and the statute, now purged of its constitutional defect, could be upheld. However, it is unlikely that Congress was thinking of such a broad category of beliefs when it enacted the conscientious objector exception. The statutory text itself says otherwise. Could the Court's inclusive interpretation of religion be distinguished from those "essentially political, sociological or philosophical" views that Congress had specifically excluded as the basis for conscientious objector status?

In *Welsh v. United States*, decided five years after *Seeger*, the Court was forced to conclude that it could not.[40] Welsh claimed conscientiously to oppose all warfare but disavowed any "religious" grounding for his beliefs. Writing for a five-vote majority, Justice Black held:

If an individual deeply and sincerely holds beliefs that are purely ethical or moral in source and content but that nevertheless impose on him a duty of conscience to refrain from participation in any war at any time, those beliefs certainly occupy in the life of that individual "a place parallel to that filled by . . . God" in traditional religious conviction.[41]

In other words, to pass constitutional muster, the statute had to be read as granting conscientious objector status to those very persons to whom Congress had explicitly denied such status! It seems the Court had to destroy the statute in order to save it, for now it granted an exemption to the draft on the basis of nonreligious objections to warfare, so long as these were sincerely held.

Within a few years of *Welsh,* Congress abolished the compulsory draft and has not renewed it. However, the question remains whether any exemption to conscription can now be granted based on conscientious objection to warfare in any form that is premised on "religious training and belief." Of course, an exemption premised on all forms of objection to warfare would nullify the compulsory nature of the draft, yet that is what the Court seems to have required. Should the United States face the necessity of resumption of conscription, Congress would have very little room to maneuver, unless the Court is willing to reinterpret the Constitution. As we shall see in the final chapter, constitutional interpretations have about them an air of finality not shared with statutory law. If the Court is unwilling to revise its own prior interpretation, the only recourse left to Congress is to propose a constitutional amendment, under the very difficult procedures of Article V.

NOTES

1. The classic discussion of this analytic task is Arthur L. Goodhart, "Determining the Ratio Decidendi of a Case," 40 *Yale Law Journal* 161 (1930). Since Goodhart published his article, legal scholars have sought fame by demonstrating the inadequacies of his thesis. One of the most accessible of these is Lief H. Carter, *Reason in Law,* 3rd ed. (Scott, Foresman, Glenview, Illinois, 1988) p. 137.
2. A good example was the Supreme Court's redefinition of its holding in *Wisconsin v. Constantineau,* 400 U.S. 433 (1971) and *Paul v. Davis,* 424 U.S. 693 (1976), discussed in Chapter 5.
3. Edward H. Levi, *An Introduction to Legal Reasoning* (University of Chicago Press, Chicago, 1949) p. 3.
4. Walter F. Murphy, *Elements of Judicial Strategy* (University of Chicago Press, Chicago, 1964) p. 93.
5. *Erie Railroad v. Tompkins,* 304 U.S. 64 (1938).
6. For a discussion of remaining federal common law jurisdiction, see Richard A. Posner, *The Federal Courts: Crisis and Reform* (Harvard University Press, Cambridge, Massachussetts, 1985) pp. 299–314.
7. Zechariah Chafee, "The Disorderly Conduct of Words," 41 *Columbia Law Review* 381 (1941).

8. Alan Freeman, "Legitimizing Racial Discrimination Through Anti-Discrimination Law: A Critical Review of Supreme Court Doctrine," in Allan C. Hutchinson, ed., *Critical Legal Studies* (Rowman & Littlefield, Totowa, New Jersey, 1989) p. 120.

9. Carter, op. cit., p. 58.

10. *Nix v. Hedden,* 149 U.S. 304 (1893). Here might be a precedent for the Reagan administration's infamous attempt to define ketchup as a vegetable for purposes of federally funded school lunch programs.

11. Carter, op. cit., pp. 31–32.

12. *Caminetti v. United States,* 242 U.S. 470 (1917).

13. *Mortensen v. United States,* 322 U.S. 369 (1944).

14. Ibid., pp. 376–377.

15. Ibid., pp. 377–378 (Black, dissenting).

16. *Cleveland v. United States,* 329 U.S. 14 (1946).

17. Ibid., pp. 22–21 (Black and Jackson, dissenting).

18. Ibid., p. 25 (Murphy, dissenting).

19. Carter, op. cit., p. 35.

20. Robert W. Gordon, "Critical Legal Histories," in Allan C. Hutchinson, ed., *Critical Legal Studies* (Rowman & Littlefield, Totowa, New Jersey, 1989) p. 90.

21. Ibid., p. 97.

22. Catharine A. MacKinnon, "Toward a Feminist Jurisprudence," in Allan C. Hutchinson, ed., *Critical Legal Studies* (Rowman & Littlefield, Totowa, New Jersey, 1989) p. 56. MacKinnon's complex discussion of the crime of rape profoundly illustrates how contending definitions of reality shape legal processes and how laws ostensibly designed to protect women from male aggression reinforce the ideological hegemony of the male definition of reality.

23. Rosemarie Tong, *Women, Sex, and the Law* (Rowman & Allenheld, Totowa, New Jersey, 1984) pp. 52–53.

24. Ibid., p. 49.

25. Gordon, op. cit., p. 97.

26. MacKinnon, op. cit., pp. 61–62.

27. *General Electric Co. v. Gilbert,* 429 U.S. 125 (1976).

28. 42 U.S.C. sec. 2000e-2(a)(1).

29. *Geduldig v. Aiello,* 417 U.S. 484 (1974).

30. 92 Stat. 2076 (1978).

31. *American Tobacco v. Patterson,* 456 U.S. 63 (1982).

32. William N. Eskridge, Jr., "Overriding Supreme Court Statutory Interpretation Decisions," 101 *Yale Law Journal* 331, 353 (1991).

33. Ibid., p. 352.

34. See generally, Mancur Olsen, *The Logic of Collective Action* (Harvard University Press, Cambridge, Massachusetts, 1971).

35. Roger H. Davidson, "Subcommittee Government: New Channels for Policy Making," in Thomas E. Mann and Norman J. Ornstein, eds., *The New Congress* (American Enterprise Institute, Washington, D.C., 1981) p. 99, and Lawrence Dodd and Bruce Opperneimer, "The House in Transition," in Dodd and Oppenheimer, *Congress Reconsidered* (Congressional Quarterly Press, Washington, D.C., 1985) p. 50.

36. *Grove City College v. Bell,* 465 U.S. 555 (1984).

37. Ibid., p. 603.

38. *United States v. Seeger,* 380 U.S. 163 (1965).

39. Ibid., p. 166.

40. *Welsh v. United States,* 398 U.S. 333 (1970).

41. Ibid., p. 340.

Chapter
7

Judicial Review and the Constitution

American law is hierarchical. We can think of law arranged into tiers, with each tier having to conform to the terms of the next higher one. In other words, any law on a lower tier that contradicted the law of a higher tier would for that reason be invalid. At the lowest tier is the common law, developed pragmatically to enable courts to resolve legal disputes in the absence of other law. While it dominated English law for centuries and American law until the turn of the twentieth century, the common law could always be superseded by legislation. Courts in the early part of the twentieth century resisted the encroachment of legislation on the common law by giving statutes the narrowest possible interpretation when they contradicted common law doctrine, but there was never any doubt that in cases of direct conflict, legislation controlled any lawsuit that came under its purview. Thus, as politics became more populist, democratic accountability could be maintained through legislative supremacy.

Of course, legislation does not spring forth out of a vacuum. Statutes frequently embody common law principles and definitions. Even when statutes depart from the common law, we have seen that the technique of the common law, stare decisis, remains a central part of judicial interpretation of statutory law. Should the judiciary interpret statutes in a way that meets with popular disapproval, correction can be affected by enacting new legislation amending the misinterpreted statute. Admittedly, there may also be many reasons for legislative inaction that do not indicate legislative approval of the courts' policies. These include lack of awareness of what the courts have done, indifference, and the power of a strategically placed minority group to block any legislative alteration of a judicial policy from which they benefit. Nevertheless, we commonly assume that democratic accountability is maintained through the possibility of legislative revision.

We are on an entirely different plane in this chapter, where we turn to the law of the Constitution. Congress did not create the Constitution; rather, all legislative authority is derived from the Constitution that created Congress. For any legislative enactment to be valid, it must conform to the terms of constitutional law. Failing that, the act of Congress is deemed void, having absolutely no legal consequences whatsoever. It follows logically that Congress may not, by a simple act of legislation, change the meaning of the Constitution. The Constitution is, according to its own terms, "the supreme law of the land," to which all other laws and authoritative acts of government must conform. For reasons we will touch on but briefly, the ultimate authority to interpret the Constitution's meaning has fallen to courts at all levels, subject to ultimate appeal to the United States Supreme Court.

Congress is not able to reverse judicial interpretations of the Constitution, for any attempt to do so would in itself be unconstitutional. Should the courts err in their reading of the Constitution, the only recourse would be to amend the Constitution under the very difficult terms of Article V or to hope that some future Supreme Court will overturn the interpretation. The fact is that amendments occur infrequently and Supreme Court revision of its own policies happens slowly, if at all. As a result, there is no immediate democratic control over constitutional decisions. This seeming paradox will require further elaboration before we examine closely the intricacies of constitutional interpretation.

A CONSTITUTIONAL REPUBLIC

Politics is a complex enterprise in which we are frequently faced with difficult value choices. Sometimes members of the community disagree over the practical definitions given to values everybody professes in the abstract, such as liberty or equality. The ways in which we define and understand these "essentially contested concepts" divide Americans into identifiable ideological groups.[1] Occasionally, even when we share a common understanding of the terms of our political discourse, our values will collide. To political conservatives, for example, the value of liberty is threatened by equality. An increase in the latter must be paid for with a corresponding decrease in the former. Such trade-offs present society with "tragic choices" in which it is impossible to pursue all values to their logical conclusion. A balance must be struck between such values, and distinct ideological groups can again be defined according to the preference given to one or the other. The tensions that exist in American politics between liberty and equality have been the impetus for volumes of passionate speeches and speculative writings. Our immediate concern is with another such tension built into American politics—that between *popular sovereignty,* manifested in democratic politics, and *constitutionalism,* manifested in judicial review.

Before we explore this, some clarification of terms is in order. By popular sovereignty, we mean the political theory that all legitimate political authority arises out of the consent of the governed. Frequently expressed in the form of social contract theory and viewing the state as an artificial creation of human beings to serve their needs, popular sovereignty tends to produce majoritarian theories of government. Contemporary proponents of popular sovereignty usually reveal an optimistic assessment of human nature that makes democratic politics a desirable possibility, one to which a community would intelligently consent. Men and women are viewed as capable of reasoned and public-spirited choice, at least enough of the time to make democratic government safe. Furthermore, since the governors are also the governed, democratic politics supplies its own corrective for errant policies. Reasonable persons, it is said, would not seek to tyrannize themselves. While popular reason might not be perfect, mistakes made by representative assemblies can be remedied by the voters once they have the benefit of direct experience with their own misguided policy.

The most optimistic of democratic theorists view human beings as capable of practicing civic virtue, by which we mean a public morality whereby each individual is able to set aside his or her private wants when acting in the role of citizen and instead pursue the interests of the community with genuine devotion. Democratic theorists often view participation in public decision making as providing an opportunity for the cultivation of such virtue. The more opportunity the citizen has to exercise responsible choice on public issues, the more he or she is drawn out from his or her private experience, enabled to make contact with his or her neighbors, and able to comprehend community needs reasonably.

A somewhat less optimistic strain of democratic thought is represented by pluralism. Perhaps human beings are not really capable of escaping their self-interested desires to the degree necessary for democratic virtue. Pluralist democracy supposes that even in the absence of a high level of civic virtue, a multiplicity of contending interest groups will balance out each other's most egoistic instincts and provide, by a sort of hidden hand, a policy approximating the best public interest. In either version, popular sovereignty is an axiomatic strain in American political thought, producing an assumption that the will of the majority ought to prevail.

Most Americans also subscribe to the value of constitutionalism, although most probably do not stop to consider how it qualifies their belief in popular sovereignty. By constitutionalism we mean the theory that government is limited by law. As the term is used here, constitutionalism does not necessarily require the presence of a written document called a constitution. The source of this supreme law can be varied. Natural law, the will of the deity, historical tradition, or human reason have all been cited as the source of "higher law" that confines legitimate political authority. Liberal writers have tended to find natural law in the reason of human beings, at least when it was not corrupted by passion. But there is the rub, for constitutionalists tend to view human reason as so fragile and human passion—the impulsive, nonrational, instinctively egoistic part of the psyche—as so powerful that reason will almost inevitably become corrupted by self-interest. To constitutionalists, human nature poses an intractable problem.

It is to restrain this self-aggrandizing conduct among individuals that government is necessary in the first place. The problem is that government will itself be administered by the same kind of self-interested individuals, who, once armed with the coercive power of the state, pose an even greater threat to our freedom and security. It is no more rational to presume enlightened political leadership than to presume an enlightened citizenry. As James Madison warned Americans, "Enlightened statesmen will not always be at the helm."[2] What leaders offer as reason in support of their political choices more often than not is merely a post hoc rationalization for selfishness. It was for this reason that the founding generation thought it important to write down constitutional restraints, so they could never be forgotten or perverted. Future generations could consult the document called the Constitution as the primary (and perhaps exclusive) source of constitutional law and hold those in power—including the equally selfish and irrational democratic majority—accountable to it.

In addition, constitutionalists tend to view society as divided into competing groups or factions. These may be defined in economic terms, as in James Madison's Federalist Paper #10, or by race, gender, religion, or a myriad of other criteria.[3] This heterogeneity enables people to abuse others in the course of pursuing their selfish wants, without tyrannizing themselves. By imposing the costs for their choice on others, the majority might escape from the self-correcting experience democratic politics requires to promote civic virtue. If human beings have a powerful tendency to act in a self-interested manner and rationalize their egoism later, all while shifting the penalties for their behavior onto weaker minority groups in the community, then civic virtue becomes a very tenuous restraint on the majority's power. Thus, fear of the tyranny of the majority is also a potent strain of American political thought, one that favors constitutional restraints on the political power a majority might wield. We value constitutionalism to protect the rights of minorities.

The trick with constitutionalism, given its countermajoritarian impact, is to enforce it. Democracy and constitutionalism, while sometimes existing in concert, or at least in uneasy truce, will occasionally be at war with one another. It is a tension built into American politics at its inception. Consider this famous passage from the Declaration of Independence:

> We hold these truths to be self-evident: that all men are created equal; that they are endowed by their Creator with inalienable rights; that among these are life, liberty and the pursuit of happiness; that to secure these rights governments are instituted among men, deriving their just powers from the consent of the governed . . . [4]

This passage is often taken as establishing the moral axioms of American society. Two criteria of political legitimacy are offered here. First, to exercise powers justly, government must reflect the consent of the people, and it must give equal weight to each of the people who consented, requiring one vote for one person. The further implication is that government decisions must be made by a majority of votes, since every vote is equal to every other vote.

In addition, however, legitimate government must secure the inalienable rights of its citizens, which are also held equally. We will, for present purposes, define rights as claims having sufficient moral content that government, that is, the majority, is obligated to respect them. To confine our notion of rights to concessions the majority gladly makes to a minority would render the concept meaningless. To be politically significant, rights must protect claims the majority would not be inclined to grant either to individuals or to minority groups, had it the choice not to. We sometimes refer to rights as having the power to "trump" the majority's will. Just as a trump card will beat any hand one's opponent holds, the presence of a constitutional right will beat the superior numbers, organization, connections, money, or votes of the majority.

However, a critical question the Declaration passes over is what would happen should a majority not consent to respect the inalienable rights held by the minority. Inevitably, occasions will arise when a minority will claim as a right something the majority does not intend to concede. Could a majority be persuaded to limit its own power out of respect for the rights of minorities? If not, how could a weak minority assert its trump card in the face of the majority's overwhelming power? Surely the electoral processes that brought the majority into power in the first place could not be depended on to protect those who lost the previous election and will likely lose the next election as well.

On those occasions when a majority—absolutely convinced of the righteousness of its cause—is moved to abuse the rights of minorities, constitutionalism will pose an unwelcomed impediment. Claims of rights are likely to be at their most controversial precisely when they are most needed. Constitutionalists, remember, doubt the majority's capacity to listen to reason and to restrain themselves. Restraints external to the voters' conscience and external to the majoritarian political processes must be found. The American solution has been complex, involving the scheme of representation in a bicameral legislature, the tendency of one faction to counterbalance the selfish schemes of another, and the separation of powers reinforced with an elaborate system of institutional checks and balances. This is the familiar constitutionalism of James Madison.[5]

Judicial Enforcement of Restraints

Our present concern is for a distinctly American innovation, the enforcement of constitutional restraints by courts in the course of resolving ordinary lawsuits, through the power of *judicial review*. We shall define judicial review as the authority of courts to evaluate the acts of government (the legislature, the executive, states, or even lower courts) in constitutional terms and, if they are found contrary to the constitution, to declare such acts null and void. It is this power that thrusts the judiciary most deeply into the political process, as courts routinely clash with other branches of government over the very rules by which our politics will be conducted. When statutes are ruled unconstitutional, decisions made by the executive branch are overturned, or states are ordered to reallocate their priorities or restructure their institutions, judicial review is frequently perceived as creating policies contrary to those favored by the majority. To add to the controversy, we should note that there is no clause in the text of the Constitution that explicitly grants to the courts such authority. Rather, it is a power courts have only inferred from the Constitution. Judicial review is itself a product of judicial review, as we shall see in later pages.

Notice that while judicial review presupposes constitutionalism, the reverse is not true. There are a number of reasonably constitutional democracies around the world that do not have judicial review. In fact, most of them do not. On the other hand, judicial review without constitutionalism is unthinkable. It should also be noted that not all judicial review is rights-protecting. Sometimes the courts are called on to resolve disputes over the boundaries separating the states' powers from those of the national government, or the Congress from the executive. However, since the most controversial examples of contemporary judicial review usually concern a claim of individual rights, we will discuss it in that context. Here is where minorities claiming rights and majorities claiming the power of self-government will clash head-on.

There are two ways in which the power of majorities is constitutionally limited. The first consists of procedural constraints, which permit the government to obtain some end provided proper procedures are observed. We can view the requirement that a law have passed both houses of Congress and be signed by the president before we are obligated to obey it as a procedural requirement. Another is the requirement that the police obtain a search warrant before they rummage through a citizen's home looking for evidence of criminal activity. Still another, should the search turn up incriminating evidence, is the requirement that punishment may be imposed only after a fair trial, including the right to confront government witnesses, the right to legal counsel, and the right against compulsory self-incrimination. These procedural rights may be asserted to force government to conform to its own rules of fair dealing with individuals.

In addition to procedural limitations are substantive prohibitions, which place some policy goals beyond the power of government or beyond the reach of majorities to pursue, even by fair procedures. The United States may not establish an official religion, no matter how much a majority might wish to do so, because the First Amendment to the Constitution says "Congress shall make no law respecting an establishment of religion." Similarly, government may not prohibit the promulgation of unpopular political or religious ideas, because the same amendment also says that Congress shall make no law "abridging the freedom of speech, or of the press." Substantive limitations create personal rights that thwart government action from occurring at all.

The nature of substantive rights must be noted closely. As individuals or as members of political factions we all make various claims on society. Most of these we call "interests," such as one's interest in securing a government job, lower taxes, protective tariff, or the benefits of some other policy. Interests are desires we press on government, successfully if we have sufficient political power. Lacking such power ourselves, we might try to garner support from others by forming political alliances. If we are unsuccessful at this pluralist bargaining, we will lose. As losers, we will not secure for ourselves the benefits we sought or might fall victim to burdens we would have preferred to avoid. In the realm of interests, it is altogether proper that minorities should lose. Such are the risks of politics.

Claims that are accorded the status of rights are different. The presence of rights reduces the risks of politics by defining certain demands as ones on which even a weak and unpopular minority cannot lose.[6] Rights are distinguished from interests by their moral content—they create reciprocal obligations on the part of the community that must be obeyed, even when it is inconvenient to do so. An act by the government that does not respect a right is illegitimate or, in terms familiar to Americans, unconstitutional. Political power is not at issue in rights disputes because rights are held equally by all members of the political community, the weak as well as the strong. It was for this reason that we referred to rights a moment ago as "trumping" the power of majorities. Rights are said to arise from correct constitutional principle, not political power.

Rights impose limits on what the majority can do to the losers of a political battle. Consider, for example, the fate of a small and unpopular religious minority. One such sect, the Jehovah's Witnesses, decline as a matter of religious conscience to salute the American flag. For this and other reasons, they became the subject of considerable popular hostility during the 1930s. With World War II approaching, their refusal to salute the flag led to widespread political repression and even outbreaks of violence.[7] In several states, children were expelled from public schools for their religious scruples. When litigation on the issue of compulsory flag salute in the public schools first reached the Supreme Court, in 1940, the Court ruled that the First Amendment's provision that, "Congress shall make no law . . . prohibiting the free exercise [of religion]," did not protect Jehovah's Witnesses from laws requiring them to salute the flag.[8]

However, three years later the Court granted certiorari to a similar case and this time ruled in favor of the Jehovah's Witnesses.[9] Instead of focusing on the narrow question of whether religiously motivated conduct was exempt from a general requirement to salute the flag, the Court considered the broader question of whether the state had the constitutional authority to require flag saluting in the first place. Regardless of the motivation of Jehovah's Witnesses, could the state coerce conformity of belief by compelling the vocal affirmation of an officially prescribed orthodoxy? This was held to violate both the establishment of religion clause and the freedom of speech provision of the First Amendment. Note the Court's appreciation of the special nature of substantive rights in our political system:

> The very purpose of a Bill of Rights was to withdraw certain subjects from the vicissitudes of political controversy, to place them beyond the reach of majorities and officials and to establish them as legal principles to be applied by courts. One's right to life, liberty, and property, to free speech, a free press, freedom of worship and assembly, and other fundamental rights may not be submitted to vote; they depend on the outcome of no elections.

This frank recognition of the countermajoritarian nature of rights was buttressed by the observation that rights are important enough to be taken most seriously when they become inconvenient or unpopular:

> [F]reedom to differ is not limited to things that do not matter much. That would be a mere shadow of freedom. The test of its substance is the right to differ as to things that touch the heart of the existing order.

Having taken a strong position on the nature of rights, the Court was equally emphatic about the right the Jehovah's Witnesses were contending for:

> If there is any fixed star in our constitutional constellation, it is that no official, high or petty, can prescribe what shall be orthodox in politics, nationalism, religion, or other matters of opinion or force citizens to confess by word or act their faith therein.[10]

The highly visible endorsement of compulsory flag salutes by President Bush as part of his successful 1988 campaign demonstrates that the freedoms of dissenters such as Jehovah's Witnesses are still precarious in majoritarian politics. Which rights citizens ought to have is a fit subject for political debate, but the emotional demagoguery surrounding the flag salute question exploited the American voter's lack of understanding of our own constitutional history and did not teach a very good lesson in civics. Events of a half century ago and in our own time reveal the same political dilemma of reconciling rights and popular sovereignty.

Two hundred years ago, Alexander Hamilton dealt with this question of reconciliation. An antifederalist writer known to us only as Brutus (said to be Robert Yates, a New York delegate to the Constitutional Convention) had charged that a judiciary independent of political control and armed with the power of judicial review would subvert the autonomy of the states by expanding national powers.[11] The proposed Constitution, Brutus charged, was vague enough to permit subjective prejudices to influence the decisions of the Supreme Court, and the people would have no recourse from politically charged judicial interpretations of the document. Such a scheme made courts, not the legislature, the ultimate governing authority.

Brutus preferred legislative interpretation of the Constitution to keep it subject to democratic control. Legislators could expand their authority only at their own electoral peril.[12] Their understanding of the Constitution would be revealed in the bills they chose to pass, since it is doubtful that legislators would ever support a bill they believed unconstitutional. Once a bill passed in the legislature, it and the constitutional interpretation it represented would be binding on the courts. Judges could not declare it void. It was in reply to Brutus that Hamilton penned Federalist Paper #78, offering two rebuttals that might initially appear inconsistent.

First, Hamilton reassured his readers that the judiciary was not an institution they should fear but was in fact "the least dangerous to the political rights of the Constitution," being always "the least in a capacity to annoy or injure them." Since the courts do not wield the coercive power of the government or the ability to bestow rewards, powers lodged in the executive, and since courts do not control the legislature's powers of law-making or appropriations, judges have no autonomous power to act on their political ambitions. Thus, wrote Hamilton, "it may truly be said [that courts] have neither FORCE nor WILL, but merely judgement."[13]

This distinction between will and judgment requires some elaboration. By "will," Hamilton referred to a choice between political alternatives, based on policy preferences. A legislature exercises will when it passes a bill, as does the president when he or she signs the bill into law or vetoes it. A constitutional convention exercises will when it chooses a separation of powers model of government over a parliamentary one or when it writes into a constitution individual rights that constrain the power of majorities. It was will that Brutus feared the judiciary would use to expand national powers at the expense of the states. We can think of will as the translation of ideological preferences into public policy, a feat accomplished through the application of political power to create preferred patterns of behavior.

What Hamilton called "judgment" was the subordinate power of applying legal standards already willed by another power to the particular case at hand. Judgment did not involve any individual discretion on the part of the judge but faithfully embodied the will of the legislature or a constitutional convention—and resolved disputes in a way determined by the willing agency. Confined to mere judgment, the court only discovered what the sovereign authority had willed. We have seen this theory of judicial discovery in Chapter 1, under the rubric of formalism. We noted there that this depiction of the judicial decision is popular with the public because it comports with the layperson's expectations of adjudication and on the bench because it diverts attention away from judicial responsibility for the choices made and serves to legitimize the decision. We have also seen that contemporary jurisprudence is skeptical of formalism, at least as an empirical description of what judges do. Brutus did not buy this theory of judicial decision making, and, one must suspect, neither did Hamilton, at least not in his heart. In Federalist Paper #80 Hamilton revealed his distrust of state judges and of the formalist view of judging by arguing that state courts could not be trusted with sole authority to interpret the Constitution because they would be prejudiced in favor of local political interests: "Thirteen independent courts of final jurisdiction over the same causes arising upon the same laws, is a hydra in government."[14] Perhaps so, but what was true for the state courts ought to have been equally true for federal courts.

Yet, Hamilton's argument demonstrates another reason for the popularity of the formalist view of judging, one we ought not ignore. Whatever its empirical merit, formalism as a normative theory does offer some basis for criticism of judges' performance, and the presence of a secure standard for criticism may impose some temperance on judges' power. Isn't that what a constitution is supposed to accomplish? If the powers of the legislator and executive are dangerous and in need of restraint, so too is the power of judges. To the degree that adjudication can be moved in the direction of formalism, we might worry less about abuses by the courts, for their choice would be more closely confined by law.

If, on the other hand, modern jurisprudence rejects formalism as an untenable empirical description of judging, we might also have to abandon it as a normative basis for criticism. Without this basis for criticism, modern formalists argue, judicial power will become dangerous indeed, turning the courts into roving commissions defining the content of public policy under the control of no one. We have already observed this problem in our discussion of statutory interpretation. In constitutional cases judicial discretion is even more disconcerting, because, as Brutus observed, there is no electoral corrective for errors or flagrant abuses. We may have to face the possibility that Hamilton's defense of judicial review is contingent on acceptance of this tenuous distinction between will and judgment.

Having reassured his audience that the courts were too confined to be a threat, Hamilton proceeded to his second argument, that judicial review was a positive good since it enabled courts to employ considerable power in defense of the citizen's rights. This argument was complex, requiring detailed discussion. Hamilton's claim, which may be doubted, was that a constitution limiting legislative authority cannot succeed without judicial review. This is true because legislators, and the majorities they represent, are not trustworthy judges of the limits of their own political authority. In making this assertion, Hamilton revealed typical constitutionalist suspicion of human nature, particularly of the average citizen's ability to remain virtuous in the face of the temptations of power, and of the average politician's ability to resist popular sentiment for unwise or tyrannical policies. But notice that first Hamilton assured us that courts were too weak to be a threat, then he described them as powerful in the defense of rights. We will have to ask how it is that Hamilton can have it both ways, if indeed he can.

Hamilton used the common law principle of agency to explain the origin of legislative power. Agency describes the relationship between persons whereby one, the principal, authorizes another, the agent, to act in his or her behalf. The agent does for the principal what he or she would do for himself or herself, had he or she sufficient time or expertise or were he or she otherwise in a position to act in his or her own interests. When he or she acts properly, the agent's decisions are treated in law as if they were actions of the principal. If the agent entered into a contract, for example, and if such was within his or her authority, then the contract would be binding on the principal's future conduct. But the scope of an agent's power is no greater that which the principal delegated to him or her. If an agent performed acts that the principal never authorized, those acts were void and would in court be deprived of all legal significance.

Hamilton's analogy is not hard to grasp. The people were the principal, the legislature was their agent. The legislature acted on behalf of the people, but only within the scope of powers they delegated to it in the Constitution. The Constitution was treated as a social contract that created the agency relationship. But should the legislature ever be tempted to exceed those delegated powers, such an act would violate the Constitution. Would the people who were suffering the abuses of a renegade legislature be without a remedy? Not so long as an independent judiciary stood ready to enforce constitutional limits on legislative power by nullifying all attempts to exceed them. Such would be the proper role of litigation between principal and agent in the common law. According to Hamilton, such was proper when issues of constitutional law were raised in suits by citizens against public officials. Were courts not equipped with the power of judicial review, the people would be helpless in the face of legislative abuse. In such circumstances, the power of the agent would exceed that of the principal, or the power of the representatives would be greater than those whom they represent. Such a proposition would be plainly absurd. Thus, even without a clause in the Constitution expressly authorizing judicial review, Hamilton found it a necessary inference from the very nature of a written constitution.

Hamilton portrayed the courts as "an intermediate body" between the people and a renegade legislature.[15] Judges stand ready to act as a barrier against encroaching political power by blocking any attempt by legislators to reach beyond the powers the people have authorized them to exercise. Contrary to Brutus's assertion, when the courts declared legislation unconstitutional, it was not because they were superior to the legislature at all, but rather because the Constitution was superior to both.

Notice that this claim makes sense only if the court that purports to enforce constitutional limits on legislative power employs pure judgment, uncorrupted by will. Were the court behaving willfully, not only would its interpretation of the

Constitution be suspect, but the danger of judicial tyranny Brutus raised would be very real. Of course, the legislature is properly willful, but only within constitutional limits. If those limits can be objectively known by judges, so that a dispassionate judgment could be made that they had been exceeded, then judicial review would not be threatening. Here, then, is the resolution of Hamilton's apparent inconsistency. Courts acting on will would be too weak to threaten the community, but when acting upon judgement courts would be powerful enough to prevent legislative tyranny.

In Federalist Paper #51, James Madison had already conceded that frequent elections were the primary defense against legislative tyranny.[16] Brutus also had suggested that legislative abuse could be prevented through the democratic processes. Why was Hamilton not satisfied with elections as the sole means for remedying legislative abuse? He would have to admit that if the legislature set on a certain policy, it would be at the urging of the people in the last election. Why do the people need a nondemocratic body like the courts to protect them from the legislature they elected? Do the people need to be protected from themselves? Or is there an important distinction between the people acting in their sovereign capacity when they adopt a constitution and the people acting in their political capacity when they elect a legislature?

There are two closely related answers to this question. Hamilton's first answer was to remind his readers of the heterogeneous nature of society, such that a majority might tyrannize a minority without imposing a great deal of pain on itself. Obviously, a weak minority has already lost at the electoral process and so cannot rely on the democratic politics to protect it from the depredations of an impassioned majority. But at times the people may, indeed, need to be protected from themselves—at least from their own ill-considered acts. Said Hamilton:

> . . . [the] independence of the judges is equally requisite to guard the Constitution and the rights of individuals from the effects of those ill humors, which the arts of designing men, or the influence of particular conjunctures, sometimes disseminate among the people themselves, and which, though they speedily give place to better information, and more deliberate reflection, have a tendency, in the meantime, to occasion dangerous innovations in the government and serious oppressions of the minor party in the community.[17]

Implicit in this passage is an important assumption about human psychology. People are to some degree capable of the kind of rational and responsible political judgment we previously called civic virtue. Were such virtue altogether beyond the reach of the human personality, constitutional democracy would be impossibly utopian. The problem of democratic politics is that peoples' rational judgment can too easily be corrupted by self-interest. It is not that people are bad: their egoism is a natural consequence of their free will combined with their self-love. Only with great effort is the community able to transcend self-interested passions, at least temporarily, as, it is hoped, they do when acting in their sovereign capacity, when adopting a constitution. A constitution sets out the rules by which the community wishes to be governed. It might be said to establish the rules of the political game, but somewhat remote from the determination of actual winners and losers. Discussion of a constitution is a particularly solemn occasion likely to bring out the best in the community's deliberate judgment. However, such virtue is short-lived, and such strenuous effort cannot be repeated often.

Once the rules are set and the game is put into play, people revert to their political capacity and begin to behave differently. It is simply expecting too much of the human personality to anticipate that people will remain rational and virtuous through the rough-and-tumble of day-to-day politics. With the allocations of material wealth, status, opportunity, and power more immediately in the balance, people descend into the kind of selfish egoism that constitutionalists instinctively fear. A community can be aided in this descent by the evil schemes of demagogues or by calamitous events, or the majority might become drunk on its own power and cease to heed its own better judgment. Minority groups become inviting targets for the displacement of burdens, while the majority seeks only to benefit itself. The community's devotion to the common good gives way to a political feeding frenzy of special interests in which only the strongest prevail. In such an environment, could a virtuous legislator say to his or her constituents, "I know what you want, and I'd love to give it to you—but I can't because it is not in the common interest, it would unjustly injure a weak minority, and, besides, it is unconstitutional"—and still expect to be returned to the legislature in the next election? Hamilton assumed not.

This is not to say that courts should be trusted always to display a virtue that is absent from the rest of society. Hamilton admitted that an "individual oppression" might from time to time emanate from the courts, but most often courts were sufficiently hemmed in by other branches of government to make willful departures from the law a futile endeavor. At least until the people, by calm and deliberate judgment, choose to alter their constitution through the difficult amending process, one calling forth a renewed sense of virtue, the constitutional decisions of the courts will remain binding on the power of the majority. Considering a constitutional amendment, the people acting in their sovereign capacity would reaffirm or reject the decision of the people in their political capacity.

Seen in this light, judicial review might be treated as an appeal from the people drunk from politics to the people sobered by reason. In the short term, the majority might resent court-imposed restraints on its power, but in the long run the majority will probably come around to seeing the wrongfulness of their ways. In other words, the reason a democratic society might rationally elect to have judicial review as a constraint on democratic choice is that it protects us from the biggest threat we face—ourselves.

Judicial Review and Democracy

In the previous section we explored the tension built into constitutional democracy. We noted that judicial review is but one of several American devices for enforcing constitutional restraints on the democratic process. There are others, of course, and although these are every bit as countermajoritarian as judicial review, they tend to be much less controversial. If the countermajoritarian role of courts frequently renders them unpopular, the judges' relative political insulation also makes them uniquely able to protect minority rights when they are threatened by popular majorities. If American society values the idea of rights and expresses that value through the adoption of a constitution, then it might find reason to be receptive to judicial review as well. Americans seem to sense this, for however controversial particular instances of judicial review might be, the practice could not long survive without popular acquiescence. This acceptance of judicial restraint on the majority's power might be a product of inertia or habit, or perhaps Americans realize at some level that all of us are minorities who might someday be potential claimants of rights against a powerful majority.

We also noted in passing the peculiar fact that the Constitution does not provide explicitly for judicial review. Before turning to the question of how courts go about interpreting the Constitution, we ought to explore further the origins of this unstated power. Searching through the text of the Constitution, the closest we will come to an explicit authorization for judicial review is the "supremacy clause" of Article VI:

> This Constitution, and all the laws of the United States which shall be made in Pursuance thereof . . . shall be the supreme law of the land; and the Judges in every State shall be bound thereby, any Thing in the Constitution or Laws of any State to the Contrary notwithstanding.

Here is a clear statement that the Constitution was meant to be binding as law, and as the highest law at that. The Constitution was controlling on all acts of government authority. This clause also settles an important federalism issue: in conflicts between the laws of a state and the laws of the United States, the former must yield to the latter, when they have been properly enacted. Notice that this clause is explicitly directed at "the Judges in every state." Whether these are state judges exclusively or state and federal judges, both of whom would be found "in every state," is unclear. What is clear is that "the Judges" are told they must resolve conflicts between state and national laws and that a state law contrary to the Constitution is invalid for purposes of adjudication. So we have a textual authorization of judicial review over the states by lower courts. We can bring these decisions under the appellate review of the United States Supreme Court by reference back to Article III, Section 2:

> The judicial Power shall extend to all Cases . . . arising under this Constitution. . . . In all cases [except a narrow original jurisdiction] the Supreme Court shall have appellate jurisdiction, both as to Law and Fact, with such Exceptions, and under such Regulations as the Congress shall make.

Judicial review over state laws is justified on textual grounds. We might also appeal to a structural theory of federalism to justify such power, since, as Hamilton noted in Federalist Paper #80, unity of interpretation of national law can be supplied only by a single national appellate court. We saw in Chapter 2 how important, yet how qualified, this unifying function of the Supreme Court can be.

What is missing so far is a justification for judicial review over the coordinate branches of the federal government, Congress and the executive. Hamilton was willing to postulate such a power as necessary to the very viability of a written constitution, since a written constitution is intended to be a practical limit on government power. But it is odd that so important a judicial role was not explicitly included in the text of the Constitution. If truly intended by the framers, would they have left judicial review to implication? Arguments similar to Hamilton's were adopted by the Supreme Court to explain its first use of judicial review, in the 1803 decision in *Marbury v. Madison*.[18] In this case a portion of the Judiciary Act of 1789, said to confer an original jurisdiction on the Supreme Court exceeding that permitted by Article III of the Constitution, was declared void. Since this was the first instance of judicial nullification of legislation, the Court had to explain how it acquired such power. The opinion of the Court, written by Chief Justice John Marshall, has provoked anxiety for generations of students of constitutional law. For our purposes, we can reduce the main argument to the following summary:

> [T]he people have an original right to establish, for their future government such principles as in their opinion shall be most conducive to their own happiness . . . The principles, therefore, so established, are deemed fundamental. And as the authority from which they proceed [the people] is supreme, and can seldom act, they are designed to be permanent.
>
> The powers of the legislature are defined and limited . . . The distinction between a government of limited and unlimited powers is abolished if those limits do not confine the persons on whom they are imposed . . . it is a proposition too plain to be contested that either the constitution controls any legislative act repugnant to it; or that the legislature may alter the constitution by an ordinary act.
>
> Between these alternatives there is no middle ground. The constitution is either superior paramount law, unchangeable by ordinary means, or it is on the level with ordinary legislative acts, and like other acts, is alterable when the legislature shall please to alter it. If the former part of the alternative be true, then a legislative act contrary to the constitution is not law; if the latter part be true, then written constitutions are absurd attempts on the part of the people to limit a power in its own nature illimitable.[19]

Chief Justice Marshall would be among the last to agree that constitutions are absurd attempts to limit a power that can never be limited. Such would run contrary to one of the most fundamental axioms of American politics and would even undermine the thesis of popular sovereignty that forms Marshall's first premise. Obviously, therefore, any act "repugnant" to the Constitution must be a legal nullity. So far, Marshall's argument has only established the theory of constitutionalism, something few Americans would reject. Translating this into judicial review was a bit more of a challenge. Surely Congress, representing the people, interpreted the Constitution when it enacted the Judiciary Act. President Washington interpreted the Constitution when he signed the bill into law. They thought the Judiciary Act of 1789 was perfectly consistent with the Constitution— otherwise, they would not have passed it. Should not the interpretation given the Constitution by the representative branches be final? How does an alleged violation of the Constitution become a judicial problem, and why is the judicial interpretation authoritative? Consider Marshall's conclusion:

> It is emphatically the province and the duty of the judicial department to say what the law is. Those who apply the rule to particular cases must of necessity expound and interpret that rule. If two laws conflict with each other, courts must decide on the operation of each.
>
> So if a law be in opposition to the constitution; if both the law and the constitution apply to a particular case, so that the court must either decide the case conformably to the constitution, disregarding the law; or conformably to the law, disre-

garding the constitution; the court must determine which of these conflicting rules governs the case. This is of the very essence of judicial duty.[20]

Marshall was comparing this case to a situation in which more than a single law might apply to a particular set of facts. Such "conflicts of law" problems are common in ordinary litigation. We noted previously several instances of conflicts of law, as when courts must choose between conflicting precedents or between the common law and a statute. Sometimes statutes contradict each other as well. When they do, the courts will generally apply the most recent statute, assuming the legislature that enacted the recent statute intended to amend or supersede the previous statute. Since both statutes originate from the authority of the legislature, and since the legislature is entitled to change its mind, there is little here that is controversial.

However, when a conflict arises between a statute and the Constitution, Marshall would have us believe the situation is similar insofar as it is an ordinary part of adjudication—requiring "mere Judgement"—for the Court to resolve the conflict by deciding which law to apply. Yet the situation is different insofar as it is the older Constitution that will govern the case, not the more recent statute. This is because the Constitution flows from a higher authority than a statute and because it is more permanently anchored than the shifting sands of ordinary politics. Anything else would "subvert the very foundation of all written constitutions."

The argument in *Marbury* is not airtight, for Marshall has neglected to tell us why it is the judicial interpretation of the Constitution, not the legislative interpretation, that must be applied to a case.[21] Indeed, we can accept Marshall's final contention that constitutional restraints cannot survive without judicial review only if we ignore the several written constitutions in force around the world without the benefits of judicial enforcement. Criticizing Marshall's circular reasoning has become a virtual rite of initiation among students of constitutional law. It is enough for our purposes to note that despite its logical and empirical flaws, the *Marbury* opinion has supplied a rationale for judicial review accepted by courts and the American public long since. What remains to be considered is the extent of the interpretive latitude courts may legitimately exercise when evaluating statutes under the Constitution.

The easy answer that must be immediately dispensed with is that no latitude is necessary, for the Constitution means just what it says. One frequently hears the argument that the courts ought to confine their activities "to interpreting the law as it exists, rather than legislating from the bench."[22] Our discussion of statutory interpretation ought to take care of any lingering belief that a legal text contains the full measure of its meaning in its explicit terms, yet formalists frequently suggest that the scope of interpretive latitude is so narrow and the rules of interpretation so obvious, that a singularly correct understanding of the text is entirely within reach. Marshall's rhetoric in *Marbury* suggested that there can be absolutely no question that the Judiciary Act of 1789 was in violation of the Constitution. One is left to wonder, then, how it was that the First Congress, containing a number of former delegates to the Constitutional Convention (including James Madison), the very people who had written the document, could have passed such a bill. The fact is that statutes as flagrantly unconstitutional as Marshall described in *Marbury* would not pass Congress. Rather, courts confront situations in which several interpretations of the Constitution are possible, and whereas Congress has preferred one interpretation, the Court prefers another.

Reading the Text

It is constitutional ambiguity that makes judicial review both necessary and controversial. As with statutes, were constitutional language absolutely pristine and unambiguous, there would be little need for adjudication, and courts could probably be eliminated from the political system. We might state as a general rule the proposition that the likelihood of constitutional litigation increases as the clarity of the appropriate text decreases. But why is the Constitution so ambiguous? Could not the framers have been more clear in relating to us their political vision? After all, the purpose of a constitution is to restrain political power, and a vague constitution that might bear multiple interpretations will not do this very well at all. But the simple fact, borne of much experience, is that some textual vagueness is inevitable in a constitution, while some of it may even be of practical value. The reasons are several. Again, we confront the disorderly conduct of words. Language is an imperfect instrument for conveying thought even among contemporaries—a fact recognized by James Madison in Federalist Paper #37:

> When the Almighty himself condescends to address mankind in their own language, his meaning, luminous as it must be, is rendered dim and doubtful by the cloudy medium through which it is communicated.[23]

The imprecision of language is exacerbated when we seek to communicate over the historical space of 200 years. Not only will the meaning of words change, but the circumstances to which those words might be applied will change in ways the authors could never have foreseen. For example, the framers of the Fourth Amendment, seeking protection against "unreasonable searches and seizures," could never have foreseen the problems associated with wire taps and electronic surveillance, yet it is their eighteenth century text, with its reference to the physical seizure of tangible things, that must be applied to these contemporary threats to individual privacy.[24]

Impressive as they were, the framers also fell somewhat short of the Almighty, so Madison had to concede additional reasons for constitutional ambiguity. Their very thoughts were often less than "luminous." Tentative or ill-conceived thought produces a vague text. For example, after a number of false starts, the delegates to the Constitutional Convention developed fairly precise ideas about how to choose a president, yet they remained uncertain about the powers he or she should hold and consequently described them in vague terms. In addition, the complex nature of political relationships sometimes defies a priori understanding. The precise division between legislative and executive powers, for example, has eluded the most profound thinkers and has had to be worked out through the experience of two centuries.

We might add further reasons for ambiguity to Madison's list. Delegates, like legislators, frequently had to compromise to arrive at a text on which all could agree. Compromise often is achieved by writing a general text and deferring to the future difficult judgments about specific details. Some omissions, the president's cabinet for example, may even have been deliberate to permit flexibility in dealing with future exigencies that could not be foreseen in 1787. It should be apparent that the most explicit constitution is not necessarily the most perfect constitution if we intend that constitution to "endure for ages to come."[25] To the contrary, ambiguity might play a positive role in drafting a constitution.

Consider the following clauses, here taken out of order from Article II, creating the office of president:

> He shall hold his Office during a Term of four years . . .
> No person except a natural born Citizen . . . shall be eligible to the Office of President . . .
> The executive Power shall be vested in a President of the United States of America.

The first of these clauses seems clear enough. Everybody knows that four years does not mean five years, and, so far at least, every president who did not secure reelection (assuming he was still eligible under the Twenty-Second Amendment) has voluntarily vacated the premises at 1600 Pennsylvania Avenue in a timely fashion. There has been no controversy over this clause because there is little room for differences of opinion concerning its meaning.

The second clause is a bit more troublesome. Did the framers intend to exclude from eligibility persons whose birth had not been "natural"? Did they intend to protect some future incumbent from succumbing to MacBeth's fallacy by ensuring he or she could never be unseated by a candidate who had entered this world by cesarean section? It is the accepted understanding of this clause that the framers meant to limit eligibility for the chief executive office to persons who were native-born citizens and exclude from consideration those who had been naturalized, but one could not be sure of this merely from a close reading of the text. One has to consult historical sources outside of Article II to know that the framers were not thinking of Shakespeare. Incidentally, this is the only place where the Constitution makes a distinction between native-born and naturalized citizens. Even so, it remains unsettled whether a candidate must have been born on American territory or whether a candidate born abroad but to American parents is a "natural born Citizen" for purposes of the Constitution. Only legislatively have we adopted both geography and parentage as independently conferring citizenship.

The third clause (actually the opening of Article II) has been the subject of considerably more controversy and litigation. The clause does settle one important question by telling us there will be only one president, rather than the plural executive preferred by some of the framers. We are also told what the chief executive's title will be. But there has long been sharp dispute over whether this clause was intended merely to describe the president's function—to execute laws enacted by Congress—or whether it conferred on the president independent powers, including all those executive in nature. The former interpretation would produce a relatively weak president largely dependent on the will of Congress. The latter, in contrast, would produce a powerful president, able to act on his or her own initiative and in sweeping fashion, without having to await legislative authorization.

The latter interpretation is today dominant, but even if we accept this theory we are still left in the dark concerning the breadth of the power granted. Does "the executive power" include the power to declare American neutrality in foreign conflicts? To dismiss executive officials without the advice and consent of the Senate? To enter into executive agreements? To impound funds appropriated by Congress? Does this clause support a claim of executive privilege, to keep from Congress information it considers vital to the legislative process? Or to keep information from the courts, when such is needed as evidence in a criminal trial? These and other controversies have occupied our attention under the executive powers clause, and some have been settled in court.[26] The answers cannot be known from the text alone, or even the text supplemented by what we know of the intent of the framers. The answer must come from political theory of what the proper role of the president should be, albeit political theory in the form of a judicial decision.

Now take another look at the first clause, the one previously treated as having a self-contained meaning. Suppose a woman were to run for the office, as will surely happen in the not too distant future. Would anyone seriously contend that she would be unqualified for the office because the framers used the male pronoun? It is doubtful that the framers even considered the possibility of a female president, but we would be more comfortable than the eighteenth century would have been in treating *he* as a generic term including all persons. In contemporary application, we see how even this relatively pristine text is in need of interpretation.

When we shift ground from government powers to human rights, our interpretive dilemma is not left behind. Consider the following, from the First Amendment:

Congress shall make no law . . . abridging the freedom of speech, or of the press . . .

No matter how clear it is that "no law" means "no law," we are still left to determine for ourselves the scope of "the freedom of speech, or of the press." We must admit that "freedom" is as ambiguous a modifier for "speech" or "press" as the framers could have found! The First Amendment cannot extend constitutional protection to every conceivable form of talking or printing. Surely a counterfeiter caught red-handed running off $20 bills in the basement cannot plead freedom of the press as a defense against prosecution. Similarly, we have to decide whether "the freedom of speech" includes speaking that provokes a violent response or speech that is offensive, obscene, defamatory, or that incites illegal behavior, or which might constitute espionage or promote prejudice against minority groups.[27]

If the Constitution protects something less than all forms of speaking and printing, it also protects some forms of conduct in addition to those using words. Speech-enhancing conduct such as picketing or protest marching deserves some level of protection. Symbolic speech, action devoid of words but often poignantly expressive of ideas, also qualifies for some protection. One recent example that generated considerable public disapproval was *Texas v. Johnson,* in which the Supreme Court held that the public burning of an American flag was expressive

conduct (as was saluting the flag in prior litigation) and so was entitled to constitutional protection.[28] Freedom of speech is of little meaning unless it includes protection for the expression of ideas the majority hates. But some authority, perhaps
one not beholden to the majority, has to decide the breadth of protection the First
Amendment offers against attempts by the powerful to coerce conformity.

It should be clear by now that the Constitution requires considerable interpretation. As with statutes, this process must be understood as interstitial rule
making by the courts. The big question still remains: How much freedom of interpretation is legitimate? A constitution that is absolutely rigid and unchanging will
soon be hopelessly outdated. One that can be bent into any shape we please will
fail at its intended purpose of restraining political power. A further issue, one con-
ceptually distinct but often debated alongside the issue of latitude, is who ultimately controls the interpretive process when the vague clauses are at issue? Political authorities, especially legislators, are the first to construe the Constitution,
but to what extent is their interpretation subject to revision by judges? Or, to put
the question in practical terms, who holds the ultimate authority to interpret the
Constitution—the democratic institutions or the nondemocratic courts?

For our purposes, we will divide approaches to constitutional interpretation
into three categories—restrained judicial review, creative judicial review, and representation-reinforcing judicial review.[29] These categories are somewhat artificial,
but they will be useful to illuminate how different schools of thought produce different interpretive theories for human rights disputes. For each, we shall be concerned with the proper role of courts as authoritative interpretive forums and how
judicial review might best be reconciled with popular sovereignty. We shall test
each theory by examining some specific instances of judicial interpretation of constitutional rights.

Remember that Supreme Court justices are not elected. During their tenure,
so long as they avoid the remote possibility of impeachment, they are largely beyond the reach of the majority. Can decisions about the fairness of policy, issues
that are ideological at their root, be made conformably to Hamilton's distinction
between will and judgment? If not, what are the limits of acceptable will in an unelected judiciary?

Restrained Judicial Review

Debate over how the Constitution should be interpreted is a fairly new academic
phenomenon. While specific interpretations of this or that clause were in the past
controversial, it is only in response to the legal realists and recent judicial innovations that debate over the grand theories of constitutional interpretation has acquired a seemingly religious intensity. Recall that the realists' attack on formalism
and its "declaratory" theory of the judicial decision exposed the discretion judges
brought to the bench. If the judicial decision was not predetermined, if the end
result was not already implied in the legal problem a case presented, then extralegal factors, including political ideology or even wholly idiosyncratic considerations, might play a substantial role in the decision. The product of such adjudication could not very well be understood as a "discovery" of the law. This frank

acknowledgment of discretion in adjudication created particularly acute problems for judicial review.

We have seen that both Alexander Hamilton and John Marshall defended judicial review on the grounds that courts were only carrying out policies mandated by the people in their sovereign capacities, that is, when they adopted or amended the Constitution. Judicial review could then be portrayed as the product of popular sovereignty and therefore as legitimate as the majoritarian procedures it counterpoised. Judicial discretion threatened to substitute the judge's policy choices for those of the people in either their sovereign or their political roles. This erosion of the linkage between judicial review and democratic legitimacy implied by realism, combined with the controversial rights activism of the Supreme Court during the 1960s and early 1970s, spawned contemporary political and scholarly interest in the grand theories of how the Constitution ought to be interpreted.

We shall begin our journey into the thickets of contemporary constitutional jurisprudence with those who are most suspicious of judicial power. Variously known in scholarly circles as "interpretivists," "originalists," or "textual determinists," members of this school of thought seek to minimize the role courts play in policy making by sharply circumscribing judges' interpretive discretion. This they accomplish by attempting to confine judicial discretion to the most "objective" standards attainable. While they reject Blackstone's reflexive discovery theory of the judicial decision, they seek to move the practice of judging as close to that model as possible, representing a kind of neoformalism. This has meant restricting judicial discretion to decide a case to a literal reading of the text or, at most, to the necessary implications of the text. In the process, they would expand the latitude granted the democratic branches in policy making, especially that of the legislature. Viewed another way, their jurisprudence maximizes the power of majorities over the community's political development, but at the cost of rights valuable to minority groups. In a sense, greater popular sovereignty is purchased at the cost of reduced constitutionalism.

Of course, where the text is literally clear, or its implications truly necessary, few would quibble with the idea that judges should follow it faithfully. What the legal realists demonstrated was the indeterminacy of legal texts, an insight begrudgingly acknowledged by contemporary interpretivists. How, then, can they find confining standards in the open texture of the constitutional text? There are two answers to this question that are somewhat at variance with each other. The first answer is to propose that when a text is ambiguous enough to support multiple meanings, judges should search through the historical record to discover how the provision was understood by those who wrote and adopted it. In the parlance of the modern debate, judges should follow the "original intent of the framers," hence the designation "originalist" to describe this theory. While the original meaning of the text might be applied to new circumstances by contemporary judges, these theorists object most vociferously to the attribution of any new meaning to the Constitution that was not entertained by its framers. Professor Mark Tushnet, a member of the Critical Legal Studies group and a critic of originalism, describes the theory succinctly: "Originalism claims that the courts should invalidate legislation only if it is inconsistent with the text of the Constitution as understood by those who wrote and adopted it."[30]

Let's consider an example. In 1983 the Supreme Court decided the case of *Marsh v. Chambers*.[31] The legislature of Nebraska, in common with other state legislatures and Congress, had for years commenced each business day with a short prayer led by a clergyman who was paid a fee from the state treasury. This practice was challenged in litigation as symbolically placing the state's seal of approval on Christian religion, thus violating the First Amendment's provision that "Congress shall make no law respecting an establishment of religion." This amendment originally applied only to acts of the federal government, but around the middle of the twentieth century the Supreme Court held that the Fourteenth Amendment that had been adopted after the Civil War made similar standards binding on acts of the states (a theory rejected by originalists but not contested here). All can agree that the First Amendment, at minimum, prevents government from establishing a church. The more difficult question is: Does a legislature make a "law respecting an establishment of religion" when it hires a chaplain to lead a daily prayer? One can stare at the text of the First Amendment for a long time without discovering an answer.

The Court's answer was that legislative prayer did not violate the terms of the First Amendment. The majority opinion, by Chief Justice Burger, explained this decision by putatively appealing to what the First Amendment's framers would say if we could present the question to them. Since we obviously cannot consult with the framers directly, Burger's approach was to draw inferences from what the historical record revealed about their thoughts on the matter. As it turns out, the First Congress had authorized the appointment of a paid legislative chaplain just three days prior to its own final action proposing the First Amendment to the states for ratification. Assuming legislators would never say one thing and do another, Burger concluded that the framers of the First Amendment did not understand it to prohibit legislative chaplains. It might be objected that the First Amendment was not yet law when the First Congress acted to authorize a chaplain. But two years later, after ratification of the First Amendment, Congress did not repeal its earlier act; in fact, it continues to hire a chaplain to this day. What the First Amendment apparently meant in 1789 it must still mean today, and so chaplains who open the legislative day with prayer do not violate the Constitution.

There is at first something beguiling about this theory of interpretation. Not only does it seem to confine judicial discretion and preserve the link between judicial review and popular sovereignty, but originalism comports with the theory of meaning most of us ascribe to a written text—that it embodies the author's intentions. However, there are a number of problems with originalism, several of which were touched on by Justice William Brennan in his dissenting opinion for *Marsh*. First, before we can confine the courts to an explication of the intent of the framers, we need some criterion that determines who counts as a member of that august group. Notice that in his *Marsh* opinion the chief justice examined the practice of the First Congress. But Congress can only propose an amendment: before it is legally binding, that proposal must be ratified by the legislatures of three-quarters of the states. Members of ratifying legislatures (or conventions) in the states must also be counted as framers. Yet, originalists seldom look beyond Congress or the Constitutional Convention in search of the framers' intent. The reason for this arbitrary selectivity may lie in the fact that consulting ratifiers as well as proposers will multiply severalfold the number of framers whose intent must be ascertained. Indeed, it is not clear why the "framers" should be limited to those who participated in the process as office holders. Popular debate, as revealed in newspaper editorials, speeches, statements of interest groups, and the like, all contribute to a climate of public opinion that influences the adoption process. Why not count the people behind such opinion as "framers"?

If we adopt a more comprehensive definition of "framer," we will face another problem that the student might already anticipate. A large number of framers—even a single framer—might have acted with a variety of conflicting intentions and reveal multiple understandings of a single text. So whose intent is definitive when the framers seem to be in disagreement, as they so often were? And what evidence of their intent is admissible? What a legislator said in committee? On the floor of Congress? Before his or her constituents? In personal correspondence, notes, or diaries? Prior to legislative action? How long afterward? What if these conflict?

The case of James Madison is instructive here. The man who authored and presented to the House of Representatives the proposal that eventually became the First Amendment should certainly qualify as a framer. Madison, at several junctures in his political career, offered a fairly strict theory of the separation of church and state, even by today's standards. He also voted in Congress in favor of the authorization of a legislative chaplain, and so appears to have accepted legislative chaplains as consistent with the Constitution. Yet privately, Madison complained that the congressional chaplain violated the First Amendment.[32] Which represents Madison's intent? As a constitutional theorist, Madison may have intended the strictest separation of religion and politics, yet as a legislator he also knew he had to respond to constituent pressures of the moment. Considerations relating solely to political survival beyond the next election weigh heavily on a politician's behavior, sometimes eclipsing better constitutional judgment. Viewed in this light, Madison's constitutional intent may not have always been revealed by his political practice. Remember, Madison was only one of almost a hundred congressmen and a few hundred framers, even by a strict definition! With such erratic behavior, discerning the intents of all the framers and combining them into some coherent theory of the First Amendment would be a challenge, to say the least.

Some originalists seek a way around this objection by arguing that subjective intents are irrelevant. What determines original intent, it is said, is how the words would have been understood by the greater society at the time of their adoption.[33] Unfortunately, we are not told how this societal understanding can be retrieved, other than through a kind of sum totaling of subjective intentions of a very large number of persons. This will be a slippery process at best, one not likely to supply objectivity to decisions nor seriously to confine judicial discretion the way originalists claim. It seems very likely that the subjective preferences of the historian must color the version of the intent of the framers he or she is able to discern.

It is noteworthy that the Court did not even purport to rely on the legislative history of the First Amendment itself to decide *Marsh*. The record of congressional debate is quite sketchy. This points to another problem—the paucity of the historical record surrounding the adoption of many of the Constitution's key provisions. We have no verbatim transcript of the Constitutional Convention. Our most reliable source for studying the convention is a notebook kept by Madison, which he subsequently edited and which was published posthumously in 1840. In his notebook, Madison related to us only summary versions of positions taken by the delegates. Records of state ratifying conventions are similarly cryptic. Even the more recent amendments proposed by Congress are accompanied by ambiguous and often contradictory historical records. The fact is that the historical record is also subject to interpretation.

Historians frequently disparage lawyers' practice of selecting from whatever records exist only the evidence that supports their desired conclusion, ignoring the rest, as "law office history," yet even the most eminent historians frequently disagree over the meaning to be attached to the historical record. It should come as no surprise by now that the need for interpretation brings with it discretion—the very evil from which originalism was to deliver us. The more insightful originalists acknowledge this, arguing that the discretion their theory permits is still more confined than any of the alternatives. This may be a fair argument, but in making it they concede at least half the battle to their opponents.

Aside from these practical difficulties, there is a peculiar logical flaw that runs through this interpretive theory: none of its proponents have demonstrated that the framers intended the meaning of the Constitution to be confined to their own specific intentions. If the framers did not intend the theory of original intent, then the theory fails to satisfy its own criterion of constitutional validity. It seems odd that Madison would have kept his record of the Constitutional Convention a secret for over half a century if the delegates' intentions were thought to be dispositive of all constitutional controversies. Nor were former framers in the habit of appealing to their original intent throughout all of the subsequent constitutional battles they fought, even among themselves. Recall Madison's acknowledgment of the Constitution's ambiguity in Federalist Paper #39, cited earlier in this chapter. Nowhere did Madison suggest that the secret of textual clarity was locked away in his colleagues' subjective intents. Surely no prudent voter would support a constitution presented in such terms. This question has been explored by Professor H. Jefferson Powell. He finds that the framers believed, when they thought of it at all, that the common law techniques of interpretation, which did not include adherence to framers' subjective intent(s), were adequate for the Constitution.[34] It was, after all, the text of the Constitution, for all its ambiguity, that was ratified, and not the framers' speeches, letters, and whatnot.

Finally, what are we to make of the framers' use of open-textured language, words capable of creative interpretation, when alternative styles of expression were surely available? They were an impressively literate group of people who were capable, at least some of the time, of considerable specificity. Was their choice of words such as "establishment of religion" deliberate? They could have said only "Congress shall not create a church," had that been the extent of their meaning. When they also chose words such as "the freedom of speech," "executive power," "cruel and unusual punishment," or "due process of law," they might have purposely building into the Constitution a certain degree of flexibility. Opponents of the originalist position frequently cite such clauses as invitations

extended by the framers to future generations to bring their own best moral judgment to bear on constitutional questions and to reinterpret the meaning of these
terms in light of subsequent experience and understanding.

We shall explore this argument and its attendant problems in the next section.
Here, we will simply note Justice Brennan's rejoinder to the majority in *Marsh,* to
the effect that originalism misapprehends the nature of the Constitution when its
proponents attempt to present it as a static document having only a singular
meaning that was fixed forever in 1789. Perhaps the framers intended a Constitution with an evolutionary meaning, often called "living Constitution," with limited
capacity to grow and be adapted to new circumstances. As Justice Oliver Holmes
wrote in the twentieth century:

> ...when we are dealing with words that are also a constituent act, like the
> Constitution of the United States, we must realize that they have called into life a be-
> ing the development of which could not have been foreseen by even the most gifted of
> its begetters. It was enough for them to realize or to hope that they had created an or-
> ganism ... The case before us must be considered in the light of our whole experience
> and not merely in that of what was said a hundred years ago.[35]

Restrained judicial review cannot be dismissed yet, however, for there is a
second theory offered for interpreting textual ambiguity. Suppose we concede
that the Constitution was purposefully written in terms capable of growth. It does
not necessarily follow that such reinterpretation should be a judicial responsibility.
After all, the Constitution derives its legitimacy from its status as an expression of
the will of the sovereign people. Perhaps they, and not nine judges in Washington,
ought ultimately to control its interpretation through democratic processes. Recall
that this was the preference of the antifederalist writer Brutus. Justice Holmes
drew a similar conclusion from his insight that legal decisions were not logically
determined.

Today, practitioners of "judicial deference" claim to be following Holmes's
lead when they argue that the courts should nullify legislation only when it violates
the Constitution in such a clear and unambiguous way that no reasonable person
could defend it. Put another way, the legislature should be permitted to adopt
whichever of several conceivable interpretations of the Constitution wins the approval of the democratic majority. So long as a rational argument could be made
in support of the interpretation chosen, the courts should defer to the legislature's
judgment. Legislators are, after all, intelligent people, capable of reading and interpreting the Constitution, at least most of the time. And they answer directly to
the voters, as judges do not.

We might apply such a theory to the facts of *Marsh v. Chambers.* The text
"Congress shall make no law respecting an establishment of religion" admits to
several interpretations. A perfectly reasonable Mr. Smith might argue that while
the First Amendment prohibits the creation of a national church, a legislature
does no such thing when it hires a chaplain. Nor is any official sanction or preference inherent in the fact that the chaplain the Nebraska legislature hired happened to be Presbyterian. Most Americans profess some religious values, and the

majority of those profess Christianity. The legislature was simply acknowledging the belief most Americans entertain in a supreme being and perhaps also the legislators' own dependence on external moral guidance. After all, the First Congress and every Congress since, as well as most state legislatures—composed mostly of reasonable persons—have had chaplains, and none of them thought the Constitution was being violated.

An equally reasonable Ms. Jones might argue that legislative chaplains do violate the First Amendment. By hiring clergy identified with a particular denomination of the Christian religion, the legislature lends to that denomination at least the appearance of favored status. The state of Nebraska, through its elected representatives, is associating itself with a distinct sect, favoring Presbyterians over others, or Protestants over Catholics, or Christians over non-Christians, or religious conscience over secularism. When they hired a chaplain, the First Congress may not have fully thought through all of the implications of the separation of church and state they obviously favored. In any event, 200 years of unconstitutional policy is still unconstitutional policy. Finally, if legislative chaplains seemed unproblematic 200 years ago, when Americans were overwhelmingly Protestant, we must today devise an understanding of church-state relations for a community in which Protestant sects have continued to multiply and to which have been added large numbers of Catholics, Mormons, and Jews. Today, the fastest-growing religion in America is Islam, but our society also contains a fair number of Hindus, Buddhists, Native American churches, and a plethora of other religious movements. Many Americans lead wholly secular lives, professing no specific religious affiliation at all. In the context of such diversity, the only neutral policy is for government to distance itself from all forms of religious belief and expression. Nebraska has failed to maintain this neutrality.

It is not contended here that both arguments are equally reasonable, nor need we take a position in favor of one over the other. This is beside the point, which is that both are plausible interpretations of the First Amendment that intelligent persons could defend with a straight face. To the deferential judge, the question is not which argument is better, but who gets to decide? In deference to democratic principles, the legislature ought to resolve this conflict. If the arguments of Mr. Smith win over those of Ms. Jones, then so be it. Judges cannot be absolutely sure that the First Amendment has been violated unless the legislature does something that neither Mr. Smith nor Ms. Jones could reasonably defend, such as requiring all citizens of Nebraska to attend weekly Presbyterian services.

Violations of the Constitution that are this palpable will be rare, and for the proponents of this theory of judicial deference that is its virtue. Since legislatures seldom act in ways that are entirely irrational, occasions for judicial nullification of policy will be infrequent. So long as it stays within the bounds of reasonable constitutional thought, the majority will have its way. Of course, there is still judicial discretion to fix the outer limits of reasonable constitutional thought, but judicial intrusions in policy will be limited to such extreme cases.

To a great extent, this deferential theory of judicial review would shift responsibility for constitutional interpretation from courts to legislatures. This would seem very democratic, but is it reasonable for a constitutional democracy? If American politics embodies a balance between democratic decision making and constitutional restraint, the deferential judge might be accused of favoring the former at the expense of the latter. This might be particularly problematic in the field of human rights, where the effect would be largely to permit whatever majority holds legislative power to determine the limits of its own authority over the lives of unpopular minorities. American history in this regard should give us pause for reflection.

Perhaps if America is committed to constitutionalism and to the protection of minority rights, the Christian majority of Nebraska should not be permitted to use its power to assert Christian hegemony over other religious groups, even when it has a plausible constitutional theory permitting it to do so. Recall also the flag salute cases discussed earlier. Justice Frankfurter, one of the most eloquent proponents of judicial deference, had to admit that a reasonable person could defend a policy of compulsory flag salutes, even over the religious objections of an unpopular minority. Notice that Frankfurter's deference was also policy making: it created a policy of legislative control over minorities, one that arguably permitted some of the most offensive sides of our national character to become law. There is simply no guarantee that the majority will always exercise its power with wisdom, tolerance, and restraint simply by confining it to policies that could be rationally defended. Nor do the procedural safeguards of federalism, bicameralism, and the separation of power always prove adequate to the task of restraining popular passions. The framers of the First Amendment realized this when they chose to put at least some degree of religious liberty completely beyond the reach of legislative politics. Otherwise, the very presence of the First Amendment in the Constitution is absurd.

The theories of originalism and deference are often combined by those suspicious of recent judicial innovations, although they do not rest together easily. In particular, anger sparked by the Supreme Court's abortion decision, *Roe v. Wade,* has led to a resurgence of popularity of such doctrines on the political right. No more passionate defender of this position can be found than Robert Bork, President Reagan's failed Supreme Court nominee. Bork has been an outspoken critic of *Roe* and similar cases that create new rights, seemingly out of whole cloth, as unwarranted intrusion by the courts into legislative policy making. To his credit, Bork is equally disdainful of theories of interpretation that creatively read policies favored by conservatives into the open texture of the Constitution.[36] Yet his critics were not satisfied with his pretensions toward a depoliticized jurisprudence. How does Bork advocate interpreting the Constitution's open texture? His answer seems to be that he would not. Instead, judges should enforce only those constitutional provisions for which clear textual meaning, or original intention, can be determined. For the remainder, he would defer to any legislative determination that could be deemed reasonable.[37] For Bork, deference was offered as a second-best position, when originalism fails. Perhaps most controversial about Bork was his willingness to extend greater latitude than most to legislatures to determine what is reasonable.

However, Bork's theory does not succeed in separating politics from constitutional adjudication. Originalism and deference are fundamentally incompatible, in that originalism supposes that a singularly correct and unchanging meaning of the constitutional text is available, whereas deference denies this and acknowledges the validity of multiple interpretations and constitutional growth. Constitutional singularity and constitutional pluralism need to be reconciled. Both are present in the Constitution, but how does the conscientious judge determine which clauses have a determinate meaning and which do not? The answer, in short, is that a clause has a sufficiently determinate meaning when the courts say so. On the other hand, they lack fixed meaning and so become subject to any reasonable legislative interpretation when the courts say so. This is indeed an odd way to depoliticize judicial decision making, for choosing when originalism is possible and when deference is necessary involves some degree of judicial discretion or, in a word not favored by Bork, politics.

In the name of a majoritarian preference, Bork would tilt the balance between popular sovereignty and constitutionalism heavily in favor of the former.[38] But notice that this choice is based on Bork's political preference for majoritarian control of policy and not on anything clearly required by the Constitution's text or by the historical record of the founding. Bork's theory of judicial review is itself based on an extratextual political theory, the very thing for which he condemns his opponents. In fact, Bork's jurisprudence is politicized root and branch. It happens that Bork's political theory consistently expands the power of government and shrinks the rights of minorities. The theory may be intellectually defensible, it may even be a politically wise course to pursue, but his critics in the Senate were quite right to be suspicious of his claims to a depoliticized jurisprudence and quite properly rejected his nomination when they found his politics anathema. Such was also a democratic choice.

Whether called interpretivism, originalism, or textual determinacy, the return to formalism fails to avoid discretion, while deference to democratic interpretations of the Constitution places the rights of minorities in jeopardy. Neither approach succeeds in separating constitutional decisions from politics. It should be noted that while these theories have in recent years been associated with conservative politics, the relationship is not necessary. In fact, for the first third of the twentieth century, an activist Court driven by a conservative laissez-faire ideology managed to resist democratic politics on economic matters, when the latter seemed to prefer welfare state policies. Then, it was primarily the political left who advocated judicial abstention.

Only after the Court's relatively recent discovery of civil rights and liberties did liberals endorse an intrusive judiciary. With the retirements of Justices Brennan and Marshall, the political balance on the Supreme Court again shifted heavily to the right, and the restraintist jurisprudence long heard from the conservative critics of the Court seemed to have suddenly taken a back seat to a conservative policy agenda in some fields. Whether liberals will now rediscover the virtues of judicial restraint remains to be seen. If the Clinton presidency succeeds in tilting the Court back toward a liberal direction, the virtues of restraint might not appeal ᴊ liberals after all, leaving it to the conservative camp. The point is, a politician's preference for judicial restraint or creativity depends largely on whose ox the Court is about to gore.

Creative Judicial Review

All agree that the goals of the Constitution include the protection of certain moral claims that are of sufficient importance to be deemed fundamental human rights. Even the will of the majority can be trumped when valid constitutional rights are at stake. But how does the Constitution state those rights? Are they confined to the specific terms of the text, as understood by those who wrote and adopted it? Or are they stated in broad and open-ended terms, capable of reinterpretation and expansion (or contraction) according to the needs of contemporary society? Does the Constitution create government power hemmed in by a few specific rights, or does it create a government of limited powers surrounded by "an ocean of rights"?[39] And who is qualified to police the majority to protect rights of minorities? The majority and their political servants? Or an elite panel of judges, distant from majoritarian politics?

Those theorists most confident in the virtue of judges and most suspicious of the passions of the majority are inclined to support a creative role for the courts in the definition and protection of minority rights. One of the most prolific spokespersons for this theory of constitutional interpretation is law professor Ronald Dworkin. While conceding that the Constitution establishes a system of majority rule for most political subjects, Dworkin accuses interpretivists and deferentialists of failing to take constitutional rights seriously. Unqualified majoritarian democracy is not the political theory of the Constitution, he asserts.[40] Restraintists cannot disagree in principle, but they are wary of judicial discretion in defining rights and so advocate a strict fidelity to the text or intent of the framers. Dworkin counters that restraintists are not practicing textual fidelity at all. Rather, it is individual rights they construe parsimoniously, contrary to the true meaning of the constitutional text and the intent of those who wrote and adopted it.

Dworkin's theory of interpretation is complex. Interpretivists view the Constitution as a set of precise instructions inherited from past generations. The Constitution is viewed primarily as a legal instrument akin to a great contract embodying the founding command of the sovereign people. But the Constitution can also be understood as a set of political aspirations that establish for the community certain moral goals and that commit future generations to the pursuit and refinement of those goals. Dworkin invites us to consider the particular nature of the instructions given. He writes:

> Suppose I tell my children simply that I expect them not to treat others unfairly. I no doubt have in mind examples of the conduct I mean to discourage, but I would not accept that my "meaning" was limited to these examples, for two reasons. First, I would expect my children to apply my instructions to situations I had not and could not have thought about. Second, I stand ready to admit that some particular act I had thought was fair when I spoke was in fact unfair, and vice versa, if one of my children is able to convince me of that later; in that case I should want to say that my instructions cov-

ered the case he cited, not that I had changed my instructions. I might say that I had meant the family to be guided by the *concept* of fairness, not by any specific *conception* of fairness I might have had in mind.[41]

The distinction Dworkin makes between a *concept* and a *conception* lies at the heart of the "noninterpretivist" case for a creative judicial review. "Conceptions" of fairness are specific rules that define fair behavior. "Don't cheat at checkers," would be an example if we stay with Dworkin's parental metaphor. If a parent instructs his or her child to avoid treating others unfairly and as an example tells the child not to cheat at checkers, perhaps it can be inferred without too much controversy that the parent intends to prohibit cheating at dominoes as well. But what about cheating on a political science examination? Or on income tax filings? Or in business? Or marriage? Might the child reasonably argue that the injunction was limited to games or, worse, only to the game of checkers? Most parents expect more from their children. We hope our offspring learn to exercise independent moral judgment and learn from our specific conceptions something about the "concept" of fairness.

By a "concept," Dworkin understands a broad category of moral injunction that includes specific conceptions—the precise examples of not cheating at checkers, dominoes, or taxes—but to which might be added numerous other examples the parent had not initially thought of, a plethora of situations in which the child is called on to define anew what it means to be fair. If the Constitution contains similar concepts, we might have to make difficult, even painful, decisions in our lives about the requirements of fairness. We may have to add new examples, or new conceptions, to the concept. We might have to subtract some if on further reflection a practice we had thought perfectly acceptable turned out to be unfair. As responsible citizens in pursuit of a fair society, we would have to be open to persuasion through reasoned argument over the boundaries of fairness. Not all our desires will fit under the concept, nor will specific choices avoid controversy. But given the vagaries of life, we would want to possess the intellectual concept of "fairness" and not just the examples the framers happened to be thinking of years ago.

Thus, clauses others call "vague" Dworkin identifies as concepts, instructions by the framers for us to do some serious constitutional soul searching. Dworkin's choice of terms to describe radically different modes of constitutional instruction, a claim he makes without historical evidence, easily lead to some semantic confusion. We can clarify his argument with a specific example. Consider the Fourteenth Amendment, adopted in 1868. Among its several important provisions is the Constitution's only explicit guarantee of equality, "nor [shall any state] deny to any person within its jurisdiction the equal protection of the laws." Absent from this clause is a precise description of what it means for persons to be equal. Obviously, individuals are not alike in every way, and it would be unjust to treat them as if they were. Distinctions have to be made between individuals of different needs and abilities or who come from different circumstances. The issue, then, is which distinctions are permissible and which are incompatible with the equality promised by the Fourteenth Amendment. As a political concept, equality has

̡en particularly volatile, especially in the twentieth century.[42] In 1868, it was agreed that the equal protection clause conferred some sort of equal status on the newly emancipated slaves. But Reconstruction thought about equality was opaque, to say the least, embellished with quixotic distinctions between civil, political, and social equality. How are we to understand the broad language of the equal protection clause?

One prominent interpretivist, Raoul Berger, has concluded from his historical research that the equality intended by the framers of the Fourteenth Amendment was confined to the rights of property ownership, contracts, and access to the judicial process.[43] In his view, any judicial expansion of equality beyond the scope of this narrow intent is an unwarranted usurpation of legislative authority. But if the framers of the equal protection clause were moved by so narrow an intent, it seems odd that they would not have said so more precisely. Their apparently deliberate use of the concept of equal protection of the laws, rather than the precise conception Berger finds, seems to set us on a course in pursuit of an equality more broadly understood. That is, it may state an aspiration of an egalitarian society, while demanding that future generations employ their best moral insight to determine how equality is to be understood and achieved. Perhaps, then, the framers intended for us to take equality into places they never dreamed of, if such made sense in terms of granting equal protection of the laws.

Consider now access to the voting booth, an application of the equal protection clause Berger firmly rejects.[44] The framers of the Fourteenth Amendment seem not to have intended any redefinition of voting rights when they adopted the equal protection clause. Hence, two years later they followed with the Fifteenth Amendment, which explicitly singles out voting rights of former slaves for constitutional protection. One condition the states commonly placed on access to the polls in the nineteenth century was the collection of a poll tax, requiring the payment of a fee prior to voting. Nothing in the text of the Constitution specifically prohibits poll taxes. A reasonable person might even defend poll taxes as a means of raising revenue and of discouraging the casting of frivolous ballots. The Fifteenth Amendment is quite clear that access to the ballot cannot be denied a citizen solely on account of race, and the Nineteenth Amendment extends similar protection against state interference on account of sex.

It might come as a surprise to many Americans that there is in the text of the Constitution no right to vote per se. Indeed, as recently as 1937, in *Breedlove v. Suttles,* the Supreme Court held poll taxes permissible under the Fourteenth Amendment.[45] So why should a state not condition voting on payment of a fee, so long as the same sum is collected from white and black, male and female, and rich and poor voters?

Critics, on the other hand, might argue that voting is a fundamental right of democratic citizenship to which no arbitrary conditions may apply. In particular, critics attack the poll tax as imposing a disproportionate burden on the poor, discouraging their electoral participation. What appears to be a nondiscriminatory tax is in reality a subterfuge to weaken the political voices of the economically vulnerable classes, which include disproportionately members of racial minority groups. By the middle of the twentieth century, Americans' understanding of equality seemed to be changing with regard to the franchise. By 1964, the Twenty-fourth Amendment prohibited poll taxes for all federal elections but did not reach state elections. By 1966, only five states continued the practice in local elections. Contemporary Americans grant that the state acts properly when it establishes reasonable voter qualifications, yet it is likely that most would deny that the ability to pay a tax is such a reasonable qualification. For all of that, without a specific textual proscription of poll taxes, how can we be sure of their constitutional status?

In 1966, the Supreme Court decided the case of *Harper v. Virginia Board of Elections,* a challenge to Virginia's poll tax.[46] In an opinion by Justice William Douglas, the Court explicitly overruled the earlier *Breedlove* opinion, finding poll taxes to violate a reinterpreted equal protection clause. Foreshadowing Dworkin, Douglas wrote:

> . . . the Equal Protection Clause is not shackled to the political theory of a particular era. In determining what lines are unconstitutionally discriminatory, we have never been confined to historic notions of equality. . . . Notions of what constitutes equal treatment for purposes of the Equal Protection Clause do change.[47]

Statements like this one send interpretivists through the roof. From their perspective, this reconstruction of the equal protection clause clearly involves the Court in policy making not warranted by the Constitution, in violation of federalism and the separation of powers between the courts and the legislature. Here we have unelected judges imposing their subjective notions of good policy on a state that has democratically chosen another. Yet, Douglas could also say, without apparent irony:

> Our conclusion . . . is founded not on what we think government policy should be, but on what the Equal Protection Clause requires.[48]

Douglas's formalist rhetoric should not be taken seriously. Even if we might approve of the egalitarian result of *Harper,* it is beside the point. If the Court can alter the meaning of the Constitution based on its perception of how society understands—or should understand—equality, perhaps it can do anything it wants, ignoring the democratic processes. Nor is there any guarantee that the Supreme Court will always define equality in a way we approve. Finally, interpretivists and deferentialists charge that when the Court expands on the meaning of the Constitution in this fashion, it cuts itself off from any plausible mandate for its decision in popular consent through the adoption of the Fourteenth Amendment. In the words of Justice, now Chief Justice, William Rehnquist:

> Judges then are no longer the keepers of the Covenant; instead they are a small group of fortunately situated people with a roving commission to second-guess Congress, state legislatures, and state and federal administrative officers concerning what is best for the country.[49]

Rehnquist's complaint should give us pause. As a prominent federal judge once wrote, "For myself it would be most irksome to be ruled by a bevy of Platonic Guardians, even if I knew how to choose them, which I assuredly do not."[50] We have seen how federal judges are chosen. It is no affront to their dignity to suggest they are not quite what Plato had in mind. A nagging issue that must be

..ced by Dworkin and others concerns the amount of political power we want to turn over to an unelected judiciary, guided only by their own moral consciences.

Can proponents of creative judicial review answer this charge leveled by interpretivists? Can they offer sufficient protection from the subjectivity of willful judges? The answer, unfortunately, has to be yes and no. Obviously, the concept of equality is not without boundaries and thus supplies some limits to judicial discretion when specific conceptions are debated. Recall also that judges are the only public officials required to explain in writing every decision made (except certiorari), and to a very critical audience. Justification of a decision as based on a conception of equality that is consistent with the Fourteenth Amendment requires an argument that would be found credible when judged by standards of legal excellence.[51] Thus, some demonstration that today's decision builds on the text, the conceptions held by the framers, judicial precedent, our developing political tradition, and contemporary moral thought will have to be offered. Perhaps judges cannot get away with just anything.

Yet these standards of legal excellence will themselves not have objective existence. Rather, they represent the shared values of a historically distinct interpretive community. As the community changes, the standards of technical excellence may not guide judges in the same way. Recall that part of the agenda of the Critical Legal Studies scholars is to expose this indeterminacy, precisely so that the community can move the process of judging in a more egalitarian direction.[52] Nor will these standards determine the specific result for any case to such a degree that the predilections of the judge can be disregarded. We can hope that they will prevent a judge from going willy-nilly wherever whim might take him or her, but within broad and ever-changing boundaries they permit substantial policy making. If noninterpretivists cannot offer the pretensions of objectivity heard from their interpretivist opponents, what they can offer might best be understood as bounded discretion. We saw in the previous section that bounded discretion is really all that interpretivists can offer as well. The boundaries of the interpretivist's discretion may be narrower, but the practical difference between interpretivists and noninterpretivists is less than their rhetoric often suggests.

Proponents of creative judicial review frequently point to the institutional checks on the courts to ameliorate interpretivists' fears. If judicial discretion is taken to extremes, the democratic process can correct the abuse. Congress can rewrite a misinterpreted statute or commence the Article V process of amending the Constitution. The president has considerable control over the administration of judicial policies. With a cooperative Senate, the president can eventually alter the political complexion of the bench through his or her appointments. Professor Michael Perry has gone so far as to propose that courts should assume a "prophetic" role in politics, one in which they consciously challenge society to correct its moral failings through creative interpretations of the Constitution. He rationalizes this expansive judicial role in part by pointing out that society retains the democratic option of rejecting the moral lesson, even through Congress's constitutional power to strip the Supreme Court of appellate jurisdiction over specific subjects.[53]

One might shudder in contemplation of the constitutional chaos Perry seems to invite. Also, whatever control Congress might exercise over the appellate jurisdiction of the Supreme Court, many scholars argue that it would be an abuse to use such power to reverse substantive judicial policies.[54] If the separation of powers requires that courts grant some level of deference to legislatures, the converse must also be true. If the political response Perry advocates were to become routine, it could spell the practical end to judicial review altogether. The momentous implications of such legislative behavior help explain why Congress has used this avenue of redress only once, just after the Civil War.[55] Since then, bills to restrict the Court's appellate jurisdiction have been offered in Congress from time to time but have failed to pass. At best, they have served as a threat that is unlikely to be carried out.

Arguments such as these can give only partial reassurance to those mistrustful of judicial policy making. When the courts seriously err, *eventual* redress is available. But this does not silence interpretivist critics, nor should it. Congress may be unable to amend a misinterpreted statute and not because the majority approves of the judicial policy. Perhaps a strategically placed minority group in Congress that benefits from the Court's decision is able to block any legislative consideration of the issue. Similarly, amending the Constitution is a slow and arduous process that can be blocked by a minority. Presidential appointment is a haphazard process that also might take many years to bear fruit. All the while, the nation suffers the ill effects of judicial policy, diminishing popular government.

There is also a theoretical inconsistency in much of the noninterpretivist literature. Most proponents of judicial creativity tend to laud the expansive human rights policies of the Supreme Court in the 1960s and, to a lesser degree, the 1970s. The Court is depicted as the protector of racial and religious minorities, women, political dissidents, defendants, prisoners, and others vulnerable to abuse at the hands of the majority. Yet, as Presidents Nixon and Reagan have shown, the Court can sometimes be substantially altered through a careful recruitment strategy. What is good for the liberal goose must also be good for the conservative gander. If noninterpretivists are comfortable with judicial intrusion into politics in pursuit of the human rights policies they approve, they must logically accept the retrenchment in human rights policies that has recently animated the Supreme Court.[56] In fact, scholars such as Perry should be positively cheering the conservative activism of the current Court as proof that the system they describe is working.

Most noninterpretivists, however, have something different in mind. They remain forgetful of the fact that the rights-expanding activism of the Supreme Court represents a brief period that is quite anomalous when considered against the broader expanse of the Court's history. More often, the Court has been closely wedded to the most established interests in society, not to the marginalized and unrepresented. We noted earlier how the Supreme Court of an earlier generation, using the same creative jurisprudence, defended the "rights" of powerful corporations to be free of welfare state regulation, long after the democratic process had abandoned the laissez-faire ideology.[57] If interpretivists cannot guarantee that the democratic process will always produce desirable results, the noninterpretivists

a similar problem regarding the judicial process. All political power may be
abused, and it must be conceded that the Court is as apt to produce poor policy as
good. Again, distinguishing the poor from the good depends on the critic's vantage
point.

Another tack taken by apologists for creative judicial review is to note the
countermajoritarian traits found in the democratic branches of government. Federalism, the separation of powers, bicameralism, state apportionment and staggered elections in the Senate, the electoral college, and the executive veto are all
provisions required by the Constitution that limit the force of majority will in the
democratic branches. Others, such as the committee system, especially the power
of committee chairs, the House Committees on Rules, on Appropriations, and
Ways and Means, or conference committees, the Senate filibuster, the seniority
system that is still largely in practice, and the phenomena of "iron triangles" or administrators "going native" are all informal developments that frequently thwart
the will of the majority.[58] Thus, it is said, judicial review is a consistent part of a
pattern of checks on the majority's power.

Viewed against this background, judicial review admittedly appears less like a
sore thumb. But the argument overlooks the fact that some of these countermajoritarian checks are at least written into the Constitution and so were
clearly consented to when the Constitution was adopted. It is hard to advance
similar claims for the more expansive versions of judicial review. The other impediments on majoritarian politics may be more amenable to democratic abolition
should the community become sufficiently annoyed by minority recalcitrance. At
any rate, it is safe to say that for all the countermajoritarian elements in the legislature and executive, they are still considerably more accountable than judges,
with their life tenure. Besides, the argument may inadvertently strengthen the interpretivist argument that the democratic process already contains sufficient opportunities for minorities to protect themselves, making extraordinary judicial intervention unnecessary. Finally, this argument erodes the earlier one that the
democratic process can correct egregious judicial errors.

Noninterpretivists are at their strongest when they forthrightly point to the
peculiar institutional advantages enjoyed by courts as protectors of rights and
openly celebrate the tension judicial review introduces into democratic politics.
Since rights claimed by unpopular minorities are most vulnerable in the majoritarian processes, federal judges' insulation from immediate political reprisal makes
courts well situated to defend them. To give the majoritarian legislature the task
of defining the validity of a minority's rights claims would raise the Hamiltonian
problem of the majority acting like a judge of its own case.[59] Those minorities who
lack sufficient numbers, finances, organization, or status to protect themselves in
the nation's legislatures frequently turn to courts to advance interests they cannot
hope to secure through pluralist bargaining. They may succeed if they can present
their case convincingly in terms of constitutional principles. The loss of a receptive forum for such claims would seriously weaken America's practical commitment to human rights. To a substantial degree, the Bill of Rights could be reduced
to a set of admonitions the majority is free to ignore.

For all of its theoretical difficulties, judicial creativity seems inevitable, as a practical matter. Most damning to the argument of interpretivists is the Constitution's text—their very lodestone. The text is frequently open-ended. Whether or not the framers consciously extended to the future an invitation to ramify moral concepts at a constitutional level, the opportunity, and perhaps the need, for such extratextual speculation is certainly present. We have already seen that even interpretivists must reach outside the text of the Constitution, if only to ignore selected parts of it, to implement their interpretative theory. How else can we understand "the freedom of speech, or of the press," "establishment of religion," "cruel and unusual punishment," "the equal protection of the law," or "due process of law" but by appealing to history and experience, mediated by our moral sense? Not only do these clauses beg for content, but consider the Ninth Amendment, which is directed specifically to the issue of constitutional interpretation:

> The enumeration in the Constitution, of certain rights, shall not be construed to deny or disparage others retained by the people.

This provision was included among the first 10 amendments adopted in 1791 to allay fears expressed by people like Alexander Hamilton and James Wilson. They had argued at the Constitutional Convention that a Bill of Rights would have a pernicious effect on individual liberty by giving credence to an interpretive theory whereby any right not specifically included in the text of the Constitution would be vulnerable to abuse by government. The amendment counters this inference, and damages the interpretivist cause, by explicitly recognizing that people have rights in addition to those that happened to be mentioned in the text of the Constitution and that these rights should also be secured. We are not told what the limits of these rights might be, but denial of their existence as part of the American constitutional scheme cannot be justified in the name of textual fidelity so long as this amendment remains part of the text. Try as they might, interpretivists cannot wish this amendment away.

Although courts are reluctant to rest a decision on the Ninth Amendment, they have been willing to boldly go where none have gone before in the creation of extratextual rights. The most controversial of these in recent years has been the right to privacy that has been a part of Supreme Court policy since 1965. In *Griswold v. Connecticut*, the right of a married couple to use a contraceptive device was said to be found in the "penumbras" that mystically surround the First, Third, Fourth, and Fifth Amendments.[60] That free speech, the right to bear arms, protection against unreasonable police searches, or compulsory self-incrimination, when taken together, suggested a right of "marital privacy" that includes sexual relations would probably come as a surprise to the framers of the Bill of Rights and perhaps even to a few noninterpretivists. In fact, marital privacy was added to the Constitution in the *Griswold* case in a judicial slight of hand only remotely confined by the text, if at all. Once created, the right was hard to contain.

Marital privacy soon became personal sexual privacy, which ultimately became reproductive freedom, including the right of a woman to terminate an unwanted pregnancy by abortion.[61] Similar doctrinal expansion became family priy, including the right to marry or to live with one's blood relatives in an extended family arrangement.[62] (Yet a changing Supreme Court paradoxically found no right to sexual freedom or personal choice that included homosexual acts.[63]) Indeed, the list of rights most Americans take for granted but have no explicit textual grounding in the Constitution is considerable.[64] One of the strongest rhetorical tactics to silence interpretivists is to list all of the rights the Court has added to the Constitution and suggest their disappearance in consequence of a narrower judicial review. This argument is what did in Robert Bork's nomination to the Supreme Court.

Yet, as attractive as many of these judicially created rights may be, critics stand on firm ground when they accuse the Court of creating a new Constitution out of whole cloth. We do well to remember the warning sounded by as profound a constitutionalist as Abraham Lincoln, over a century ago:

> ... the candid citizen must confess that if policy of the government, upon vital questions, affecting the whole people, is to be irrevocably fixed by decisions of the Supreme Court, the instant they are made, in ordinary litigation between parties, in personal actions, the people will have ceased to be their own rulers, having, to that extent, practically resigned their government, into the hand of that eminent tribunal.[65]

Abortion has proven especially controversial, giving rise to several proposals to amend the Constitution or to strip the Supreme Court of appellate jurisdiction over the subject. To date, none of these responses has been successful. Presidents Reagan and Bush sought to reconstruct the Supreme Court according to an interpretivist/deferentialist model, hoping to overturn the *Roe* decision. A recent decision by the Supreme Court—by the vote of one justice—has claimed to affirm the basic right to secure an abortion, while also narrowing the right substantially by permitting states to erect impediments to its exercise.[66] As the Bush presidency came to an end, the Court seemed to be within one vote of an interpretivist victory on the issue of abortion.

In the long run, the promise of the intrepretivist model is sharply to curtail or, if consistently followed, to eliminate from constitutional law all such rights, not just abortion, that were not explicitly envisioned by the framers. What would the American constitutional system look like without judicially created extratextual rights? If this right of personal privacy were eliminated, we would enhance the majority's control over policy, but at what cost? We ought to consider the implications of this policy, since its chances for success seem only diminished, not eliminated, by the election of President Clinton. Indeed, should Republicans regain the White House in 1996, it may well be with an explicit promise to curtail judicial activism further.

Consider the 1927 case of *Buck v. Bell*.[67] Carrie Buck was a retarded women institutionalized by the state of Virginia. She was the daughter of a similarly institutionalized woman and herself the mother of a child who, it later turned out, was of average intelligence. At the time, Virginia law permitted the superintendent of state institutions to compel the sterilization of such "defective persons" as Buck on the theory that heredity may play a role in determining intelligence and a reduction in the population of dependent persons would alleviate the burdens such people pose to society. With the aid of interested third parties, Buck filed suit to enjoin the state, claiming a constitutional right to refuse a compulsory tubal ligation.

Since there is in the Constitution no explicit right to procreate or to avoid unwanted medical procedures, this policy was challenged under the open-textured Fourteenth Amendment. Buck's argument was that the fairness required by that amendment's due process clause must include a right to bear a child. Notice that validation of the notion of fairness urged by Buck required the Court to consult some sort of moral code beyond the text of the Fourteenth Amendment. But the Court, in an opinion by the father of all deferentialists, Oliver Wendell Holmes, dismissed Buck's claim:

> We have more than once seen that the public welfare may call upon the best citizens for their lives. It would be strange if it could not call upon those who already sap the strength of the State for these lesser sacrifices, often not felt to be such by those concerned, in order to prevent our being swamped with incompetence. It is better for all the world, if instead of waiting to execute degenerate offspring for crime, or to let them starve for their imbecility, society can prevent those who are manifestly unfit from continuing their kind. . . . Three generations of imbeciles are enough.[68]

In brief, no matter how weak the scientific theory behind such a eugenics policy, no matter what moral reservations it may raise, and no matter what personal hardship is inflicted on individuals like Buck, if a reasonable person could possibly defend such a policy as fair, the majority must be permitted its choice. How could we test the reasonableness of such a defense? Note carefully Holmes's rhetoric. He seems unable to identify with Buck as a fellow human being capable of having rights. She is instead depicted as a "degenerate," who "sap[s] the strength" of the community, who is "manifestly unfit from continuing [her] kind," and who threatens to "swamp" society in "incompetence". She is, in short, a subhuman being, incapable of parental yearnings. Holmes's disregard of Buck as a fellow human endowed with inalienable rights reflected the common prejudice of his day and to some degree our own. The very ubiquity of such prejudice, already manifested in Virginia's legislative policy, no doubt enhanced the seeming rationality of compulsory sterilization, making deference more palatable to Holmes's colleagues.

We ought to think long and hard before we attribute to society the wisdom or moral authority to define a whole class of human beings as unworthy and therefore fit for elimination. Once society has taken that step, the choice between passive elimination through severing the fallopian tubes or more active policies of mass extermination becomes much easier to discuss. It was not until 1942, against the background of Nazi eugenics policies, that this position was reevaluated and procreation declared a fundamental constitutional right.[69] Notice that the same jurisprudence that created the right to abort a pregnancy also created the right to bear a child. It might be possible to save one right and eliminate the other, but not with interpretivist or deferentialist arguments advocated by recent presidential candidates.

Buck v. Bell is admittedly an extreme case from fairly long ago. It stands as a warning, however, that democratic societies are capable of their own tyrannies.

ecially where the interests of small and disfavored minorities, like the victims of mental retardation, are at stake, majorities are capable of being as inhumane, as unfeeling, and as despotic as any autocrat. Contemporary examples of indignities inflicted on individuals by democratic politics also abound. Consider *Moore v. East Cleveland.*[70] An urban zoning ordinance typical of many cities restricted Inez Moore's neighborhood to single-family occupancy homes. A family was defined by the ordinance solely in terms of the nuclear family of parents and children. Moore shared her house with her adult son, his son, and a second grandson, the orphaned cousin of the first. So far as we know, Moore and her family were otherwise decent, law-abiding citizens. Yet, Moore was convicted of violating the zoning ordinance. Her conviction was overturned only after the Supreme Court, building on earlier precedents, created an extratextual right of family integrity that permitted blood relatives to live together free of interference from the state.

It must be said that the ordinance in question was not enacted specifically with Moore in mind. It was intended only to regulate community development and preserve the character of residential neighborhoods. Once the ordinance was in place, political authorities were probably just too distracted by other concerns to be sensitive to Moore's needs. A single widow with two grandchildren is easy to ignore. Courts are unique in that they must respond to suits such as Moore's, despite her relative powerlessness. Without such creative judicial review, who could protect the right of Ms. Moore to offer domicile to her grandchildren? Who do we trust with the power to control the most intimate aspects of our lives, other than ourselves? Perhaps judges will not always do a good job at answering such questions, but litigation provides a structured forum in which individuals can appeal over the heads of the majority when they can present their claim in a constitutionally convincing manner. We should tamper with this opportunity only with the utmost care.

Representation-Reinforcing Judicial Review

We have surveyed two schools of constitutional thought. The first maximizes popular control over policy, but at significant cost to individual rights. The second offers greater hope for the protection of individual rights, but risks at least a partial despotism of nine justices insulated from democratic accountability. Americans have a penchant for compromise, perhaps combined with a cultural aversion to driving any theory to its logical conclusion. It should come as no surprise that a compromise position on judicial review is available, one that seeks to keep the best of both theories with a minimum of risks to popular government or minority rights. Inconsistency is the risk of compromise, however, and sometimes those who offer a middle course find themselves fighting a two-front war. Such has been the fate of those who have tried to make judicial review safe for democracy by confining it to a role that facilitates the representative process or at least checks its occasional self-destructive tendencies.

For the first third of the twentieth century, conservative noninterpretivists on the Supreme Court succeeded in promoting from the bench a policy of economic laissez-faire. This was accomplished through very questionable interpretation of the due process clauses of the Fifth and Fourteenth Amendments and of congressional power to regulate "commerce among the several states," granted in Article I. These policies came to a conclusion after 1937. The Roosevelt administration's eventual triumph over the Court served as a reminder that even the Supreme Court cannot hold back sustained popular opinion too long. Thereafter, the Court promised to uphold economic regulations if they passed Holmes's test of reasonableness, which they always did. But if obstructing democratic control over economic development was no longer an acceptable judicial function, what role should courts now play? Could judicial review be exercised in such a way as to make it more compatible with democracy?

The first explicit attempt at such reconciliation was soon offered by Justice Harlan Fiske Stone in an otherwise unimportant case called *United States v. Caroline Products Co.*[71] A manufacturer of an adulterated dairy product unsuccessfully challenged federal regulation of its wares on due process and commerce grounds. The Court adopted a deferentialist approach to the case and upheld the regulation as a reasonable exercise of legislative authority. In what has become undoubtedly the most celebrated footnote in American jurisprudence, Stone wrote:

> There may be a narrower scope for the operation of the presumption of constitutionality when legislation appears on its face to be within a specific prohibition of the Constitution, such as those of the first ten amendments. . . .
>
> It is unnecessary to consider now whether legislation which restricts those political processes which can ordinarily be expected to bring about repeal of undesirable legislation, is to be subject to more exacting judicial scrutiny under the general prohibitions of the fourteenth amendment than are most other types of legislation. . . .
>
> Nor need we inquire whether similar considerations enter into the review of statutes directed at particular religious . . . or racial minorities . . . whether prejudice against discrete and insular minorities may be a special condition, which tends to seriously curtail the operation of those political processes ordinarily thought to be relied upon to protect minorities, and which may call for a correspondingly more searching judicial inquiry. . . . [citations omitted][72]

The first of these paragraphs merely recited Alexander Hamilton's thesis that legislation contrary to specific prohibitions in the Constitution was invalid and would be declared so by courts. More interesting was Stone's example of specific prohibitions, the Bill of Rights. These provisions are in fact among the least specific clauses the Constitution has to offer, where the formalist theory of judicial review is hardly adequate. Yet Stone may have been suggesting that given its institutional insulation, the judiciary could play a useful role in American politics if it increased its attention to civil liberties issues. If so, he confined the Court to those issues that could be attached to some provision of the text, in repudiation of freewheeling invention under the due process clauses. Until then, civil liberties cases had appeared before the Supreme Court only sporadically. Today they are a staple of the Court's docket.

The next two paragraphs offer more innovative possibilities, suggesting that judicial review could be put into the service of democratic government by remedying failures in the representative process. In other words, the Court should ace Holmesian deference in most areas of policy, upholding any legislation at could be reasonably defended as consistent with constitutional authority. Hence, economic regulation would be viewed as a reasonable exercise of Congress's power to "regulate commerce among the several states," even where the economic motive might seem subordinate to other goals.[73] Different rules should apply, however, when the conditions specified in this footnote are present. Here, we could expect the courts to be more interventionist or more likely to overrule legislative policy. Courts may even be more creative in formulating some kinds of rights.

The second paragraph, for example, suggests that sometimes the democratic branches might not play politics by democratic rules, as when they seek to close off the channels of debate and decision making to certain ideas or weaken participation by certain groups. We seldom defend democratic government with the argument that the majority is endowed with superior wisdom. Were that true, constitutionalism would be unnecessary. Rather, we point out that the governors and the governed are the same people, so that when mistakes are made, the effects of bad policy are quickly felt by the electorate and remedied through the same democratic process that produced them in the first place. In that way, democracy can be seen as having a built-in feedback loop that monitors and self-corrects errors in the decision-making process. But this presupposes that reigning ideas can be tested through open criticism and debate. If the popular channels of public discussion are blocked to dissident ideas, the electorate may never learn of its mistakes, nor ever have the opportunity to consider an alternative policy. The *Caroline* footnote suggests that the nonmajoritarian judiciary may be able to play an important role in protecting democracy from itself by overturning legislation that impedes future democratic decision making.

Freedom of speech and press cases are obvious examples. During the periods immediately following each of the world wars, repressive legislation was popular with a frightened electorate anxious to equate political dissent with subversion. Critics of public policy were silenced in the name of national security, all with the apparent blessing of the electoral majority. But what kind of security does a democracy obtain when it violates its own premises? Speech acceptable to the majority is seldom in danger, but without dissent even mainstream thought cannot be critically tested through democratic debate. During the 1960s, with dissenting politics on issues of race relations and the Vietnam War on the increase, the Court became quite protective of speech and press rights. Of course, the *Caroline* rationale is directly applicable only to the expression of politically relevant ideas. The Court, however, chose not to attempt to distinguish political speech from other forms of expression that may be harder to fit under the *Caroline* footnote. Judicial review became quite protective of many unpopular forms of cultural expression.

Similarly, voting rights might be a legitimate area for judicial intervention under the *Caroline* doctrine. Where the majority is able to enact any policy that disenfranchises certain populations or dilutes their voting strength, the effect may be to shift the pain of bad policy onto those who cannot affect change. Reform of such measures will be unavailable through ordinary electoral politics. Only courts may be able to remedy the resulting defects in the representative process. The *Harper* case invalidating poll taxes, discussed previously, could find some justification in this theory. Similar issues of access to the ballot, legislative malapportionment, and association for collective advocacy, including public interest litigation, became the Court's business under this theory.[74]

The third paragraph suggests another way courts might facilitate representative government, by offering special protection to "discrete and insular minorities." This idea requires some elaboration. Somebody loses something in any political contest, and democratic theory holds that ordinarily it should be the minority. Obviously, not every minority who lost in the democratic branches should be able claim judicial protection from policies chosen by the majority, for that would spell the end of all democratic politics. Rather, Stone suggested that *some* minorities might lose too often, and for the wrong reasons, and might in consequence become the special wards of the courts. When the interests of such groups appear to have been unduly sacrificed by legislative majorities, the courts ought to be more willing to intervene. Clearly, much of the work of the federal courts in the past 40 years has been to examine closely policies that imposed unfair disabilities on vulnerable minority groups.

The immediate challenge of such a theory is to identify those groups the courts need to protect. Some groups might be so weak, because of their small numbers or geographic dispersion, that they lose political contests perennially. Now suppose a politically weak, unassimilated, and readily identifiable group were to be singled out for abuse in the popular political processes. We might find them routinely denied the fair hearing and respectful consideration accorded to other groups in the legislative arena because they are victims of prejudice. Ultimately, their political clout may be less than zero, as political leaders hoping to appeal to more assimilated voters heap abuse on unpopular minority groups, often in subtle ways. The practice of "wedge politics," so called because it seeks explicitly to divide society into categories of "us" and "them" for electoral advantage, is an old and disreputable feature of American politics. Sometimes, the affront is even more direct, at the behest of a majority openly contemptuous of minority aspirations and willing to penalize a population for who they are.

Race provides the paradigm example. Many a politician, including some recent candidates for national office, have successfully appealed to racial antagonism to garner favor with white voters. Documenting the corrosive effects of racial prejudice on American democracy would fill a book in itself. National, religious, cultural, or political minorities might also be targeted by demagogues hoping to exploit popular fears. Recall the earlier example of the Jehovah's Witnesses. Gender or sexual orientation also define disempowered groups who have been victimized by popular prejudice and who might lack sufficient political strength to protect themselves in democratic policy making. Women actually constitute a slight majority of the population but have historically been excluded from the centers of decision making, a disability well illustrated by the Senate's recent hearings on the nomination of Justice Clarence Thomas. We saw in Chapter 6 evidence of general neglect of the mentally ill, a group unrepresented, largely out of sight, and easily

oked. In the future, we might have to identify additional minority groups in
d of protection, perhaps including some not so "discrete and insular." Persons
ao are HIV-positive, for example, might become the next victims of public hys-
teria, while persons accused or convicted of crime have always been inviting targets.

Beyond the clear examples of race and ethnicity, it may be difficult to identify
"discrete and insular minorities." The admission of newer groups to such status
will necessarily be a controversial exercise of judicial discretion. The courts will
have to decide, without textual guidance, who qualifies for such privileged access
to judicial shelter. Granting some groups greater protection than others may seem
to critics to run afoul of the concept of "equal justice under law" that is promised
on the frieze of the Supreme Court building and that has long been an American
aspiration.

Once identified, however, the argument that such persons can rely only on
courts to protect them from more powerful majorities is a powerful one that can
be traced back to Alexander Hamilton. Of course, the minority group must be
able to articulate convincingly its grievance in the rhetoric of constitutional rights.
We saw earlier that rights are a special form of claim, one the majority is obligated
to respect. Experience teaches us that the majority may be more willing to listen
to rights claims made by those groups who enjoy the majority's sympathy.[75] Those
who are objects of the majority's contempt will likely find their claims falling on
deaf ears in the legislative arena. Courts may be able to compel equal consideration for such groups by preventing the most egregious forms of discrimination or
neglect, but not without importing into the Constitution a contested sociology.

Similarly, the *Caroline* footnote suggests a hierarchy of rights, so that courts
will be more hospitable to some rights claims than others. There has, in fact, been
a dualism between rights of expression, religious freedom, or privacy on one hand
and rights of property on the other. Since 1937, courts have not been so solicitous
of the latter despite textual indications supported by historical evidence that the
framers took such rights very seriously. It might be true that the wealthy minority
can take care of itself all too well in the legislative arena and is therefore in no
need of special judicial protection, but this position is also impossible to ground in
the text of the Constitution. Instead, it reflects a judicial choice regarding the desired structure of the political system that is extratextual in origin and that reflects
a substantive political theory to which not all Americans subscribe. Hence, it will
be as controversial as similar choices inherent in both interpretivist and noninterpretivist theories of constitutional interpretation.[76]

From the interpretivist perspective, neither a hierarchy of preferred rights
nor the selection of certain minority groups for recognition as "discrete and insular minorities" can be justified in terms of the constitutional text or the intent of
those who adopted it. Any such policy involves the courts in the wholesale rewrit-
ing of the Constitution and is an unwarranted invasion of the democratic
processes. Interpretivists are apt to complain, rather, that the nature of democratic politics is itself a subject the Constitution has left to the majority's determination, within the confines of reasoned judgment. Denial of free expression rights to
those who would advocate antidemocratic doctrines of fascism or Leninism, for

example, would not be altogether unreasonable and so should be a choice left to the majority to make.[77]

Similarly, membership in the community should be left to the wisdom of the legislative process. If it chooses to exclude some groups from the fullest privileges of membership, it should be allowed to do so, except where the purpose of the distinction is merely to discriminate, for example, against blacks for the sake of racial exclusion. The historical concern of the framers of the Fourteenth Amendment should confine its application to discrimination by race, or at most by nationality. It should not become a vehicle for judges to shape participation in the affairs of the community in ways that are anathema to the majority of its members.

On the other hand, when viewed from the perspective of the noninterpretivist, representation-reinforcing judicial review does not offer enough protection for human rights. The theory treats the Constitution primarily as a document that protects decision-making procedures, while ignoring its substantive limits on the choices that may be made through those procedures.[78] Important rights other than ones connected to political participation or claims peculiar to discrete and insular minorities are left exposed to the tides of majoritarian politics. Personal privacy rights, including reproductive freedom or family integrity, would still be left in the hands of the majority. Claims under the establishment of religion clause would be hard to place under this theory. Even the right of free expression might not be inclusive enough were it limited to speech and press useful for democratic participation. After all, the First Amendment's text makes no distinctions among kinds of speech or press that are protected. Expression that is of only scientific or artistic interest is nonetheless valuable and possibly vulnerable to majoritarian taste. The theory of evolution or the photographs of Robert Mapplethorpe may not sway elections but may be personally liberating to those who value them.

The theory of representation-reinforcing judicial review in reality requires an unelected judiciary to choose a particular theory of representative democracy and reinforce *it*, to the exclusion of others. It treats the Constitution as having already determined the kind of representative democracy the United States should be, but without any textual basis. The theory does not remove judicial discretion, nor can it provide a demonstrably correct, or even necessarily the most workable, balance between democracy and constitutionalism.

For all of that, the theory appears to have been extremely influential. It is worth noting that traces of the theory actually predate the *Caroline* case. It was none other than Oliver Wendell Holmes, together with fellow judicial restraintist Louis Brandeis, who first advocated a more interventionist form of judicial review in free speech cases.[79] Neither justice ever articulated a theory of preferred freedoms to explain why their approach to judicial review differed in free speech cases. They seem to have realized in some inchoate sense, however, that their usual policy of judicial deference made sense only when the democratic process was functioning properly, and that proper functioning of the democratic system required substantial protection for dissident political expression, even if compelled by courts.

After the *Caroline* case, explicit appeals to the footnote soon fell out of favor on the Supreme Court. Yet the thinking behind the footnote seems to have influenced

t in its most secretive decision making—the granting of certiorari. We
m Chapter 2 that civil liberties issues seem to be a kind of cue, signalling
ter likelihood that certiorari will be granted. Especially during the extraordi-
ary decade of the 1960s, the Court appeared to be unusually sensitive to democratic participation rights as well as egalitarian claims by the marginalized groups in
society. In the scholarly literature, the current spate of jurisprudential theorizing
was largely initiated by Professor John Hart Ely, whose fine book, *Democracy and
Distrust,* is an extended elaboration of the *Caroline* footnote and a defense of
much of the judicial policies associated with the tenure of Chief Justice Earl Warren, to whom the book is dedicated.[80]

As we move into the 1990s, however, it appears the Court has lost much of its
taste for protecting minorities or democratic procedures. The success of Presidents Reagan and Bush in redirecting the Supreme Court was substantial. If the
rhetoric of some recent Supreme Court appointees and their supporters can be
taken seriously, we should expect the courts to move more in the direction of interpretivism and deference to the legislative process. It appears more likely, however, that an increasingly conservative, and politically inspired, Supreme Court is
intent on taking constitutional politics into a different direction. Decisions of the
1990–1991 term, from which the voice and vote of Justice Brennan was absent,
suggested that in some fields of constitutional law the Court will waste little time
worrying about precedents, the text, or other obstacles to the fulfillment of a
conservative policy agenda.[81] As we have noted elsewhere, the direction President
Clinton will take the Court remains yet to be seen. If he is determined to alter the
direction of the Court from its recent course, he will have to combine considerable political skill and no small amount of luck in the appointment process.

NOTES

1. Kenneth M. Dolbeare and Linda J. Medcalf, *American Ideologies Today* (Random
   House, New York, 1988), especially Chapter 2.
2. Federalist Paper #51, in James Madison, Alexander Hamilton, and John Jay, *The Federalist* (Modern Library, New York, 1937) p. 57.
3. Ibid., p. 55.
4. Merrill D. Peterson, *The Portable Jefferson* (Viking Press, New York, 1975) p. 235.
5. James Madison, Alexander Hamilton, and John Jay, *The Federalist Papers* op. cit., see
   especially Madison's #10 and #51.
6. Political theorists disagree over whether rights are absolute in the sense that they can
   never be overcome by the interests of the majority or whether they are defeasible but
   only if the majority can meet some higher level of justification. This is a complex argument, but happily not necessary to make our point. We will proceed on the simpler assumption that rights create perfect trumps and always defeat political power. For a
   criticism of this view, see Mary Ann Glendon, *Rights Talk: The Impoverishment of Political Discourse* (Free Press, New York, 1991).
7. The story is told well in Peter Irons, *The Courage of their Convictions* (Penguin, New
   York, 1990). See Chapters One and Two.
8. *Minersville School District v. Gobitis,* 310 U.S. 586 (1940).
9. *West Virginia v. Barnette,* 319 U.S. 624 (1943).

10. Ibid., pp. 638–639, 642.
11. Brutus, Letter #XI, in Herbert J. Storing, ed. *The Anti Federalists,* selected by Murray Dry (University of Chicago press, Chicago, 1985) p. 165.
12. Storing, op. cit., Letter #XV, p. 187.
13. Alexander Hamilton, Federalist #78, op. cit., p. 504.
14. Alexander Hamilton, Federalist #80, op. cit., p. 516.
15. Alexander Hamilton, Federalist #78, op. cit., p. 506.
16. James Madison, Federalist #10, op. cit., p. 51. Hamilton agreed in #78, p. 503.
17. Alexander Hamilton, Federalist #78, op. cit., p. 508.
18. *Marbury v. Madison,* 5 U.S. 137 (1903).
19. Ibid., pp. 176–177.
20. Ibid., pp. 177–178.
21. William Van Alstyne, "A Critical Guide to *Marbury v. Madison,*" 1969 *Duke Law Journal* 1.
22. See remarks of George Bush, in "Candidates State Positions on Federal Judicial Selection," 72 *Judicature* 77 (Aug/Sept 1988).
23. James Madison, Federalist #37, op. cit., p. 230.
24. *Katz v. United States,* 389 U.S. 347 (1967).
25. *McCulloch v. Maryland,* 17 U.S. 316, 415 (1819).
26. *Myers v. United States,* 272 U.S. 52 (1926), *United States v. Belmont,* 301 U.S. 324 (1937), *Train v. City of New York,* 402 U.S. 35 (1975), *United States v. Nixon,* 418 U.S. 683 (1974).
27. *Chaplinsky v. New Hampshire,* 315 U.S. 568 (1942), *Feiner v. New York,* 340 U.S. 315 (1951), *Cohen v. California,* 403 U.S. 15 (1971), *Miller v. California,* 413 U.S. 15 (1973), *New York Times v. Sullivan,* 376 U.S. 254 (1964), *Brandenburg v. Ohio,* 395 U.S. 444 (1969), *R.A.V. v. St. Paul,* 112 S. Ct. 2538 (1992).
28. *Texas v. Johnson,* 491 U.S. 397 (1989).
29. We will employ the traditional terms for our first two categories. The third term comes from John Hart Ely, *Democracy and Distrust* (Harvard University Press, Cambridge, Massachusetts, 1980) p. 73ff. This book is a sophisticated but accessible contribution to contemporary debate about judicial review that the ambitious student would find helpful.
30. Mark Tushnet, "Constitutionalism and Critical Legal Studies," in Alan S. Rosenbaum, ed., *Constitutionalism: The Philosophical Dimension* (Greenwood Press, New York, 1988) p. 153.
31. *Marsh v. Chambers,* 463 U.S. 783 (1983).
32. Ibid., pp. 807–808 (Brennan, dissenting).
33. Robert H. Bork, *The Tempting of America: The Political Seduction of the Law* (Free Press, New York, 1990) p. 144.
34. H. Jefferson Powell, "The Original Understanding of Original Intent," 98 *Harvard Law Review* 885 (1985).
35. *Missouri v. Holland,* 252 U.S. 416, 433 (1920).
36. Bork, op. cit., p. 223ff.
37. Bork, op. cit., p. 166–167. See also, Robert Bork, "Neutral Principles and Some First Amendment Problems," 47 *Indiana Law Review* 1, 8, 10–12 (1971).
38. Ibid., pp. 140, 258.
39. Edward S. Corwin, "The Basic Doctrine of American Constitutional Law," 7 *Michigan Law Review* 247, 248 (1914).
40. Ronald Dworkin, *Taking Rights Seriously* (Harvard University Press, Cambridge, Massachusetts, 1977) pp. 132–33.
41. Ibid., p. 134.

Kenneth M. Dolbeare and Linda J. Medcalf, *American Ideologies Today: From _eopolitics to New Ideas* (Random House, New York, 1988) pp. 19–22 and succeeding chapters.

43. Raoul Berger, *Government by Judiciary: The Transformation of the Fourteenth Amendment* (Harvard University Press, Cambridge, Massachusetts, 1977).

44. Ibid, p. 191.

45. *Breedlove v. Suttles,* 302 U.S. 277 (1937).

46. *Harper v. Virginia Board of Elections,* 383 U.S. 663 (1966).

47. Ibid., p. 669.

48. Ibid., p. 670.

49. William H. Rehnquist, "The Notion of a Living Constitution," 54 *Texas Law Review* 693, 698 (1976).

50. Learned Hand, *The Bill of Rights* (Antheneum, New York, 1977) p. 73.

51. See, for example, Owen M. Fiss, "Objectivity and Interpretation," 34 *Stanford Law Review* 739 (1982). Fiss uses the term "bounded objectivity," at 745, to describe this restraint, but this seems to misstate just what it is that has to be bounded. The use here of "bounded discretion" more accurately describes the problem.

52. See, for example, Mark Tushnet, "Critical Studies and Constitutional Law: An Essay on Deconstruction," 36 *Stanford Law Review* 623 (1984), and Tushnet, "Following the Rules Laid Down: A Critique of Interpretivism and Neutral Principles," 96 *Harvard Law Review* 781 (1983).

53. Michael J. Perry, *The Constitution, The Courts, and Human Rights* (Yale University Press, New Haven 1982) p. 128.

54. See, for example, "Silencing the Oracle: Carving Disfavored Rights Out of the Jurisdiction of Federal Courts," in Laurence Tribe, *Constitutional Choices* (Harvard University Press, Cambridge, Massachusetts, 1985) p. 47ff.

55. Ex parte *McCardle,* 74 U.S. 506 (1869).

56. See, for example, *Rust v. Sullivan,* 111 S. Ct. 1759 (1991), which seems to indicate a reevaluation of abortion as a constitutional right as well as a retrenchment in free speech rights; *Arizona v. Fulminante,* 111 S. Ct. 1246 (1991), permitting the admissions of coerced confessions into evidence at trials, if supported by corroborating evidence, casting doubt on the life expectancy of *Miranda v. Arizona,* 384 U.S. 436 (1966) the symbol of Warren Court activism, and *United States v. Leon,* 468 U.S. 897 (1984), eroding the protections offered by the exclusion of evidence seized by the police in violation of the Fourth Amendment.

57. The most notorious examples include *Lochner v. New York,* 198 U.S. 45 (1905), overturning legislation limiting the work week; *Coppage v. Kansas,* 236 U.S. 1 (1915), overturning collective bargaining legislation; *Hammer v. Dagenhart,* 247 U.S. 251 (1918), overturning child labor legislation; *Adkins v. Children's Hospital,* 261 U.S. 525 (1923), overturning minimum wage legislation; and *Schecter Poultry Corp. v. United States,* 295 U.S. 495 (1937), largely gutting the National Industrial Recovery Act, the centerpiece of the Roosevelt administration's New Deal.

58. See, for example, Jesse Choper, *Judicial Review and the National Political Process* (University of Chicago Press, Chicago, 1980) pp. 12–29.

59. Hamilton, Federalist Paper #78, op. cit., p. 508, Dworkin, op. cit., p. 142, Choper, op. cit., p. 64, Perry, op. cit., p. 147.

60. 381 U.S. 479 (1965). Only Justice Goldberg, in a concurring opinion, rested heavily on the ninth amendment.

61. *Eisenstadt v. Baird,* 405 U.S. 438 (1972), *Roe v. Wade,* 410 U.S. 113 (1973).

62. *Zablocki v. Redhail,* 343 U.S. 374 (1978), *Moore v. East Cleveland,* 431 U.S. 494 (1977).

63. *Bowers v. Hardwick,* 478 U.S. 186 (1986).

64. In addition to these rights, and the right to vote noted above in *Harper v. Virginia Board of Elections,* we might add such rights as the presumption of innocence and to demand proof beyond a reasonable doubt in criminal prosecutions, re *Winship,* 397 U.S. 358 (1970); to associate with others for political discussion and advocacy, *De Jong v. Oregon,* 299 U.S. 353 (1937); *NAACP v. Alabama,* 357 U.S. 449 (1958); to travel from one state to another, *Crandall v. Nevada,* 73 U.S. 35 (1868); *Shapiro v. Thompson,* 394 U.S. 618 (1969); and, perhaps most critical, to retain one's citizenship, in many respects the right to have rights, *Afroyim v. Rusk,* 387 U.S. 253 (1958); nor is this a complete catalogue of extratextual rights.

65. Abraham Lincoln, "First Inaugural Address," March 4, 1961, in Richard N. Current, *The Political Thought of Abraham Lincoln* (Bobbs-Merrill, Indianapolis, Indiana, 1967) pp. 175–76.

66. *Planned Parenthood of Pennsylvania, v. Casey,—U.S.—*(1992). In this holding, Chief Justice Rehnquist and Justices Scalia, White and Thomas would have overruled *Roe v. Wade* outright. Justices O'Connor, Souter, and Kennedy, perhaps taking judicial restraint more seriously than the presidents who appointed them, felt obligated by considerations of stare decisis to leave the core right of *Roe* intact. Only Justices Blackmun and Stevens stood squarely behind *Roe v. Wade.*

67. *Buck v. Bell,* 274 U.S. 200 (1927).

68. Ibid., p. 207.

69. *Skinner v. Oklahoma,* 316 U.S. 535 (1942).

70. *Moore v. East Cleveland,* 431 U.S. 494 (1977).

71. *United States v. Caroline Products Co.,* 304 U.S. 144 (1938).

72. Ibid., p. 152, N.4.

73. See, for example, *Heart of Atlanta Motel v. United States,* 379 U.S. 241 (1964) and *Katzenbach v. McClung* 379 U.S. 294 (1964), both upholding the 1964 Civil Rights Act as valid commercial regulations under the commerce clause of Article I.

74. *Baker v. Carr,* 369 U.S. 186 (1962), *Reynolds v. Sims,* 377 U.S. 533 (1964), *NAACP v. Alabama,* 357 U.S. 449 (1958), *NAACP v. Button,* 371 U.S. 415 (1963).

75. John Hart Ely, *Democracy and Distrust: A Theory of Judicial Review* (Harvard University Press, Cambridge, Massachusetts, 1980).

76. *Kovacs v. Cooper,* 336 U.S. 77, 94–95 (1949) (Frankfurter, dissenting).

77. *Dennis v. United States,* 341 U.S. 494, 525 (1951) (Frankfurter, concurring).

78. "The Pointless Flight from Substance," in Laurence Tribe, *Constitutional Choices* (Harvard University Press, Cambridge, Massachusetts, 1985) p. 11.

79. *Abrams v. United States,* 250 U.S. 616 (1919) (Holmes, dissenting), *Gitlow v. New York,* 268 U.S. 652 (1925) (Holmes, dissenting), and *Whitney v. California,* 274 U.S. 357 (Brandeis, dissenting).

80. John Hart Ely, *Democracy and Distrust: A Theory of Judicial Review* (Harvard University Press, Cambridge, Massachusetts, 1981).

81. During the 1990–1991 term, the Court overruled no less than five of its own recent precedents, all in the field of criminal law, and frequently on its own initiative. See *Payne v. Tennessee,* 111 S. Ct. 2597 (1991), permitting the state to introduce evidence of the victim's character in capital murder trials, overruling *South Caroline v. Gathers,* 490 U.S. 805 (1989). Neither party requested a reconsideration of *Gathers.* See *McClesky v. Zant,* 111 S. Ct. 1454 (1991), limiting prisoners' access to federal habeas cor-

proceedings. Chief Justice Rehnquist had a year earlier requested such reform m the legislature, but when Congress declined to take action the Court made its own policy. Also see *Arizona v. Fulmante,* 111 S. Ct. 1246 (1991), holding the admission of a coerced but corroborated confession into trial to be a "harmless error," overruling *Chapman v. California,* 386 U.S. 18 (1967); *Wilson v. Seiter,* 111 S. Ct. 2321 (1991), shifting the focus in Eighth Amendment challenges to prison conditions from the state of the institution to the administrator's state of mind; and *Riverside v. McLaughlin,* 111 S. Ct. 1661 (1991), allowing a delay of 48 hours between arrest and preliminary hearing, repudiating previous requirement of a "prompt" hearing. In *Payne,* Chief Justice Rehnquist suggested that precedents were entitled to less respect when they were five to four decisions over "spirited" dissents—apparently meaning any dissent in which the Chief Justice joined.

A Brief Epilogue

The three theories of constitutional jurisprudence surveyed in Chapter 7 each provide some guidance for the exercise of judicial review. Each prescribes a proper role for the judiciary, especially for the Supreme Court, in American politics. Each theory seems to be consistent in certain ways with the Constitution and with the political traditions of the United States. Each offers certain advantages, yet each begs certain questions, rests on certain shaky assumptions, and bears certain risks. Most important, each has certain political consequences that may substantially alter the lives of different groups in society. They should be evaluated in light of the institutional arrangements and processes discussed in earlier chapters.

We have seen that courts do not, contrary to popular assumptions, apply law to disputes in a mechanical, simple, or objective way. No theory of constitutional interpretation succeeds in removing politics from the judicial decision, nor can one theory be shown to be more correct than another. At least none are so obviously preferable as to silence the proponents of competing doctrines. We face here a dilemma: the ideal of a government checked by law requires that law be autonomous from politics. Yet, it is this autonomy that much of this book has challenged, because the relationship of law to politics is itself political. The persistence of the notion of reflexive formalism in judicial opinions, political rhetoric, and media punditry has infused public discussion of judicial politics with considerable confusion, and no small amount of hypocrisy.

The appropriate question for debate is not whether courts ought to make policy, for they must, but rather what kind of policy ought courts be making? We saw in Chapter 7 that this question is really about the kind of political regime the United States ought to cultivate. Pure majoritarian democracy has never been our choice, and probably for good reason. The politics of rights creates a certain amount of safe space within which minorities may flourish, including political and dissidents so necessary to vital democratic politics. We have recognized sometimes begrudgingly, from the beginning of our national existence, and we have sought to establish some protective cover for the diversity that has always characterized American society.

On the other hand, excessive diversity poses a danger of undermining the sense of community, of shared experiences, values and purposes on which democratic politics also depends. It is doubtful that many Americans wish to impose on society the deadening conformity that must result from an unqualified majoritarian rule. Nor is it likely that a significant number would advocate the dismemberment of American society into a multiplicity of autonomous communities that remain foreign to each other. Between these extremes lies a vast array of choices we might make regarding the proper balance between diversity and community. Although this question has always been with us, the expansive role courts play in this debate is a fairly recent development in American politics. Even so, in an era in which multiple minorities of all kinds are demanding more recognition, it is a role our courts are not likely to shed easily.

In the contemporary political context, those who fear conformity have tended to describe themselves as liberal and have tended to applaud judicial "protection" of human rights. Those who fear diversity have tended to call themselves conservatives and have been appalled by judicial "usurpation" of the majority's discretion to form the kind of community it finds most conducive to its own happiness. The former tends to approve of the expansive theories of constitutional interpretation described in Chapter 7, while the latter tends to prefer the restrained theories of judicial review. These alignments are neither perfect nor inevitable, but the debate has surely been shrill.

What both sides share is an interest in how the courts are shaped. We saw in Chapter 2 that the system of federal courts we know took about a century to develop. Since the end of the nineteenth century, changes in judicial structure have been of a more incremental nature, but even these have often been controversial. Consider the seemingly simple decision of the 1980 split of the large Fifth Circuit, encompassing the southernmost states from Texas to Georgia and Florida, into the new Eleventh and now smaller Fifth Circuits. Groups on both sides of the civil rights controversy that has characterized American racial politics for half a century expressed a profound interest in the issue, and did not keep their mutual suspicion a deep secret for the two decades the fight waged.[1] Questions over jurisdiction or procedure also generate interest beyond what their technical nature would at first seem to merit.

Similarly, the recruitment of judges has excited considerable interest by various factions who expect to be affected, directly or indirectly, by the decisions federal courts are likely to make in the near future. Students may recall the very visible confrontations that accompanied recent appointments to the Supreme Court. However, the lower federal bench also shapes our politics, and if appointments to the district and appellate courts have been less visible, their politics has been no less intense. Thus, we have devoted a considerable amount of attention, two chapters, to the question of judicial recruitment. It is quite doubtful that either the structure or the staffing of courts would attract much political attention were judges mere oracles of the law who set forth to discover the correct solution to the suit before them. The American public may be more astute than much judicial rhetoric gives them credit for.

At the beginning of this book, we promised that there would be no simple solutions to the question, What is the proper role for courts in American society? Perhaps we have delivered on that promise better than any other. This should not surprise us, for politics is an inherently difficult and risky enterprise. We wager our happiness, our wealth, our very lives on decisions made with only limited understanding of the issues involved, and with no reliable forecast of their consequences. And we are doomed to live with the consequences of our imperfect knowledge. As psychotherapist Sheldon B. Kopp has written, "We must live within the ambiguity of partial freedom, partial power, and partial knowledge."[2] It is a safe bet that such conflicts will be a lasting part of our political life. Our salvation—if salvation exists at all—may rest not in this or that theory of constitutional interpretation, but in the fact that the debate continues.

We conclude our journey with an invitation to the student to continue the debate, but also with a note of existential anxiety. The exasperated student at this point might be tempted to put the subjects we have surveyed as far out of mind as possible. Such a reaction is as understandable as it is futile. In fact, none of us can avoid the dilemmas we have posed. We can participate actively in the political process, with all its tensions and ambiguities, pursuing justice as we are best given to understand it. Or we can remain passive recipients of decisions made by others, whose commitment to justice may be weak. Either way, the issues raised here will remain a part of each of our lives.

If the American Constitution has not given us a "machine that would go of itself," it has given us a structure within which our differences may be resolved, including our differences about the structure itself, it is hoped for the betterment of us all.[3] Its continued success depends on informed, thoughtful, and committed citizens. Students about to assume the mantle of citizenship will embark on life's journey with uncertain guidance from others. Perhaps this book has offered some assistance. The student may not agree with all of the assessments offered here, but no matter. If some light has been shed, the effort has been worthwhile.

NOTES

1. See generally, Deborah J. Barrow and Thomas G. Walker, *A Court Divided: The Fifth Circuit Court of Appeals and the Politics of Judicial Reform* (Yale University, New Haven, 1988).
2. Sheldon B. Kopp, "An Eschatalogical Laundry List: A Partial Register of the 927 (or was it 928?) Eternal Truths", in Sheldon B. Kopp, ed. *If You Meet the Buddha on the Road, Kill Him!* (Science and Behavior Books, Ben Lomand, California, 1972) p. 166.
3. James Russell Lowell, "Address to the Reform Club of New York," quoted in Michael Kammen, *A Machine that Would Go of Itself* (Alfred A. Knopf, New York, 1986) p. 18.

Index